A Textual History of Christian-Muslim Relations

A Textual History of Christian-Muslim Relations

Seventh–Fifteenth Centuries

Charles Tieszen

Fortress Press
Minneapolis

Cover image: "The Baptism of Christ," from The Chronology of Ancient Nations by
Muhammad b. Ahmad al-Biruni, 1307. Or Ms 161 fol.140v (gouache on paper).
Bridgeman Art Gallery.
Cover design: Laurie Ingram

Library of Congress Cataloging-in-Publication Data
ISBN: 978-1-4514-9026-8

The paper used in this publication meets the minimum requirements of American
National Standard for Information Sciences — Permanence of Paper for Printed
Library Materials, ANSI Z329.48-1984.

Manufactured in the U.S.A.

This book was produced using Pressbooks.com, and PDF rendering was done by
PrinceXML.

Contents

Publication Credits

The following publishers are acknowledged for the permission to reproduce material in this book.

Chapter 1

Paul J. Alexander, *The Byzantine Apocalyptic Tradition* © 1985 by the Regents of the University of California. Used with permission of the copyright holder via Copyright Clearance Center.

John of Damascus on Islam: The "Heresy of the Ishmaelites" by Daniel J. Sahas, copyright © 1972 by E.J. Brill, Leiden, Netherlands. Used by permission of Koninklijke Brill NV, Leiden.

Chapter 2

Theodore Abu Qurrah, translated by John C. Lamoreaux, copyright © 2006 Brigham Young University Press. Used by permission.

Defending the "People of Truth" in the Early Islamic Period: The Christian Apologies of Abu Ra'itah. Copyright © 2006 Koninklijke Brill NV, Leiden. Used by permission of the publisher.

Chapter 3

Chapter 4

Chapter 5

Muslim-Christian Polemic During the Crusades, edited by Rifaat Ebied and David Thomas, copyright © 2005 Koninklijke Brill NV, Leiden. Used by permission of the publisher.

Joseph Kenny, "Saint Thomas Aquinas: Reasons for the Faith against Muslim Objections," Islamochristiana 22 (1996): 31-52. Used by permission of *Islamochristiana*.

Muslim-Christian Polemic During the Crusades, edited by Rifaat Ebied and David Thomas, copyright © 2005 Koninklijke Brill NV, Leiden. Used by permission of the publisher.

From Thomas F. Michel, *A Muslim Theologian's Response to Christianity*, © 1985 Caravan Books. Used by permission of the publisher (www.scholarsbooklist.com).

Daniel Sahas, "Captivity and Dialogue. Gregory of Palamas (1296-1360) and the Muslims," *Greek Orthodox Theological Review* 25 (1980). Copyright 1980 © Hellenic College, Inc. Used by permission of Holy Cross Orthodox Press.

Chapter 6

From Jean-Marie Gaudeul, *Encounters and Clashes: Islam and Christianity in History*, vol. 2 (Rome: Pontificio Istituto di Studi Arabi e Islamici, 1984). Used by permission of Pontificio Istituto de Studi Arabi e Islamici.

The Complete Philosophical and Theological Treatises of Nicholas of Cusa (2 vols.), translated by Jasper Hopkins (Loveland, CO: The Arthur J. Banning Press, 2001). Used by permission of the publisher. Can be found online at www.jasper-hopkins.info.

Acknowledgements

A book like this depends on the generosity of numerous people. Many publishers gave their permission for selections of texts to be published here. Brandin Francabandera took time from his family holiday to acquire sources at libraries I was unable to visit personally. Jonathan Ingram faithfully reads nearly everything I write and offered helpful perspective on this manuscript, while Will Bergkamp, Esther Diley, and Lisa Gruenisen at Fortress Press were consistently organized, cheerful, and encouraging. The generosity of these individuals made writing this book possible.

I am also grateful to many Muslim, Christian, and Jewish friends—some of whom I know only through their medieval writings, others from living and thriving friendships—who not only put faces to inter-religious studies for me but also help to make me a better person. I cannot live life well without them. I hope they are not disgraced by some of the negative medieval perspectives featured in this book.

At the very beginning of this project, my son, Brahm, learned to say the word "team." As toddlers do, he repeated the word frequently and would often bounce into my office to say that he, his mother, and I were a team. It is true—and not simply because Sarah, my wife, cared for Brahm during times when I researched and wrote (though she often did). In fact, I cannot be who I am without Brahm and Sarah. I am deeply thankful for all of their help and for picking me to be on their team.

Finally, I conceived of this book with students and professors in mind. In this light, I happily dedicate it to my teachers: Professors Cindi Strong, Tim Tennent, Todd Johnson, and especially to my doctoral father, David Thomas.

Introduction

Voices in the History of Christian-Muslim Relations

The history of Muslims and Christians encountering and engaging one another is a story of great complexity and nuance. It resists just one interpretation and forces those who wish to accurately understand the history to consult a variety of sources and perspectives. Consider, for instance, the story told to us by the eleventh-century mosque of Bab al-Mardum, hidden among the web of narrow streets in Toledo, Spain.[1] Travellers who visit the little structure today, having recuperated from a steep descent down the Calle de las Descalzas, may enter the mosque and gaze in wonder at its blind arcades, multi-lobed arches, and—most notably—nine ribbed domes that clearly pay homage to the Grand Mosque of Córdoba.[2] A closer look, however, reveals another influence: the columns supporting the mosque's domes predate the structure by many centuries. In fact, they are Christian columns from a period

---

1. For a detailed description of the structure, see Susana Calvo Capilla, "La mezquita de Bab al-Mardum y el proceso de consagración de pequeña mezquitas en Toledo (s. XII–XIII)," Al-Qantara 20, no. 2 (1999): 299–330 and Jerrilynn D. Dodds, María Rosa Menocal, and Abigail Krasner Balbale, The Arts of Intimacy: Christians, Jews, and Muslims in the Making of Castilian Culture (New Haven: Yale University Press, 2008), 112–22. See also, Calvo Capilla, "Reflexiones sobre la mezquita de Bab al-Mardum y la capilla de Belén de Toledo" in Entre el califato y la taifa: Mil años de Cristo de la Luz (Actas del Congreso Internacional, Toledo, 1999) (Toledo, Sp.: Asociación de Amigos del Toledo Islámico, 2000) and Calvo Capilla, "La capilla de Belén del convent de Santa Fe de Toledo: ¿Un oratorio musulmán?" Tulaytula 11 (2004): 31–73.
2. Ibid., 46; Marianne Barrucand and Achim Bednorz, Moorish Architecture in Andalusia (Köln, Ger.: Taschen, 2007), 88; Dodds, Menocal, and Balbale, The Arts of Intimacy, 116.

when Visigoths ruled Spain. The mosque of Bab al-Mardum was formerly a Christian church, and the builders who constructed it repurposed the church's columns for their mosque.

Using scraps of the former church in the mosque's construction was, of course, practical and resourceful. But the irony, however deliberate it may or may not have been, should not be missed. With the new mosque complete, Muslim worshippers (or even passersby) not only saw a triumphant mosque where a church once stood, but they might have also noticed that Christian pillars were now supporting Muslim domes. There is no evidence to suggest that anyone viewed the new mosque in this way, but if the architectural submission was noticed, then it could have reminded onlookers of a reversal of fortunes: the eighth-century shift from Christian to Muslim control of Toledo. Might the eleventh-century mosque with its Christian pillars tell a story that reopened a very old wound?[3]

Moving past these Christian columns by walking around the structure's perimeter, a relatively enormous apse adds to the mosque's story. Less than a century after the mosque was completed, Christian armies recaptured Toledo. Then, having passed into the hands of the Knights of St. John, the mosque was reconverted to a church, the Cristo de la Luz, in 1183. The apse most clearly marks this retransformation; at first glance, it is an extension sympathetic to the original tastes of the mosque's designers. Indeed, it remains honest to the Muslim architecture by employing the same style of foundation, brickwork, and cornice. Likewise, it retains the blind arcades, lobed arches, and ceramic roof tiles.[4] In this sense, the original structure and its addition maintain architectural symmetry. The church's apse carries on where the mosque left off, a testament to cooperative

---

3. The conquest of Toledo by Muslim armies in the eighth century was swift and required little military effort. According to some sources, the city was abandoned before the Muslims' arrival. In any case, the power shift may have gone almost entirely unnoticed by rural dwellers, though those remaining in urban centers like Toledo would have faced changes, perhaps even architectural ones, more squarely. See Richard Hitchcock, *Muslim Spain Reconsidered: From 711–1502* (Edinburgh: Edinburgh University Press, 2014).

4. Alejandro Lapunzina, *The Architecture of Spain* (Westport, CT: Greenwood, 2005), 130.

architecture, mutual dependence, and a history of coexisting relationships between Muslims and Christians.

And yet there is still more to this little mosque-turned-church story. Stepping back from the Cristo de la Luz's beautiful design, perceptive onlookers may notice that the twelfth-century Christian addition—the apse—is grossly out of scale when compared to the rest of the structure. Indeed, the apse is so much larger that it appears to consume the tiny mosque. Once more, the irony of such disproportion must not be missed, for the apse may have stood in some minds as a statement of triumphalism. The Christians who commissioned the church's reconversion to a church could have simply destroyed it and built a fresh structure. A more powerful statement, however, would be to repurpose what was already there. Thus, the vanquished mosque becomes the stuffed and mounted animal in the victorious Christian hunter's den.[5] Where Christian capitals once served Muslim domes, a mosque is now subservient to a church, a symbol of receding Muslim control of Spain. Again, we have no evidence that anyone viewed the church in this way, but the perspective gives way to the suggestion that, perhaps at least to some, the reconverted structure represented contempt. However medieval Christians and Muslims looked upon the church-turned-mosque-turned-church, does the Cristo de la Luz tell a story of subjugation or mutual appreciation? And what of the many kinds of stories that lie in between perspectives of subjugation and appreciation?

Traveling north of the Cristo de la Luz to the library of El Escorial near Madrid, one finds another curious story. In this case, it is told by a manuscript of the *Books of Chess, Dice, and Board Games* commissioned in the thirteenth century by Alfonso X, King of León and Castilla.[6] In it, descriptions of games are accompanied by

---

5. Dodds, Menocal, and Balbale, *The Arts of Intimacy*, 121.

6. Alfonso X, el Sabio, *Libros de acedrez, dados, e tablas* (late-thirteenth century), MS T.I.6 (facsimile), Biblioteca Monasterio del Escorial, Madrid (henceforth MS T.I.6); reproduced as *Libros del ajedrez, dados, y tablas*, 2 vols. (Madrid: Edilán, 1987). A detailed description and analysis of this text is Sonja Musser Golladay, "*Los libros de acedrex dados e tablas*: Historical, Artistic and Metaphysical Dimensions of Alfonso X's *Book of Games*" (PhD diss., The University of Arizona, 2007). See also, Olivia Remie Constable, "Chess and Courtly Culture in

exquisite miniatures illustrating various chess problems and game situations. The miniature concluding the section on chess depicts a red-bearded Muslim in his tent hosting a blond Christian nobleman. The tent bears a *basmalah* ("In the name of God, the Most Gracious, the Most Merciful") in blue *kufic* script and is topped with a green pendant.[7] Both men rest on striped cushions positioned on either side of a chessboard, the remaining pieces of which suggest that the match is nearly complete.[8]

Like the Cristo de la Luz, this medieval miniature dramatizes the history of Christian-Muslim relations in many ways. In one sense, Muslims and Christians could frequently be at odds with one another, sometimes to a violent degree. Indeed, the characters in the manuscript illumination are playing a mock game of war while being sheltered by the cool shade of a war tent. The Muslim wears a large, sheathed sword, and his two lances stand outside near a tent flap. Close examination of the chessboard reveals similar tension. The Christian's pieces are severely depleted. Cornered, he faces imminent checkmate in exactly eleven moves.[9] The Muslim looks on, fully expecting his decisive victory.

In an entirely different sense, one can look past the war tent and mock battle at what may very well be two friends enjoying one another's company, wiling away an afternoon over a friendly match of strategy and intellect. In fact, the Muslim is depicted reaching with his left hand towards a carafe and drinking glass. With his right hand he appears to motion for his companion to take a drink, and the Christian seems to gesture appreciatively in response.[10] It is a

Medieval Castile: The *Libro de ajedrez* of Alfonso X, el Sabio," *Speculum* 82, no. 2 (April 2007): 301–47.

7. Golladay transliterates the inscription as "Bismillahir-Rahmanir-Rahim," i.e., *bismi-llahi al-rahmani al-rahimi* ("In the name of God, the Most Gracious, the Most Merciful"). See Golladay, 956n682.

8. For a detailed description of this particular miniature, comprising folio 64r of the manuscript and illustrating chess problem 103 (its corresponding text appears on folios 63r and 63v), see ibid., 366–68, 956–58. For a transcription of the accompanying text, see ibid., 1338–39.

9. "The dark pieces play first and give checkmate to the white King in eleven moves with the same players, neither more nor less" (*Los prietos iuegan primero e dan mathe al Rey blanco en onze uezes con los sus iuegos mismos ni mas ni menos*). MS T.I.6, fol. 63r and Golladay, 1338.

10. Golladay, 956 and 956–57n685. We cannot be sure as to the players' true identities. Some

rather harmonious scene, reminiscent of frequent instances of inter-communal cohesion, cooperation, and the prosperous exchange of ideas. What story does this miniature tell us? Can the history of Christian-Muslim relations be described as one of mutual enmity or friendly encounter? Alongside the Cristo de la Luz, what stories are left untold, and what perspectives remain unconsidered by the miniature?

An examination of religious treatises yields similarly complex stories. On the one hand, we find authors like Eulogius, the ninth-century Christian priest from Córdoba who, in a treatise recounting the alleged acts of Christian martyrs, looked at those embracing Islam and wrote that they were taking a "cup from a rotten sewer" (*cloacae putrientis poculum*).[11] On the other hand, we can also find those like the ninth-century Muslim caliph al-Ma'mun who, as we are told in a supposed account of his debate with a Christian monk, announced to his opponent: "This is a court of justice and equity: none shall be wronged therein. So advance thy arguments and answer without fear, for there is none here who will not speak thee well. . . . Let everyone speak who has the wisdom to demonstrate the truth of his religion."[12] Even in the context of theological treatises like these, we see a dichotomy of contempt and respect, not to mention the myriad of perspectives that overlap and lie in between those extremes. The history of Christian-Muslim relations demands careful study.

As a point of departure, the study of Christian-Muslim relations in this book begins by consulting sources coming from within the genre of theological literature—texts written by Christians about Islam or by Muslims about Christianity. These include texts devoted to religious apologetic or polemic, theological treatises, responses to theological questions, and accounts of theological debates. Other

suggest the Christian is Alfonso X and the Muslim Ibn al-Ahmar, but textual evidence may suggest that the Christian is an unknown prisoner of war playing a game with his captor. See ibid., 957–58.

11. Eulogius, *Memoriale sanctorum*, II.7.2 in Ioannes Gil, ed., *Corpus scriptorium muzarabicorum*, 2 vols. (Madrid: Instituto Antonio Nebrija, 1973).

12. Quoted in Alfred Guillaume, "Theodore Abu Qurra as Apologist," *The Muslim World* 15 (1925): 46.

valuable sources—archaeology, poetry, general histories, legal texts, travel literature, and so on—will be left to other books. As a result, this study cannot entirely characterize the history or trajectory of Christian-Muslim relations, but it should provide readers with a helpful introduction to the ways in which Christians and Muslims reflected theologically about each other. In addition, since much of the content within the texts I introduce forms the basis for the discussions that take place between Christians and Muslims in our contemporary society, readers are also given a foundational understanding of the key themes of theological engagement in present-day Christian-Muslim dialogue. Thus, like al-Ma'mun, I attempt to let as many voices speak as possible so that we can begin to understand the history of Christian-Muslim relations with greater clarity.

In what follows, then, the reader is given brief introductions to authors and their religious treatises in order to set them in proper context and draw the reader's attention to some of the key theological topics presented in the texts. This is followed by a selection of important passages taken directly from the texts, which allow the texts to tell us their stories instead of us merely reading *about* them. A select bibliography at the end of the book provides recommendations for secondary literature that may be helpful for pursuing the topics, the history, or the primary sources even further.

This format helps us to achieve two goals. First, it helps introduce readers to primary sources, and second, it helps them encounter the major theological issues that emerge from those sources. It must be said that many introductions to the history of Christian-Muslim relations rarely give the reader an opportunity to read extended sections from an actual medieval text. At times, brief passages are quoted or titles are referred to, but readers are left without hearing medieval authors speak for themselves. Of course, interested readers can consult the many available modern editions of these texts (some of them in translation), but this can be a daunting task; many editions will be inaccessible to someone beginning his or her study of

Christian-Muslim relations. In short, while readers may learn something *about*, say, John of Damascus or Abu 'Isa al-Warraq in historical overviews, in this book they read John and al-Warraq in their own words. Just as importantly, readers discover, in turn, the theological topics medieval authors were concerned with and where those fit in the overall context of Christian-Muslim engagement. As a result, the book can be used to initiate conversations about how Christians and Muslims discuss, disagree, and attempt to communicate the theological distinctions of divine unity, Trinitarian theology, Christology, soteriology, anthropology, revelation, or the use of Scripture.

This study unfolds over the course of six chapters that are arranged chronologically. I begin in the seventh century with *The Apocalypse of Pseudo-Methodius* and move gradually forward to the fifteenth century, ending with texts by Nicholas of Cusa. Roughly speaking, the book covers the medieval era. Of course, narrowing the range of writings to specifically theological ones in this period leaves a wide variety of texts from which to choose. Why this particular collection? The texts included here are some of the most important ones, forming the foundations of how Christians and Muslims engaged one another theologically. Some of them may appear in translation elsewhere, but they are collected together here because, as a whole, they represent many of the most essential texts for those who wish to understand the history of Christian-Muslim theological engagement and the fullest range of theological issues that arise from this history. Further, the theological topics that emerge from these texts continue to appear in present-day works about Christian-Muslim dialogue. Helping readers to encounter this collection of primary sources will help them form the groundwork for more study in the field.

In the conclusion, I map the ground the book covers by charting some of the literary topoi of Christian-Muslim theological engagement. Here, many of the common theological themes found within the texts are highlighted and given brief analysis. This is followed by a small glossary of some of the more obscure terms encountered in the texts.

A Few Words on Transliteration and Format

In most English works devoted to Islamic studies, a system of transliteration using Latin characters represents Arabic letters and vowel markings. Although these systems vary, many incorporate a dot or macron above or below a letter to indicate a long vowel or a particular Arabic letter with no real equivalent in English. In this book, a simplified system of transliteration is used whereby Arabic words are italicized and rendered into English without dots or macrons. The Arabic letter *ayn* is represented with a ' and the *hamza* is represented with a '. Common Arabic words or names such as Muhammad, caliph, or Qur'an are left unitalicized. In Arabic proper names, the patronymic form "ibn" is abbreviated to "b." unless it appears as the first part of a name (e.g., "Ibn Hazm"). A similar system of transliteration is also applied to other languages that would normally require specific diacritical marks.

The texts selected are originally found in previously published editions. Some of these were published over a century ago, and others come from editions that were published in countries such as the United Kingdom. In each case, every attempt is made to retain the original publication's spelling and grammatical formats. This explains why, for example, an American spelling of a word is found in one text while a British spelling of that same word may be found in another text.

In some cases, punctuation has been altered in order to ease the reader's job in following the text. Finally, asterisk dividers (***) are used to indicate where sections of texts have not been included or in order to distinguish between the end of my introduction to a text and the beginning of a text.

1

Between Heresy, Adaptation, and The End
of The World

Early Christian Responses to the Rise of Islam
(Seventh to Eighth Centuries)

The Apocalypse of Pseudo-Methodius (ca. 640–692)

Author unknown
Language: Syriac
Source: Paul J. Alexander, *The Byzantine Apocalyptic Tradition*
(Berkeley: University of California Press, 1985), 36–51.

Some of the earliest Christian responses in writing to the rise of Islam come
to us in the form of apocalyptic reflection, a genre of writing in which, for
Christian authors, biblical prophecies are applied to current events in such a
way that the latter become harbingers for the end of time and God's final
judgment. One of the best known of these kinds of texts is The Apocalypse
of Pseudo-Methodius, *so named because its author was not really the*

Methodius, bishop of Olympus, who died in 312. Instead, he was likely an Eastern Christian in the late-seventh century posing as Methodius so that he could foresee the Arab advance (referred to as "Ismaelites"). He views their arrival in the context of the eschatological prophecy in the biblical book of Daniel. According to this book, four kingdoms hold sway over the peoples of the earth, culminating with the kingdom of the Greeks. In The Apocalypse of Pseudo-Methodius, *Muslims appear as an interlude to the sequence of these four kingdoms.*

The Apocalypse of Pseudo-Methodius *was an extremely popular text, so much so that it was translated from its original Syriac into Greek and many other languages spoken and read by early-medieval Christians encountering Islam. Like other apocalyptic works, it provided Christian readers with an explanation for the rise of Islam and located its purpose in the Christian sacred text. In this case, the cause of Islam was Christian sin; Muslims were used by God as a form of judgment. As a result, the text could also nourish the reader's hope that righting his or her ways would bring an end to Islamic rule, which in turn would signal the return of God's blessing.*

***

For there is no people or kingdom under heaven that can overpower the kingdom of the Christians as long as it possesses a place of refuge in the life-giving Cross, which is set up in the center of the earth and possesses its power over height and depth. Also the bars of Hell which are the tyrants of impiety [or: heathendom] cannot prevail over this kingdom of the Christians. Thus runs the true saying of Our Savior who spoke to Simon [Matt. 16:18]: Which is the power of kingdom or people below heaven that is mighty and strong in its power and will be able to prevail over the great power of the Holy Cross in which the kingdom of the Greeks, that is of the Romans, possesses a place of refuge? The blessed Paul wrote to the Thessalonians in the second letter when he warned them: Do not be frightened by quick and vain rumors saying: Behold, the day of the Lord Jesus has come [2 Thess. 2:2]. As long as this kingdom which possesses an abiding place of refuge is the center, the Son of Perdition will not be revealed for that something which is in the center is the priesthood and the kingship and the Holy Cross. And this kingship of the Christians overpowers all kingdoms of the earth, and by it all leaders and all authority will be paralyzed and come to nought and all its people will be left destitute, and by it they will be conquered and through it they will come to nought.

***

Because of [Christian sin] God will deliver them to the defilement of the barbarians. And heroic men will be buffeted by the punishment of distress. . . . And the veil of silence will spread over all men, and all inhabitants of the earth will sit in surprise and in consternation. And the route of [the Arabs'] advance will be from [the inhabitants] and by them, and what is small will be reckoned like big and mean like noble. And their commands will cut to pieces like that which is in swords [i.e., steel]. . . . For these cruel barbarians are not human beings but are sons of desolation and upon desolation their faces are set upon the sword. They are despoilers and for destruction they will be sent . . . And they will be cruel and murderers and bloodthirsty and destroyers and a testing furnace for all Christians.

***

. . . There will be sought . . . those who blaspheme [i.e., those Christians who apostatize] concerning the sacred mysteries and deny the Messiah and ignorant men in whom is not the wisdom of God. They will be servants of that one [Muhammad?] and their false words will find credence. And concerning anything that is said to them they will comply. And true men and clerics and wise men and good men will be held in contempt in their eyes and they will be like dung, for they will be subjected to the punishment of the Ismaelites. And they will be distressed until they abandon hope for their lives. And honor will be lifted from the priests, and the divine liturgy and living sacrifice will cease from the Church. And at that time priests will be like the people, and their corpses will be thrown like mud upon the roads without burial. And throughout those days blows of wrath will be sent upon men, two and three in one day. And a man will go to sleep in the evening and will wake up in the morning and will find outside his door two and three oppressors and they will ask tribute and money.

***

And they will blaspheme and say: There is no deliverer for the Christians. Then suddenly there will be awakened perdition and calamity as those of a woman in travail, and a king of the Greeks will go forth against them in great wrath, and he will be aroused against them like a man who shakes off his wine, and who [plots] against them as if they were dead men. He will go forth against them from the sea of the Cushites and will lay desolation and ruin in the desert of Jethrib and in the habitation of their fathers. And the sons [allies?] of the king of Greece will seize the places of the desert and will destroy with the sword the remnant that is left of them in the land of promise. And fear of all those around them will fall upon them. They and their wives and their sons and their leaders and all their camps and the entire land of the desert of their father will be given into the hands of the kings of the Greeks, and will be surrendered to desolation and destruction and to captivity and murder. And their servitude will be one hundred times more severe than their yoke had been.

***

And all the wrath of the ire of the king of the Greeks will be completed upon those who denied. And there will be peace on earth the like of which ha[s] never existed, because it is the last peace of the perfection of the world. And there will be joy upon the entire earth, and men will sit down in great peace and the churches will arise nearby, and cities will be built and priests will be freed from the tax, and priests and men will rest at that time from labor and tiredness and torture, because that is the peace of which He said in His gospel: There will be great peace the like of which never existed, and men will sit down in repose and will eat and drink and rejoice in the joy of their heart, and men will take wives and wives will be given to men [Matt. 24:38].

On Heresies, chapter 100 (ca. mid-eighth century)

John of Damascus (ca. 675–ca. 754)
Language: Greek
Source: Daniel J. Sahas, *John of Damascus on Islam: The "Heresy of the Ishmaelites"* (Leiden, Neth.: Brill, 1972), 132–41.

On Heresies, *usually referred to by the Latin title* De haeresibus, *is a Greek text written sometime after 743 as the second part of a larger work titled* The Fount of Knowledge *(in Greek,* Pege gnoseos*). As its title suggests, the focus of the work is a list of heresies, the hundredth and last chapter of which is devoted to Islam.*

John of Damascus, a Melkite Christian born in Damascus sometime around 675, wrote the text. His father held a high-ranking position under the Muslim ruler Mu'awiya and, for a time, Umayyad caliphs employed John as well. Facing restrictions upon Christians employed by Muslims, John retired to the Monastery of Mar Saba near Jerusalem where he resided until his death in the mid-eighth century.

Though John wrote other important works, On Heresies *is significant as one of the earliest known Christian texts to give significant attention to Islam. It influenced later Christian writing on Islam for centuries. Specifically, many of the themes John treats—attacks upon the legitimacy of Muhammad's claim to prophethood and his alleged debauchery, the historicity of the Qur'an, and defenses of the Trinity and Christology—provide inspiration for many later Christian works devoted to Islam.*

***

There is also the still-prevailing deceptive superstition of the Ishmaelites, the fore-runner of the Antichrist. It takes its origin from Ishmael, who was born to Abraham from Hagar, and that is why they also call them Hagarenes and Ishmaelites. They also call them Saracenes, allegedly for having been sent away by Sarah empty; for Hagar said to the angel, "Sarah has sent me away empty." These, then, were idolaters and they venerated the morning star Aphrodite, whom notably they called [*Chabar*] in their own language, which means "great"; therefore until the times of Heraclius they were, undoubtedly, idolaters. From that time on a false prophet appeared among them, surnamed [*Mamed*], who, having casually been exposed to the Old and the New Testament and supposedly encountered an Arian monk, formed a heresy of his own. And after, by pretence, he managed to make the people think of him as a God-fearing fellow, he spread rumors that a scripture was brought down to him from heaven. Thus having drafted some pronouncements in his book, worthy [only] of laughter, he handed it down to them in order that they may comply with it.

He says that there exists one God maker of all, who was neither begotten nor has he begotten. He says that Christ is the Word of God and his spirit, created and a servant, and that he was born without a seed from Mary, the sister of Moses and Aaron. For, he says, the Word of God and the Spirit entered Mary and she gave birth to Jesus who was a prophet and a servant of God. And that the Jews, having themselves violated the Law, wanted to crucify him and after they arrested him they crucified his shadow, but Christ himself, they say, was not crucified nor did he die; for God took him up to himself into heaven because he loved him. And this is what he says, that when Christ went up to the heavens God questioned him saying: "O Jesus, did you say that 'I am Son of God, and God'?" And Jesus, they say, answered: "Be merciful to me, Lord; you know that I did not say so, nor will I boast that I am your servant; but men who have gone astray wrote that I made this statement and they said lies against me and they have been in error." And God, they say, answered to him: "I knew that you would not say this thing." And although he includes in this writing many more absurdities worthy of laughter, he insists that this was brought down to him from God.

***

We ask, "How is it that your prophet did not come this way, by having others bearing witness to him, nor did—as in the case of Moses, that God gave the Law to him while the people were looking and the mountain was in smoke—God give him as well, as you claim, the scripture in your presence so that you, too, have an assurance?" they reply that God does whatever he pleases. "This" we say "is what we also know; but how did the scripture come down to your prophet, this is what we are asking." And they answer that, while he was asleep the scripture came down upon him. Then we say to them in jest that . . . since while asleep he received the scripture . . . he did not have a sense of this even taking place.

***

When we again ask them, "How is it that, although in your scripture he commanded not to do anything or receive anything without witnesses, you did not ask him, 'You first prove with witnesses that you are a prophet and that you came from God, and which scripture testifies about you,'" they remain silent because of shame. Since you are not permitted to marry a woman without witnesses, neither to purchase something, nor to acquire property—you do not even condescend to have an ass or an animal without witnesses—you have women, and properties, and asses and everything else through witnesses; and yet, only your faith and your scripture you have without witness. And this is because the one who handed it down to you does not have any certification from anywhere, nor is there any one known who testified about him in advance, but he, furthermore, received this while asleep.

***

Again we respond to them: "Since you say that Christ is Word and Spirit of God, how do you scold us as *Associators*? For the Word and the Spirit is inseparable each from the one in whom this has the origin; if, therefore, the Word is in God it is obvious that he is God as well. If, on the other hand, this is outside of God, then God, according to you, is without word and without spirit. Thus, trying to avoid making associates to God you have mutilated Him. For it would be better if you were saying that he has an associate than to mutilate him and introduce him as if he were a stone, or wood, or any of the inanimate objects. Therefore, by accusing us falsely, you call us *Associators*; we, however, call you *Mutilators* . . . of God."

***

"How is it that you rub yourselves against a stone by your [*Chabathan*] [i.e., *al-Ka'bah*], and you express your adoration to the stone by kissing it?" . . . They claim that the stone is of Abraham. . . . This, then, which they call "stone" is the head of Aphrodite, whom they used to venerate [and] whom they call [*Chaber*], on which those who can understand it exactly can see, even until now, traces of an engraving.

***

This [Mamed], as it has been mentioned, composed many idle tales, on each one of which he prefixed a title, like for example the discourse of The Woman, in which he clearly legislates that one may have four wives and one thousand concubines if he can, as many as he can maintain beside the four wives; and that one can divorce whomsoever he pleases, if he so wishes, and have another one. He made this law because of the following case: [Mamed] had a comrade named Zaid. This man had a beautiful wife with whom [Mamed] fell in love. While they were once sitting together [Mamed] said to him: "Oh you, God commanded me to take your wife." And he replied, "You are an apostle; do as God has told you; take my wife." Or rather, in order to tell the story from the beginning, he said to him: "God commanded me [to tell you] that you should divorce your wife;" and he divorced her. Several days later he said, "But now God commanded me that I should take her." Then after he took her and committed adultery with her he made such a law: "Whosoever wills may dismiss his wife. But if, after the divorce, he wants to return back to her let someone else marry her [first]. For it is not permitted for him to take her [back] unless she is married by somebody else. And even if a brother divorces [his wife], let his brother marry her if he so wishes." This is the type of precepts that he gives in this discourse: "Till the land that God gave you and beautify it; and do this and in this manner"—not to say everything obscene, as he did.

On the Triune Nature of God (755 or 788)

Author unknown
Language: Arabic
Source: Margaret Dunlop Gibson, *An Arabic Version of the Acts of the Apostles and the Seven Catholic Epistles from an Eighth or Ninth Century Ms. In the Convent of St Catharine on Mount Sinai, with A Treatise On the Triune Nature of God with Translation, from the Same Codex* (London: C. J. Clay and Sons, 1899), 2–36.

The author of this text is unknown, but may have been associated with a monastery like the Monastery of St. Catherine on Mount Sinai, which preserves the only known manuscript of the work. The text refers to a date, claiming that Christianity has existed for seven hundred and forty-six years. Using the Alexandrian calendar, the text may be dated to either 755 or 788, depending on whether the author began his count from the incarnation or the crucifixion. Margaret Gibson, who provides a transcription and English translation of the work (though she neglects to transcribe nearly a quarter of the manuscript), applies to it a slightly misleading title (in Arabic, Fi tathlith Allah al-wahid), especially since the work gives a great deal of space to matters of Christology and soteriology, in addition to the lengthy prayer at the beginning (Samir Khalil Samir promises a forthcoming Arabic edition of the text along with an English translation by Mark Swanson).

The text is enormously significant, because it is one of the earliest apologies for Christian doctrine to appear in Arabic and to come from an

Islamic milieu. Furthermore, it is an early example of Christian use of the Qur'an and Islamic patterns of speech in the defense and explication of Christian belief. For example, the text begins like all Islamic texts do, with a basmalah *("In the name of God, the Most Gracious, the Most Merciful") that, in this case, is appropriately Christianized. Even more significantly, the author refers to the Torah, the Psalms, the Prophets, and the Gospels as books that were "sent down"* (al-manzila), *a concept and title applied to the Qur'an* (al-Tanzil). *Similarly, the author refers to the Gospel as "a guidance and a mercy"* (hudan wa-rahmatan), *which is a phrase also applied to the Qur'an (e.g., Qur'an 31:3). Furthermore, the text quotes qur'anic passages and makes frequent reference to the notion of Christ as a word and spirit from God (e.g., Qur'an 4:171)—a common feature of Christian texts devoted to Islam—but uses it in support of Trinitarian doctrine.*

At times the author seems to address Muslims directly, suggesting it functioned as an apology for Christian doctrine that was meant to be read by Muslims. But the features described above would have also made the text useful to Christian readers rethinking the presentation of their faith—either in the context of apology or perhaps even catechism—in an environment increasingly influenced by Muslims and Islam.

★★★

In the name of the Father, and of the Son, and of the Holy Ghost, one God. O God, we rejoice in Thy mercy in truth and right. Praise be to God before whom nothing was, and who was before everything, after whom there is nothing, and He is the heir of all things, and to Him all things return, who by His knowledge kept the knowledge of all things, and nothing but His work is sufficient for this, in whose knowledge is the end of all things, and He counts everything by His knowledge. We ask Thee, O God, by Thy mercy and Thy power to put us among those who know Thy truth and follow Thy will and [fear] Thy wrath and adore Thy excellent names in Thy sublime attributes. Thou art the compassionate, the merciful; seated upon the throne Thou art worthy; Thou art higher than the creatures and Thou fillest all things. Thou doest good and art not done good to; Thou judgest and art not judged; Thou art rich towards us and we are poor towards Thee. Thou art near to those who approach Thee; Thou answerest those who call on Thee and implore Thee. Thou, O God, art Lord of all things, God of all things, Creator of all things. Open our mouths, loosen our tongues, soften our hearts, and open our breasts to the praise of Thy noble and high and great and blessed and holy name. Verily there is no god before Thee, and no god after Thee. To Thee [shall we] return; Thou art the Almighty. To Thee be the praise, O God, who dwellest in light, Creator of the angels and the spirit that they may adore Thy name, Thy holy name, for the message of Thy name and for the authority of Thy power; and they do not weary of Thy majesty and Thy holiness, saying, Holy, holy, holy is the mighty Lord, who filleth the heavens and the earth with His honour. Verily they adore Thee, and set their seal to one Lord, that men may know that the angels adore God and His Word and His Spirit, one God and one Lord. We worship Thee, our Lord and our God, in Thy Word and Thy Spirit.

***

We do not distinguish God from His Word and His Spirit. We worship no other god with God in His Word and His Spirit. God shewed His power and His light in the Law and the Prophets and the Psalms and the Gospel, that God and His Word and His Spirit are one God and one Lord. We will shew this, if God will, in these books which have come down to him who wishes intuition and perceives things and knows the truth and opens his breast to believe in God and His Scriptures.

***

It is written also in the beginning of the Law, which God sent down to His prophet Moses on Mount Sinai, "In the beginning God created the heavens and the earth." Then he said, "The Spirit of God was upon the waters." Then He said, by His Word, "Let there be light," and there was light. Then He said, "Let there be firmament," and there was a firmament, which is the lower heaven. Then He said, "Let the earth bring forth the grass and the green herb and the tree with fruit and other things, and let the earth bring forth the living soul of wild beasts, and cattle and lions, and creeping things," and it was so. Then He said, "Let the waters bring forth every creeping thing that hath life, and every fowl that flieth in the heavens of their kind and sex," and it was so. Then He said, "Let us create man after our own image and likeness." So God shewed in the beginning of the book which He sent down to His prophet Moses, that God and His Word and His Spirit are one God, and that God, may He be blessed and exalted! created all things, and gave life to all things by His Word and His Spirit. We do not say three Gods . . . but we say that God and His Word and His Spirit are one God and one Creator. This is like the disc of the Sun which is in the heaven, and the rays which issue from the Sun, and the heat which comes from the Sun, each from the other. We do not say that these are three suns, but one Sun, and these are three names not to be distinguished from one another. Also . . . like the mouth and the tongue which is in the mouth, and the word which issues from the tongue; so is our saying about the Father and the Son and the Holy Ghost. By it the prophets prophesied, and said, "The mouth of the Lord hath spoken." This all is the proof of our faith in the Father and the Son and the Holy Ghost. We know God to be one Lord in His Word and His Spirit. And in Him we adore and praise the Word of God and His Spirit.

***

We do not say that God begat His Word as any man begets; God forbid! but we say that the Father begat His Word as the Sun begets rays, and as the mind begets the word, as the fire begets heat; none of these things existed before what was begotten of them. God, may His name be blessed! never existed without Word and Spirit, but God was ever in His Word and His Spirit; His Word and His Spirit were with God and in God before He made the creatures. We do not say how this is. Verily everything relating to God is majesty and might. As no man can understand anything of God, neither can he understand the Word of God and His Spirit.

***

You will find it also in the [Qur'an], that "We created man in misery, and we have opened the gates of Heaven with water pouring down, and have said, And now are ye come unto us alone, as we created you at first." He said also, "Believe in God, and in His Word; and also in the Holy Ghost, but the Holy Ghost has brought it down a mercy and a guidance from thy Lord," but why should I prove it from this and enlighten [you] when we find in the Law and the Prophets and the Psalms and the Gospel, and you find it in the [Qur'an], that God and his Word and His Spirit are one God and one Lord? Ye have said that ye believe in God and His Word and the Holy Ghost, so do not reproach us, O men! that we believe in God and His Word and His Spirit: and we worship God in His Word and His Spirit, one God and one Lord and one Creator.

***

And say not that God is removed from His place, or that there is of Him one thing without another: God forbid! but we say that God is all complete in Heaven, and all complete in the Christ, and all complete in every place. Seest thou not the Sun which God created . . . and light to the people of the world, that it is in heaven, and in the wadys [i.e., a dry riverbed] and the mountains and on the hillsides and the seas? It is not divided and it is not removed from place to place, but wherever it wills it exists as it wills; it fills all things with its majesty and its might and there is nothing more glorious than it.

***

God was more merciful than the merciful amongst His creatures. He appointed One who should preside over their salvation and their redemption from the temptation of Satan and his error. When the prophets of God saw this, that the children of Adam were lost, and that the Devil had conquered them, and that no man could save the race of Adam from error and destruction, the prophets and apostles of God entreated God and asked Him to come down to His creatures and His servants and to preside in His mercy over their salvation from the error of the Devil.

★★★

What shall I shew and make clear from this prophecy about the Christ, when the prophets prophesied and said that He is God and Lord and Saviour? It is He who came down from heaven a Saviour to His servants. The throne is not divided, for verily God and His Word and His Spirit are on the throne, and in every place complete without diminution. The heavens and the earth and all that is therein are full of His honour.

★★★

God destroyed him and put him beneath Him in his disobedience through what he intended. God sent from His throne His Word which is from Himself, and saved the race of Adam and clothed Himself with this weak conquered Man through Mary the good, whom God chose from the women of the ages. He was veiled in her, and by that He destroyed the Evil One, and conquered and subdued him and left him weak and contemptible. He boasts not over the race of Adam, for it was terrible grief when God conquered [the Evil One] by this Man with whom He clothed Himself. If God were to destroy Satan without clothing Himself with this Man by whom He healed him, Satan would not have found grief and remorse.

★★★

The Christ was born of Mary the pure by the Holy Ghost without any man touching her, God of God and Light of His Light, His Word and His Spirit, perfect Man in soul and body without sin. Mary remained a virgin after she gave Him birth. If the Christ had not been God of God and Light Mary would not have remained a virgin after she had given Him birth; but she gave birth to the Light of God and His Word, mercy and guidance and salvation to His creatures. He saved Adam and his race from the error of Satan. He raised up Adam from his stumbling and healed his wound and repaired his affliction and mended his rupture and liberated him and his race from the hands of Satan. He put an end to his darkness and wandering and broke off our hearts from the service of the Devil. He crucified sin by His cross, and by His death killed the Death which Adam had inherited by disobedience. He brought to light the Resurrection, He raised up truth and righteousness and guidance by His mercy and His favour towards men, and towards the creatures of God.

***

And the Christ wrought signs, the work of a God, that men might know from His work that He is God of God and Light. Thus the Christ said to the children of Israel, "If ye believe not in Me, believe in My work which I do." The Christ created, and no one creates but God. You will find in the [Qur'an], "And he spake and created from clay like the form of a bird, and breathed into it, and lo! it was a bird by permission of God." He forgave trespasses, and who forgives trespasses but God? He satisfied the hungry, and no one does that nor provides food but God. You will find all this about the Christ in your Book.

***

The Christ went up to Heaven, and Heaven was not divided, and sat at the right hand of the Father. He put His enemies who were disobedient to Him below His footstool, and below the feet of those who believe in the Christ. Thus you will find in the [Qur'an], "I have appointed Thee and raised Thee up to Myself, and have purified Thee from those that are unbelievers. I will make those who follow Thee above the unbelievers until the day of resurrection." Say not that we believe in two Gods, or that we say there are two Lords. God forbid! Verily God is one God and one Lord in His Word and His Spirit.

***

He is the Lord who came to us from Zion, and turned away error from us, and was a Saviour to us and a Deliverance from the Devil. No intercessor could lead us from error and no angel from among the angels of God, and none could save us from the Devil nor from his snares, until our Lord came to us from Zion. He was born of the race of David the prophet, as God has promised him; He saved us with power and authority and guided us to the light of God and He fulfilled the obedience [due] to Him; He was mercy to His creatures.

**

The Maiden is the Virgin who is of the race of Adam. She gave birth to the Christ, Emmanuel, God of God, and mercy to His creatures. We do not hear of one man from Adam till this our day who was called "God with us" or who was called the Word of God. He was born of a Virgin without any man touching her. Is not He the Christ? And do they not lie regarding what God has bestowed on creatures in the Christ?

**

What is the punishment of him who falsifies the word of God by the tongues of His prophets? Let us fly for refuge to God from this and ask Him to make us of those who believe His word and the word of His prophets. Verily this is mercy and favour from God and grace for well-being. Then fear God and follow the word of the Christ. Do not doubt Him.

**

We do not know that any of the prophets came down with a new law from Zion save the Christ with the Gospel, a guidance and a mercy, and a proof of the work of obedience to God. The perfection of the work is by purity of spirit and the approach of the soul to God, and temperance in the world and longing for the next world. This is the perfection of knowledge and of worship which God desires from men without their disliking it. Thus said the Christ, "I am not come to destroy the example of Moses but to fulfill it, and to give myself a ransom for many." In truth He has redeemed us from death and sin and the error of Satan. To Him be praise and thanks for this.

**

[After extensive references to biblical prophecies that the author argues refer to Christ:] We do not know that God looked upon the earth or mixed with the people except when He appeared to us in the Christ, His Word and His Spirit. He veiled Himself in flesh, He who is not of us. Men saw Him and He mixed with them. He was God and Man without sin. It was He who knew the paths of good and of knowledge and judgment, and who taught them and made them spring up to those who follow His command and His word. The speech of the Christ was the speech of light and life, as the Apostles said to Him, "Thy speech is the speech of light to those who go and call on Thee." Let us ask God in His mercy to make us of those who follow the commands of the Christ and let us believe in Him as the prophets prophesied about Him and preached about Him.

***

God and His Word and His Spirit are one God in Heaven and earth and in every place. This is the proof of what God's prophets said about it of old time. Verily he who believeth not in God and His Word and His Spirit, one God, hath not kept the faith in God and hath not accepted the word of God's prophets, when they speak about everything that He sent down to them, that God's Word is His strength and His wisdom, and that the Holy Ghost is the life of everything.

***

[The Christ] burneth up sins and killeth them by means of forgiveness, as fire burneth thorns and destroyeth them and one sees no trace of them. Sins and trespasses are like thorns. The Christ said in the Gospel, "Verily, verily I say unto you that he who is not born of water and Spirit shall not enter the kingdom of Heaven"; but he who is born of water and Spirit is he who is baptized in the name of the Father and the Son and the Holy Ghost, one God and one Lord. Let it not take thee aback when thou hearest, "the Father and the Son and the Holy Ghost." Verily the Father is God; the Son is the Word which is from God; and the Holy Ghost is the Spirit of God through whom He sanctifieth everything; as water cleanseth the defilement of the body, so the Holy Ghost cleanseth the defilement of souls and spirits and purifieth them from sins and trespasses, so that he who is baptized in faith is cleaner than when he was born from his mother's womb, he has no sin and no iniquity.

***

He that believeth and is baptized is saved and delivered and pardoned; he who believeth not hath not been baptized, and there hath been decreed against him contempt and remorse. Praise be to God who hath delivered us from the Dragon and his error, and saved us from our sins and trespasses by the immersion of baptism and our faith in the Christ, the Word and the Light of God.

Christianity in the Language of Islam

Developing Christian Theology in Islamic Contexts
(Eighth to Ninth Centuries)

On the Characteristics of the True Religion
(late-eighth or early-ninth century)

Theodore Abu Qurrah (mid–eighth century–ca. 816)
Language: Arabic
Source: John C. Lamoreaux, *Theodore Abu Qurrah* (Provo, UT: Brigham Young University Press, 2005), 55–57.

Theodore Abu Qurrah was a Melkite Christian, at one time bishop of Harran near Edessa in present-day Turkey, and one of the earliest Christians to write in Arabic. A sizedisable portion of his texts that remain extant—some in Arabic and others in Greek—are devoted to the challenge of Islam, though Abu Qurrah rarely mentions the religion specifically. Instead, he makes references to Muslim tenets and frequently makes use of Islamic thought-forms and patterns of theological discourse.

In the text below, Abu Qurrah identifies characteristics that distinguish the true religion (Christianity) and make it superior to his opponents' religions, probably Jews and Muslims. That the latter are likely opponents seems clear given Abu Qurrah's attacks upon Muhammad's parochial ministry (he spoke only Arabic and was sent only to Arabs) and his apparent lack of miracles that might confirm the nature of his prophethood.

Indeed, a common feature of many early-medieval texts written by Christians in Islamic milieus is an intention to help readers discern the true religion in a context of competing truth claims. Texts like this could discourage Christian conversion to Islam by giving Christian readers reasons to cling to their faith at a time when the religion was beginning to grow in influence. Though an author's intended audience is always a matter of debate in texts like those included in this book, any Muslims who may have read a text like the one from Abu Qurrah below would perhaps reconsider their theological allegiances.

***

My friends, every religion and all who believe in the resurrection as a day of judgment agree with us on this point: There is just one religion that God wants human beings to have, and it is according to the dictates of this religion that he judges them on the day of the resurrection, with no one entering paradise except through it. Come, let us examine together, in a sincere manner, the characteristics of this religion. As for us, the community of Christians, we know that the true religion of God, which he wants human beings to have, has three characteristics.

The first characteristic is that God sends his messengers to all the nations of the world. This we know for the simple reason that we have no doubt that God is just and that it would not befit his justice if he were to judge all the nations of the world on the day of the resurrection without having sent his messengers to them. Indeed, if he were to do so, he would no longer be just. If someone suggests that God judges human beings according to the dictates of a religion that he communicated via messengers to just some, that person attributes unfairness to God. If God only sent messengers to some nations and neglected others but then judged them all by the same standard on the day of the resurrection, there is only one thing to which we could compare him—may he be blessed and exalted! Imagine a man who has fifty slaves in fifty hamlets. When it comes time to sow the fields, he sends to some and commands them to sow. To the others, however, he does not send. When it is time for the harvest, he sends to all his slaves and assembles them. He then judges all of them together according to the amount of grain they have, punishing those who did not sow—and his punishment is harsh, continual, and never ending, and is accompanied by his command that the punishment not be lifted from them as long as he lives. Who does not recognize that the one who does this is unfair? May God be exalted above this, and may he know that we are not among those who say such things of him!

The second characteristic is that the messengers God sends must be able to perform wonders and signs. These attest that the one doing them is God's messenger. Such was the case with the miracles and wonders Moses performed in Egypt in Pharaoh's presence. These attested that he was God's messenger. Because of them, Pharaoh's people will have no defense before God on the day of the resurrection for neglecting to follow Moses, what he said, and what he brought from God. Indeed, if God had not given the messengers that he sent to human beings the ability to perform wonders, he would not have on the day of the resurrection any just reason to charge them with having declared his messengers liars, with not having accepted them and put their trust in them, and with rejecting what they brought. In short, if God—apart from wonders—were to punish the nations that did not accept his messengers, he would no longer be just. There is only one thing to which we could compare him. Imagine a man who has fifty slaves in fifty hamlets. To his slaves in his hamlets he sends messengers with a letter on which there is no seal. His slaves refuse to have anything to do with his messengers and do not accept his letters, saying to them, "We shall not accept your letters. If they were authentic, our master would have put his seal on them." When it reaches their master that his slaves disregarded his messengers and declared his letters false, he is angry at them and punishes them harshly, commanding that the punishment not be lifted from them as long as he lives. This too is among the most horrid and unfair things that one could do. May God be exalted above it!

The third characteristic is that God's messengers must instruct the nations to which they are sent in their native tongues, so that those nations might understand them and receive what they bring. Why is this? If God were not to give the messengers he sends to human beings the power to address them in an understandable manner, he would not have a just claim against them on the day of the resurrection should they declare his messengers liars and not believe and accept their message. In short, if God were to punish the nations that did not accept his messengers, notwithstanding that those messengers had addressed them in an unintelligible fashion, he would no longer be just. There is only one thing to which we could compare him. Imagine a man who sends a foreign messenger to his slaves in his hamlets, commanding them to come. The messenger goes and delivers the message of their master. In that they do not understand him and comprehend his message, they end up staying where they are. When news of this reaches their master, he is angry at them and punishes them harshly, commanding that the punishment not be lifted from them as long as he lives. This too is among the most horrid of things that one could do and one of the most loathsome things that could be said of God. May he be exalted above it!

The true religion of God, which alone he accepts on the day of the resurrection, must combine in itself these three characteristics we mentioned: its messengers must have gone forth to all the nations of the world; they must have performed among them signs and wonders; and they must have addressed each nation in its own tongue. If it has these three characteristics, those who do not accept God's messengers have no excuse or defense on the day of the resurrection. It is clear that not one of the peoples of the world can say that there is in the world a religion whose messengers went forth to all the nations of the east and the west, with wonders and signs, and addressed each nation in its own tongue—with a single exception, that most famous of religions, about which all the nations of the world, to the ends of the earth, know and have heard, namely, the Christian religion. Its messengers, the apostles of Christ, went forth to the ends of the earth, to the east and to the west.

On the Trinity
(late-eighth or early-ninth century)

Theodore Abu Qurrah (mid-eighth century–ca. 816)
Language: Arabic
Source: John C. Lamoreaux, *Theodore Abu Qurrah* (Provo, UT: Brigham Young University Press, 2005), 175–93.

In this treatise, Abu Qurrah begins by identifying different types of people and their motivations for accepting or rejecting a religion. Using arguments based on reason, he concludes that most embrace a religion because of deception or desire, with the exception of Christians. This discussion forms the basis of Abu Qurrah's main concern: a defense of Trinitarian belief and an attempt to clarify the Trinity for those who are, in Abu Qurrah's estimation, confused by the doctrine.

As noted, ninth-century Christians like Abu Qurrah faced the need to re-articulate their beliefs for a new context and in a new language. This was especially important in regard to the mounting pressure to convert and perhaps to confusion over the doctrine that distinguished Christianity from the religions around it. A fresh presentation of the Trinity, then, would not only nourish beleaguered Christians but also potentially challenge any Muslims who might read it as well.

***

What I have said thus far is a prelude to persuading those whose minds are confused when Christians speak of the Father, Son, and Holy Spirit as three hypostases and one God and when they say that each of these hypostases is in itself fully God. Those who are confused about this doctrine say that it cannot be so, but that rather it must be either that not one of these hypostases be called God in that there is just one God or that each of these hypostases be God, in which case it would be said that there are three gods. Our response to those who say this: . . . we find that [the Scriptures] mention the Father as God, the Son as God, and the Holy Spirit as God. They do not speak of three gods, however, but warn us sternly to speak of just one God. Through faith we would accept what these scriptures have to say, even if our minds had not found a way to confirm it, for we have defined faith as being "as certain about what is beyond our understanding as we are about what is comprehended by our understanding."

***

I want those who deny Christian doctrine to know that some names refer to persons and others to natures. Names that refer to natures include "man," "horse," and "ox." Names that refer to persons include "Peter," "Paul," and "John." If you want to count many persons with one nature, you must not predicate number of the name that refers to the nature. If you do, you attribute to the persons different natures. How so? If you want to count Peter, James, and John (three persons with a single nature, that being man), it is not right to predicate number of man, that is, their nature, and say that there are three mans. If you do, you cause their single nature, to which the name "man" refers, to be different natures and do something foolish. In the same way, the Father, Son, and Holy Spirit are three persons with one nature (that being God). If you count them, you must not predicate number of the name "God," which is the name of their nature. If you do, you cause their single nature, to which the name "God" refers, to be different natures and fall into manifest error. Again, everyone knows that, when you count Peter, James, and John, number must not be predicated of man. Know this:

Peter is a man, but man is not Peter; James is a man, but man is not James; John is a man, but man is not John. Since man is not Peter, or James, or John, when you count Peter, James, and John, you must not predicate number of what is not numbered. In the same way, know this: The Father is God, but God is not the Father; the Son is God, but God is not the Son; the Spirit is God, but God is not the Spirit. When you count the Father, the Son, and the Holy Spirit, you must not predicate number of the name "God" and speak of three gods. If you do, you have predicated number of what is not numbered. Rather, you must count three persons and one God. This is because "person" is a logical name and does not belong essentially to just one of them. Rather, the name "person" is predicated of the Father and of the Son and of the Holy Spirit, and of every angel, human being, and animal, as well as of every other indivisible entity. The logical name was introduced solely that number might be applied to it, for it is not right for number to be applied to their common name, that by which their nature is named, which name belongs essentially to it—otherwise, it would follow that there are different natures, as we have already said. Nor is it right for number to be applied to the particular, non-logical, name of each of them—otherwise, number will make each of the numbered entities to be all of them. How so? If you say, "Here, Peter, James, and John are three," you make each one to be the three of them. So also, if you say, "In heaven, the Father, Son, and Holy Spirit are three," you make each one to be the three of them. For this reason, it is necessary that number be applied to the logical name, which is predicated of each of them (that is, of a person) and that we say that Peter, James, and John are three persons, but that the name "man" remain singular, neither diffused nor multiplied.

Notwithstanding what we have said, the Father, Son, and Holy Spirit are not like three men, divided in terms of place or differing in form, will, or state. Indeed, if things that are many agree in these respects, they are said to be one in the respect in which they agree, while those that differ in these respects are counted as many. You can say, "I and you are one in form, since we agree in it; I and you are one

in will; I and you are one in state." You can also say, "I and you are
not one in form, since we differ in it; I and you are not one in will;
I and you are not one in this state." (And the same holds for other,
similar respects.) Human beings are divided in place and differ in all
that we mentioned. As for the Father, Son, and Holy Spirit, however,
not one is in a place that the others are not in, not one has a form
that the others do not have; and the same holds for will and state. If
even one of these characteristics makes those that agree in it to be
one, even if they are many, how much more is it necessary for the
Father, Son, and Holy Spirit to be one, since they are not separated
in place and agree in all these respects as well as in others like them.
The Father, Son, and Holy Spirit resemble, rather, three lamps in a
dark house. The light of each is dispersed in the whole house, and the
eye cannot distinguish the light of one from the light of the others
or the light of all from the light of one. So also, the Father, Son, and
Holy Spirit are one God, even though each is fully God. That said,
the divine unity of the Father, Son, and Holy Spirit is incomparably
more pure, lofty, and real than both the light of the lamp and every
other refined entity among created beings, even the most refined.
Again, imagine that three men stand and recite a poem together and
that you are outside listening. You hear only a single poem, but you
do not doubt that each of them recited the complete poem, nor could
you say, "I heard three poems." This is the case even if in the voices
of the men there is some difference. As for the Father, Son, and Holy
Spirit, there is no difference among them at all, no difference that has
an effect on the hypostasis of one of them—other than that each is
different from the other. Indeed, it is even more appropriate that they
be one God, even if each is fully God. We find that people predicate
unity of nature of the name that refers to the nature, not only in
things that are refined, but also in things that are coarse. How is that?
If three pieces of pure gold were placed before you, you would say
that each of the three is fully gold and would not say that the three
are three golds, but rather that they are one gold. If this is so, then it
is even more appropriate that number not be predicated of the name

of the nature of the Father, Son, and Holy Spirit, nor that it be said that they are three gods.

***

. . . Certain foolish people ask Christians: Was it three or one that created the world? If you say three, they consider this loathsome. If you say one, they consider the other two hypostases nullified. Their minds' twisted logic impels them to their souls' destruction. To them we respond: It is one that created the world, and to say this does not prevent each of the other hypostases from being creator. If you would understand this, listen: You say: "The tongue of the prophet Moses spoke truth," and are right to do so. You say, "The prophet Moses spoke truth," and are right to do so. You cannot say, "The prophet Moses and his tongue spoke truth," for Moses spoke through his tongue. You say, "The sun gives light to human beings," and are right to do so. You say, "The rays of the sun give light to human beings," and are right to do so. You do not say, "The sun and its rays give light to human beings," for the sun gives light through its rays.

***

In the same way, one says, "The Father created the world" and "The Son created the world." One does not say, "The Father and the Son created the world," for the Father created the world through his Son. It is as St. Paul said, "In these last days God has spoken to us by his Son, through whom he created the world." It is also as the evangelist John said in his gospel concerning the Son (calling him "the Word"), "In the beginning was the Word, and the Word was with God, and the Word was God. He was with God; all things were made through him, and apart from him nothing was made." We do not think that the tongue and the mind or the rays and the sun . . . are more closely united than the Father and the Son—and this, because of the refinement of the divine essence, which is unimaginably more refined than the most refined creatures.

***

. . . The Son is to the Father as the . . . rays are to the sun and speech to the mind, notwithstanding that we hold the Son to be a full hypostasis—and this, because the divine nature is too refined to be found to have change with regard to any of its hypostases, as we have just said. For this reason, St. Paul called the Son "the light of the Father's glory," when he said, "In these last days God has spoken to us by his Son, through whom he created the world. He is the light of the Father's glory and the form of his essence." He also called him "the wisdom of God" and "his power" when he said, "Christ is the wisdom of God and his power," comparing him to God in the same way that the fire's heat is like the fire, for heat is the fire's power. So also, the evangelist John called him "Word" when he said, "In the beginning was the Word, and the Word was with God." Why did these two theologians refer to Christ with these names? It was not because Christ was not a hypostasis and fully God. Rather, it was to teach us the following: even as the annexed noun and the noun to which annexation is made are not said to do something, notwithstanding that each is said to do it by itself, so also, the Father and the Son are not said to create, even if each is said to create by itself. Be that as it may, these two theologians were loathe to predicate attributes that would induce those who hear to the conclusion that the Son does not have a hypostasis and that he is not fully God like the Father, even as each of these annexed nouns has not a hypostasis and is not called by the name of the noun to which it is annexed. For that reason, each of them also called the Son "God." John the evangelist said, "In the beginning was the Word, and the Word was with God, and the Word was God." He thus called him both "Word" and "God." St. Paul, too, said, "From the Jews, according to the flesh, Christ appeared, he who is God over all, who has praises and blessings." By saying this, John and Paul divested him of the attribute "Son" and indicated that it need not be said that both he and the Father created something; at the same time, by calling him "God," they taught that he is a full hypostasis and denied that the divine nature was subject to composition or that change was to be found with regard to each of its hypostases. All the theologians dealt in a similar fashion with the Holy Spirit: they annexed him to the Father in the same way that they annexed the Son to the Father, but then they said that he is a complete hypostasis like the Father and the Son. Now then, the Son and the Spirit are to the Father as such annexed entities are to that to which they are annexed. The holy church thus says that the Father created and that each of the others created, but does not say that they created together. On the one hand, in that the church teaches that the Son is fully God and that the Spirit is fully God, even though they are annexed to the Father in this manner, she hypostatically counts the Son and the Spirit with the Father and speaks of the Father, Son, and the Holy Spirit; and thus, by counting the Son and the Spirit hypostases with the Father, she has gone beyond the limit of those annexed entities, none of which are hypostatically counted with that to which they are annexed. On the other hand, in that the church teaches that the Father, Son, and Holy Spirit are one God—in the ways we mentioned earlier, even as the sun and its rays and its light are one sun, and so on—she says that the Father, Son, and Holy Spirit created [sing.] the world but does not say that they created it. Similarly, she says "Father, Son, and Holy Spirit have mercy [sing.] on me," but does not say, "Have mercy [pl.] on me." (Other similar examples could be cited.)

***

The ignorant ask the Christians: "Tell me. Do you deny every God other than the Father? Do you deny every God other than the Son? Do you deny every God other than the Holy Spirit?" If the Christian says, for instance, "I deny every God other than the Son," they respond, "The Father and the Holy Spirit, then, must not be God." If, however, the Christian says, "I do not deny every God other than Christ," they respond, "You have, then, multiple gods." Those who ask this must examine these matters in a subtle fashion and recognize that their question is crass. This will be clear to you from what follows. Imagine that a full gospel is placed before you and you are asked, "Do you believe in this gospel?" You respond, "Yes." It is then asked, "Do you deny every gospel other than it?" You answer, "Yes," even though you know that there are in the world an innumerable number of gospels. If the questioner were then to single out each of those gospels and ask about it, you would say, "I deny every gospel other than this." It does not follow from your words that each of those gospels is not a full gospel, for the gospel through which the Holy Spirit speaks is one. Similarly, you say, "I deny every God other than Christ," but your words do not entail that the Father and the Holy Spirit cease being each a full God. Here's why. When asked about the gospel placed before you, you were asked not about its hypostasis, but its essence (that is, its words, through which the Holy Spirit spoke), for the name "gospel" is not distinct to that book to the exclusion of others. Similarly, when asked, "Do you deny every God other than Christ," you were not asked about his hypostasis, even if the question hints at it, but only his nature, for the name "God" is not distinct to Christ to the exclusion of the Father and the Spirit. The name "God" is the name of a nature, not a hypostasis, even if the question hints at it, but only his nature, not a hypostasis, as we established above. For that reason, you can rightly say, "I deny every god other than Christ," without having the Father and Spirit cease from being each God. The question, instead, is equivalent to asking, "Do you deny every divine nature other than Christ's nature?" This you answer in the affirmative, and your answer is true, in that the Son's divine nature is the nature of the Father and the Spirit.

***

As we have already said, you must know that the divine nature is not subject to composition and that change has no effect on any of its hypostases; rather, it is wholly and purely simple, no divine hypostasis being able to have added to it anything that can have an effect on it. I want those of you who deny the Son and the Spirit for fear of believing in three gods to answer me this: Does God have a Word? If you say that he does not, you have both made him mute and made human beings better than him. There is no escape: you must say that God has a Word. We then ask: With regard to the Word of God, is he a part of God? If you say that he is a part of God, you ascribe parts to God and introduce composition into his nature, which cannot be;

nor can you say that God's Word is in God as form is in matter or anything else similar to that, for all this is excluded from God . . . You are thus compelled to make the Word a full hypostasis and to say that he is fully God. (The same can be said of God's Spirit.) We then say to you: God and his Word and his Spirit are one God even as a person and that person's word and spirit are one person; and the Word of God is God, in that the divine nature is not subject to composition or anything like composition, such as is the case with creatures. Now then, the Son is to God as a person's word is to that person, and the Spirit is to God as a person's spirit is to that person, even though the Word of God is God and the Spirit of God is God—and this, because of how exalted the divine nature is above composition and the like. Accordingly, God and his Word and his Spirit are not said to be other than one God, even as a person and that person's word and spirit are not said to be other than one person. Do you not see that a person's word is related to a person as the Word is related to God, and the same holds for the Spirit, though in a manner that is incomparably more exalted than is the case with an individual created being—and this, notwithstanding that the Son and the Spirit are fully God in the manner we have explained?

***

Thus, the Son is to God as the arm is to a person, and the Spirit is to God as the finger is to a person. Even as a person and that person's arm and finger are one and not three persons, so also God and his Son and Spirit are one and not three gods, even though both the Son and the Spirit are each fully God—and this, because of what we have explained about how the divine nature transcends division, composition, and the like.

***

As for those who believe in both the Torah and the gospel, as well as in the books that stand between these, let them not deny that the Father, Son, and Holy Spirit are one God, even if each is fully God. . . . They should know that they are required to accept the testimony of the scriptures that the Son and the Spirit are each fully

God. They should not let their intellects induce them to ignore the testimony of scripture, with the result that they say that it is not right that the Son is God and the Spirit is God and that both of them, along with the Father, are one God.

On Our Salvation
(late-eighth or early-ninth century)

Theodore Abu Qurrah (mid-eighth century–ca. 816)
Language: Arabic
Source: John C. Lamoreaux, *Theodore Abu Qurrah* (Provo, UT: Brigham Young University Press, 2005), 129–49.

In this third and final text from Abu Qurrah, we see a series of Christological and soteriological arguments deployed in what is likely an attempt to respond to Muslim objections. Abu Qurrah begins by asserting that humans have no way to make amends for their sin. In order to exact justice for sin and accomplish salvation, Christ, the Son, must experience the pain of the crucifixion. With this in mind, Abu Qurrah goes on to discuss the means by which the Son resides in a body and a lengthy proof that God has a Son.

Topics like the nature of sin and its relationship to humanity, salvation, and the work of Christ lay at the center of what distinguishes Christian from Muslim doctrine. Thus, a text like this, written in Arabic, helped to reveal the ways in which early-medieval Christians like Abu Qurrah rethought the distinctions of their faith in Muslim contexts.

***

. . . The penalty God imposed for any sort of disobedience is hanging over the heads of those who have fallen into that disobedience: those who have been disobedient are not in any way able to pay for themselves the required penalty and they have absolutely no escape from it.

***

Given what we have said, we human beings might expect one of two things from God: either he will forgive our sins freely and mercifully remit the penalty we owe for them, or he will demand—and justly so—that we give him full payment, in which case we go to eternal damnation.

***

The only way for human beings to escape their sins is for there to be some just cause, through which the law might be upheld. Further, the one who says this, if he were to allow that it is possible, he would have to conclude that there is no one who will not share with him in forgiveness through God's mercy, which is not so sparing that it does not encompass both the believer and the unbeliever—if in fact it abounds apart from some just cause.

***

The eternal Son, who was begotten of the Father before the ages, who shares the Father's essence and is his equal, in his mercy came down from heaven to Adam's seed and took up residence in the womb of the Virgin Mary, who had been purified through the Holy Spirit. He took from her a body that he fashioned for himself, along with a mind and a soul, and became a human being from the Holy Spirit and from the pure Virgin. He went forth into the world and allowed himself to experience the punishment that each of us merited because of our sins, namely, being beaten, being humiliated, being crucified, and experiencing death. If he had not become incarnate, there would have been no way for him to experience such pains, for in his divine essence he is neither seen nor touched, nor is he affected by suffering, pain, or harm. By becoming incarnate, however, he made it possible for himself to experience such suffering by exposing his body to it. His back he allowed to be beaten by whips, his head to be struck, his face to be spat upon, his hands and his feet to be nailed, his side to be pierced by a lance. He truly underwent these sufferings in his body, although none of them reached through to his divine nature. It is thus that he accomplished our salvation.

***

It is through this eternal Son alone, who endured and underwent for us these pains in his body, which he subjected to them, that we have forgiveness of sins. It is through his pains alone that we are delivered from the punishment we merit because of our sins. There is no way for anyone to have their sins forgiven or to be delivered from punishment for sin except through these pains that befell this Son.

***

All this, my friends, Christ accomplished for us through what he undertook to suffer for us, through his crucifixion and through the pains experienced in the body that he assumed from the pure Mary. It is thus that his summons is called the "gospel," that is, the "good news," for it proclaims to humanity the good news about how Christ saved them from that from which they were unable to save themselves. We give praise to Christ for his immeasurable grace.

***

[Perhaps you will say:] My friend, you have established that there is no way for [our sins to be forgiven except] through the pains that this [Son] experienced [and] allowed himself to suffer as [a ransom from the punishment] each of us merited [through sin]. It remains for you to explain [how this] Son, who is God and equal [to God], [was able to] be contained by a body, so as to be touched [by pains that would not otherwise have found] a way to befall him. To this, [we respond]: Notwithstanding that [God] is uncontained, uncircumscribed, and without limit, [he willed]—may he be blessed!—to appear to his creatures, by [manifesting his deeds and words to them] from a place appropriate for them. It was his kindness and beneficence that led him to do this for them. Indeed, if he had not done so, their minds would have been distracted . . . and they would have had neither peace nor repose . . . and their being agitated will not lead them . . . to grasp the one [through whom alone] they have rest.

This is [why] he made himself a throne and sat on it in heaven, from the time that he first created them: not because he needed a throne on which to sit but because they needed [to understand] the place of his dwelling, that they might worship [him in it] and that he might give them commands from it.

***

All the prophets thus agree that God sits on a throne. I do not [suppose that the people] of faith will disagree with the prophets about God's sitting on a throne. At the same time, none [of them] can say that because of his sitting [on a throne he is not everywhere in heaven]. Rather, all of us know that [God is in every place] and that he [fills the whole of heaven], notwithstanding that he shows himself to his angels [in heaven] only from the throne . . . it is to that place that the angels lift praise [to God] because of his residing there—and they do not do this in ignorance.

Similarly, we know that the eternal Son is in every place, that he is limited by nothing, that nothing contains him, and that he need not reside [in any particular] place. That said, the eternal Son—may he be blessed!—out of mercy, because of our need [for a savior], [took up residence in] the body he took from the pure Virgin Mary and [was subjected to] suffering and pain, which, when they befell him, ransomed us from the curse of the law. . . . He resided in it out of mercy, and this [body] became for us analogous to the throne in heaven, [for] the body, through the action of the divinity [which was joined to it through the purest and most exalted manner of union], [allowed] itself to suffer calamities as a ransom for human beings.

***

Perhaps you will say that the throne is pure while the human body is not its equal in this regard. We respond: In terms of its creation, the throne is not more pure than humanity. Indeed, both you and we say that God did not create anything more honorable than the human being. God did not abhor residing in the most honorable part of his creation. Rather, because of its precedence, this human creation was a fitter place for God to reside than the whole of creation: the impurity God abhors is sin alone.

As for the body that he took from Mary, no motion toward sin ever entered it. It is as St. Paul said, "He was like us in everything except for sin." Again, the prophet Isaiah said of him, speaking in the voice of the Father, "My sinful people led him to death. I shall requite the wicked for his burial and the rich for his death, for he had done no sin and no deceit was found in his mouth."

***

Christ's body is "the sun of righteousness," even as the prophets said. Similarly, Christ's body is to the divinity as the sun's body is to the light. Even as God created the light on the first day and then created the body of the sun on the fourth day and made that light he had created on the first day to take up residence in it, so also this body taken from Mary became the dwelling place of the divinity: from it, its light shone forth, and it manifested its deeds and words to the angels and to the whole of creation. This body was not taken from the Virgin Mary until the Holy Spirit had purified her of all stains of sin. The eternal Son took it from her as something immaculate, pure, and cleansed, ready for the divinity to reside in it. After the divinity took up residence in it, it became a fount, from which there flowed all the exalted features of the divinity, such as righteousness, wisdom, and might. Nonetheless, the eternal Son held back the glory of his divinity and did not manifest it in his body, since he was dwelling among human beings. [The eternal Son] let human actions such as eating, drinking, sleeping, and so on, be manifested in it, so that Satan might not recognize him and might make bold with him, so that through the people who obey him there might befall him those pains, the befalling of which was salvation from our sin and the nullification of Satan's just claim, which was against Adam, through his willingly entering into obedience to him. When he had completed his mission in this regard and had handed over his humanity for our sakes, he raised it on the third day and made flow from it all his glory. In it, he then ascended in glory to heaven, where with it he sat on the throne on which he had been before becoming incarnate. From there, those who love him await his coming in that body, on the clouds, with his angelic hosts, that he might judge the living and the dead and reward everyone for what they have done.

The Disputation of Patriarch Timothy I
with Caliph al-Mahdi (782/783)

Patriarch Timothy I (ca. 740–823)
Language: Syriac
Source: Alphonse Mingana, "Timothy's Apology for Christianity," in *Woodbrooke Studies: Christian Documents in Syriac, Arabic, and Garshuni*, vol. 2 (Cambridge, UK: W. Heffer and Sons Limited, 1928), 1–162.

The Nestorian Patriarch Timothy I was born in what is now northwestern Iraq. Consecrated a bishop and later catholicos-patriarch, Timothy functioned as both an ecclesiastical and diplomatic figure. In the latter role, he interacted with ʿAbbasid caliphs, one of which was the eighth-century Caliph al-Mahdi.

Timothy leaves behind him a small corpus of texts, most of which are letters in which we see his ecclesiastical and diplomatic skills at work. Among these letters, one of the most important for the study of Christian-Muslim relations is a Syriac account of an audience he had with al-Mahdi (referred to as "King" in the text) for the purpose of theological debate. This debate occurred over the course of two days, covering such theological themes as Christology and the Trinity and more mundane matters of religious practice (for example, circumcision and the direction of prayer). In addition, of particular interest is the discussion of Muhammad's significance for Christians, both as a prophet and as an anonymous biblical figure. In their discussion, both Timothy and al-Mahdi demonstrate familiarity with one another's Scripture.

The account of the disputation was popular among various Christian communities, judging by manuscript witness and translations from a wide range of periods. It also functioned as a source for other Christian works devoted to Islam. While many Christian apologetic and polemical texts were read—not necessarily by the communities they attacked (in this case,

45

Muslims) but by their fellow-believers—Timothy's disputation demonstrates that inter-religious discussion did indeed occur and was not uncommon in the history of Christian-Muslim relations.

***

Our God-loving King . . . said to me: "How is it that you accept Christ and the Gospel from the testimony of the Torah and of the prophets, and you do not accept Muhammad from the testimony of Christ and the Gospel?" And I replied to his Majesty: "O our King, we have received concerning Christ numerous and distinct testimonies from the Torah and the prophets. . . . These . . . show us Jesus Christ in a clear mirror and point to Him. So far as Muhammad is concerned I have not received a single testimony either from Jesus Christ or from the Gospel which would refer to his name or to his works."

And our benevolent and gracious King made a sign to mean that he was not convinced, then he repeated twice to me the question: "Have you not received any?" And I replied to him: "No, O God-loving King, I have not received any." And the King asked me: "Who is then the Paraclete?" And I answered: The Spirit of God." And the King asked: "What is the Spirit of God?" And I replied: "God by nature; and one who proceeds, by attribute; as Jesus Christ taught about Him." And our glorious King said: "And what did Jesus Christ teach about Him?" And I answered: "He spoke to His disciples as follows: 'When I go away to Heaven, I will send unto you the Spirit-Paraclete who proceedeth from the Father, whom the world cannot receive, who dwelleth with you and is among you, who searcheth all things, even the deep things of God, who will bring to your remembrance all the truth that I have said unto you, and who will take of mine and show unto you.'"

And our King said to me: "All these refer to Muhammad." And I replied to him: "If Muhammad were the Paraclete, since the Paraclete is the Spirit of God, Muhammad, would, therefore, be the Spirit of God; and the Spirit of God being uncircumscribed like God, Muhammad would also be uncircumscribed like God; and he who is uncircumscribed being invisible, Muhammad would also be invisible and without a human body; and he who is without a body being uncomposed, Muhammad would also be uncomposed. Indeed he who is a spirit has no body, and he who has no body is also invisible and he who is invisible is also uncircumscribed; but he who is circumscribed is not the Spirit of God, and he who is not the Spirit of God is not the Paraclete. It follows from all this that Muhammad is not the Paraclete. The Paraclete is from heaven and of the nature of the Father, and Muhammad is from the earth and of the nature of Adam. Since heaven is not the same thing as earth, nor is God the Father identical with Adam, the Paraclete is not, therefore, Muhammad.

". . . The Paraclete searches the deep things of God, but Muhammad owns that he does not know what might befall him and those who accept him. He who searches all things even the deep things of God is not identical with the one who does not know what might happen to him and to those who acknowledge him. Muhammad is therefore not the Paraclete. Again, the Paraclete, as Jesus told His disciples, was with them and among them while He was speaking to them, and since Muhammad was not with them and among them, he cannot, therefore, have been the Paraclete. Finally, the Paraclete descended on the disciples ten days after the ascension of Jesus to heaven, while Muhammad was born more than six hundred years later, and this impedes Muhammad from being the Paraclete. And Jesus taught the disciples that the Paraclete is one God in three persons, and since Muhammad does not believe in the doctrine of three persons in one Godhead, he cannot be the Paraclete. And the Paraclete wrought all sorts of prodigies and miracles through the disciples, and since Muhammad did not work a single miracle through his followers and his disciples, he is not the Paraclete."

***

"If he were mentioned in the Gospel, this mention would have been marked by a distinct portraiture characterising his coming, his name, his mother, and his people as the true portraiture of the

47

coming of Jesus Christ is found in the Torah and in the prophets. Since nothing resembling this is found in the Gospel concerning Muhammad, it is evident that there is no mention of him in it at all, and that is the reason why I have not received a single testimony from the Gospel about him."

And the God-loving King said to me: "As the Jews behaved towards Jesus whom they did not accept, so the Christians behaved towards Muhammad whom they did not accept." And I replied to his Majesty: "The Jews did not accept Jesus in spite of the fact that the Torah and the prophets were full of testimonies about Him, and this renders them worthy of condemnation. As to us we have not accepted Muhammad because we have not a single testimony about him in our Books." And our King said: "There were many testimonies but the Books have been corrupted, and you have removed them." And I replied to him thus: "Where is it known, O King, that the Books from which you have learned that the Books which we use have been corrupted? If there is such a book let it be placed in the middle in order that we may learn from it which is the corrupted Gospel and hold to that which is not corrupted. If there is no such a Gospel, how do you know that the Gospel of which we make use is corrupted? . . . To tell the truth, if I had found in the Gospel a prophecy concerning the coming of Muḥammad, I would have left the Gospel for the [Qur'an], as I have left the Torah and the Prophets for the Gospel."

And our King said to me: "Do you not believe that our Book was given by God?" And I replied to him: "It is not my business to decide whether it is from God or not. But I will say something of which your Majesty is well aware, and that is all the words of God found in the Torah and in the Prophets, and those of them found in the Gospel and in the writings of the Apostles, have been confirmed by signs and miracles; as to the words of your Book they have not been corroborated by a single sign or miracle. . . . Since signs and miracles are proofs of the will of God, the conclusion drawn from their absence in your Book is well known to your Majesty."

***

And our gracious and wise King said to me: "What do you say about Muhammad?" And I replied to his Majesty: "Muhammad is worthy of all praise, by all reasonable people, O my Sovereign. He walked in the path of the prophets and trod in the track of the lovers of God. All the prophets taught the doctrine of one God, and since Muhammad taught the doctrine of the unity of God, he walked, therefore, in the path of the prophets. Further, all the prophets drove men away from bad works, and brought them nearer to good works, and since Muhammad drove his people away from bad works and brought them nearer to the good ones, he walked, therefore, in the path of the prophets. Again, all the prophets separated men from idolatry and polytheism, and attached them to God and to His cult, and since Muhammad separated his people from idolatry and polytheism, and attached them to the cult and the knowledge of one God, beside whom there is no other God, it is obvious that he walked in the path of the prophets. Finally Muhammad taught about God, His Word and His Spirit, Muhammad walked, therefore, in the path of all the prophets.

"Who will not praise, honour and exalt the one who not only fought for God in words, but showed also his zeal for Him in the sword? As Moses did with the Children of Israel when he saw that they had fashioned a golden calf which they worshipped, and killed all of those who were worshipping it, so also Muhammad evinced an ardent zeal towards God, and loved and honoured Him more than his own soul, his people and his relatives. He praised, honoured and exalted those who worshipped God with him and promised them kingdom, praise and honour from God, both in this world and in the world to come in the Garden. But those who worshipped idols and not God he fought and opposed, and showed to them the torments of hell and of the fire which is never quenched and in which all evildoers burn eternally.

"And what Abraham, that friend and beloved of God, did in turning his face from idols and from his kinsmen, and looking only

49

towards one God and becoming the preacher of one God to other peoples, this also Muḥammad did. He turned his face from idols and their worshippers, whether those idols were those of his own kinsmen or of strangers, and he honoured and worshipped only one God."

***

And our King said to me: "You should, therefore, accept the words of the Prophet." And I replied to his gracious Majesty: "Which words of his our victorious King believes that I must accept?" And our King said to me: "That God is one and that there is no other one besides Him." And I replied: "This belief in one God, O my Sovereign, I have learned from the Torah, from the Prophets and from the Gospel. I stand by it and shall die in it."

***

And our victorious King said: "And what did impede the Prophet from saying that [three-lettered titles given to various chapters in the Qur'an] clearly referred to God, His Word and His Spirit?" And I replied to his Majesty: "The obstacles might have come from the weakness of those people who would be listening to such a thing. People whose ears were accustomed to the multiplicity of idols and false gods could not have listened to the doctrine of Father, Son, and Holy Spirit, or to that of one God, His Word, and His Spirit. They would have believed that this also was polytheism. This is the reason why your Prophet proclaimed openly the doctrine of one God, but that of the Trinity he only showed it in a somewhat veiled and mysterious way, that is to say through his mention of God, and of His Spirit and through the expressions 'We sent our Spirit' and 'We fashioned a complete man.' He did not teach it openly in order that his hearers may not be scandalized by it and think of polytheism, and he did not hide it completely in order that he may not deviate from the path followed by Moses, Isaiah, and other prophets, but he showed it symbolically by means of the three letters that precede the Surahs."

On the Proof of the Christian Religion
and the Proof of the Holy Trinity (ca. 815–825)

Abu Ra'itah al-Takriti (ca. late-eighth century–ca. 830)
Language: Arabic
Source: Sandra Toenies Keating, *Defending the "People of Truth" in the Early Islamic Period: The Christian Apologies of Abu Ra'itah* (Leiden, Neth.: Brill, 2006), 82–144.

Little is known about Abu Ra'itah. From the writings left to us, it appears that he was from the Christian city of Takrit near Baghdad and among the first generations of Arabic-speaking Christians. Some have suggested he was a Jacobite bishop, but the evidence that exists indicates only that he was a theologian.

Living at a time when there was increasing pressure for Christians to adapt to the world of Islam and even convert, Abu Ra'itah wrote his theological treatises—among the first to do so in Arabic—as a means for articulating Christian doctrine in a world influenced by the language and religion of Islam. This first text by Abu Ra'itah, one of his earliest, is another example of a treatise that functioned as a means for helping readers discern the true religion. In this effort, Abu Ra'itah covers a broad range of theological topics including the Trinity and Christology as well as matters of Christian practice. Of particular interest here are the arguments at the beginning of the treatise that focus on the reasons one might have for belonging to a religion.

***

Since it has been shown that the Christian law differs from [these] six kinds [of false reasons to belong to a religion], it remains that the characteristic of it, the inherent property belonging to it, is that it is evident and demonstrated to be above every religion by the confirmation of the Lord of the Worlds, Who confirmed with it those who proclaimed [the Christian law] through signs and miracles and clear proofs which led all of the peoples to accept it willingly.

51

So [motivation for] the peoples' acceptance of the Christian religion is clear: in spite of the diversity of their inclinations and the break from their origins [such an acceptance necessitated], [in spite of] differences in their values, great distance between their lands, the divergence of their intentions, not to speak of their [diverse] practices and word usages, [they accepted it] without [prompting by] worldly desires or fear, without aspiring to a known afterlife, without approval and embellishment, without licentiousness or permissiveness, without collusion to revive the prestige of [one's heritage] in order to attain what is hoped for.

***

. . . He has adorned [them]—His company [of Apostles], namely, gave life to the dead in His name, they opened [the eyes] of the blind by His permission and healed the lepers by His strength, and [performed] other wonders by His power and visible and perceptible marvels that no one is able to reject, be he king or servant, high-born or low-born, educated or ignorant, wise or foolish. They proved the authenticity of their proclamation by these true signs, and were able, because of these, to dispense with its authentication through embellished and affected speech, practiced style, with setting aright what is absurd, joining together what is unknown, and explicating what is obscure, because the word is able to be rejected without difficulty and refuted, even when it [has reached] the greatest [level of] credibility and clarity. But it is not possible to deny and reject the signs and wonders in [one's] heart, even if the tongue denies them because of prior envy or hatred.

***

For this is the customary practice of God, from the first to the last [peoples], in the establishment of His religion and erecting His banner and affirming His proof for His creation: correction through signs and clarification through miracles, which are not comprehended by creaturely understanding and are not located in the memory of a created heart; [it is] not in the many opinions, nor eloquent speech, nor the strength and courage [of human beings], as I have described.

Since this has happened, it is not justified to battle Christianity and to remain firm [against it] with unswerving opinions and eloquent speech, because they are incapable of attaining the essence of its truth and reaching the utmost limit of its veracity, as I have [already] described before this. [In fact,] the place [where] the elucidation [necessary] to reach the utmost limit of its veracity [is found] is in the signs and wonders which humble obstinate difficulties [in the search for the truth] and overcome hardness of heart or uncertain comprehension and perception of a being which is being described in itself. Can an opinion, that is, [any] statement, be certain [and] complete in comprehension? Our statement (that is, a description of our opinion) is incapable of attaining a description of something whose description cannot be attained, nor the perception of it in its essence or the knowledge of this or the confession of it.

A clear indication and an evident proof confirming our teaching and the correctness of what we say is what we have said about the leaders of Christianity and what we have taken from the Old and New Books of God, which confirms the truth of their proclamation by what we have described of the signs and wonders, without [resorting to] opinion or analogy.

The First Risalah *on the Holy Trinity* (ca. 815–828)

Abu Ra'itah al-Takriti (ca. late-eighth century–ca. 830)
Language: Arabic
Source: Sandra Toenies Keating, *Defending the "People of Truth" in the Early Islamic Period: The Christian Apologies of Abu Ra'itah* (Leiden, Neth.: Brill, 2006), 164–215.

In this risalah (letter or treatise), Abu Ra'itah builds on his exposition of Trinitarian doctrine in earlier works. Much time is spent defining important terms related to the Trinity, and Abu Ra'itah makes extensive use of analogy, Aristotelian logic, and scriptural proofs in a complex defense of one of Christianity's central tenets.

Of particular concern for Abu Ra'itah is the need to give readers a means by which to defend their belief in a Trinity in unity before those who might disagree with them and to ensure that such a defense stands up to rational criticism (hence the repetition of the phrase "If they say . . .").

***

Do you say that "one" may only be spoken of in three ways: either as genus, or as species, or as number? No one among you who is reasonable will regard this as an innovation.

***

If you say, "How are you able to describe God as 'one in number' neither [as] a part, nor as a perfect [whole]?," it should be said to you: We describe Him as one perfect in *ousia*, not in number, because He is in number (that is, in *hypostaseis*) three. [This] description of Him is perfect in both ways: When we describe Him as one in *ousia*, then He is exalted above all His creatures, be it His perceptible or His intellectually comprehensible creation—nothing is comparable to Him, nothing is mixed with Him; He is simple, without density, incorporeal, His *ousia* approaches everything closely without blending or mixing.

And [we describe Him] in number because He encompasses all of the species of number. For number can only be counted in two species: even and odd. These two types are included in the three *hypostaseis*. In whatever manner we describe Him, nothing is equivalent to His perfect description. So you know: We describe God as one, [but] not as you describe Him. This is the beginning of our statement on this.

***

. . . They will . . . ask us: "How can a single thing be continuous and divided [simultaneously]? Do you not understand what you describe?" . . . On the contrary, . . . we only describe [God] by continuity in *ousia*, and by dissimilarity in the individuals, that is the *hypostaseis*. If they refuse this description because it is obscure to them, and say that this is contradictory because the one whose *ousia* is other than his *hypostaseis*, and whose *hypostaseis* are something other than his *ousia* cannot be described because it is contradictory and not appropriate, it should be said to them: Have we described [God's] *ousia* as other than His *hypostaseis* as you have described?

If they say: "Nonetheless, you meant this when you assert that the manner of [God's] unity is different from the manner of His division, and the manner of His division is different from the manner of His unity," it should be said to them: The issue is not as you think it is. We only describe [God] as unified in *ousia* and divided in the *hypostaseis*, and [God's] *ousia* is His *hypostaseis*, and His *hypostaseis* are His *ousia*, as with the placement of three lights in one house.

None of us thinks that we mean three lamps, rather, we mean their light, even though God, blessed is He, is above every analogy. For the lights are three and one—they are identical with each other. They are three because each one of them is self-subsistent and enduring in its being, even if there is no obstruction in the space between it and the other lights, and [they are] one, because they are all united in light. And the demonstration of this (that they are one and three [simultaneously]) is that each one of them is not the others in the proper state of its being. Because, were one of these lamps to be removed from the house, its light would be removed with it, and nothing of it would remain.

If they say: "Is it possible that the three lights exist apart from three lamps? In this way, you describe the three *hypostaseis* as having a source, like [the] source of the lights of the lamps previously mentioned," then it must be said to them: . . . When we briefly described the lights, which are above all of the senses and all knowledge, we are not compelled to describe each one of them as having a cause. Rather, one of them is the cause of the other two, without beginning and without time. And the two are related to the one in a substantial, natural relation. And both are something perfect from something perfect, just as Eve and Abel, who are from Adam, are something perfect from something perfect. And the two of them are related to Adam by a substantial relation. They are one in humanity, and three in *hypostaseis*.

The *ousia* of the Godhead is the three *hypostaseis*, and the three *hypostaseis* of the *ousia* of the Godhead are the *ousia*. For the difference between the *ousia* [and] the single *hypostasis* is like the difference between a whole thing and one of its properties, because its difference lies in the plurality of what it consists of, not in the *ousia*. So the whole of humanity (that is, all humans) is not differentiated, as Moses to Aaron (that is, the individuals), except it consists of a plurality.

***

If they say: "If these three *hypostaseis*, according to you, occur in the *ousia*, then each one of them is described by a proper attribute of [one of] the others: begetter, or begotten, or processing, so that there is no difference between one and the other," they should be answered: By my life! If each one of them were not a perfect *hypostasis*, particularized from the others by a property, then each one of them would exist just as you have described. However, when each one of them exists as a perfect *hypostasis*, bound by its property which differentiates it from the others, then none of them are required to take on the attribute of the other as a property. Rather, each one of them is recognized by its own property: the Father by His Fatherhood, and the Son by His Sonship, and the Spirit by His Procession from the Father.

And the difference of their properties is not something which makes its *ousia* different, like Adam and Abel and Eve, whose *ousia* is one with no difference in it, because all of them are human beings.

***

If they say: "If the three *hypostaseis* described by you as divine have the same relationship to each other according to your account as Adam and Abel and Eve, then what obstacle stands between you and describing them as three gods, just as Adam and Abel and Eve are described as three human beings?," then they should be answered: It is only permitted to describe Adam and Abel and Eve as three human beings on account of the difference which exists between them. It is absolutely not possible that [a difference] like [this] exists in these three [divine] *hypostaseis*.

If they say: "What is this difference which separates Adam and Abel and Eve from each other, of which nothing like it exists in these *hypostaseis* you described as divine? Clarify it for us, so that we can know it," then they should be answered: We shall clarify it for you, since you have asked us this. Their first difference is that they have a beginning and an end. Some of them are older than the others in existence, because they became beings at different times, and lived earlier and later [than the others].

Further, they require completely separate places, so that their bodies can grow. And they are different in power and in ambition, because they are not equal in power and ambition. They are endowed with difference in even more than what we have mentioned: the difference of each one of them within himself, so that there is scarcely [a] blink of an eye, or a moment [when] he is peaceful. For this and similar [reasons], Adam and his wife and his son are described as three human beings.

As for the One Who is in agreement in all of His affairs, Who is harmonious in all of His states, [both] earlier and later, but utterly first [and] only, before and after, above the need of a place on account of He being spirit and the immateriality of His *ousia*, without difference in His power and without variation in His will, nor in His operations: one *ousia*. How is it possible to describe one whose state is this as three gods?

***

If they say: "How is it possible that you describe God with these attributes of continuity and division simultaneously? Is it not the case that continuity is anticipated by a division, or a division is preceded by continuity?," it must be said to them: . . . Tell us about the sun and its light and its heat: Is it continuous, one part with another part, or is it separate and not continuous? Or does it have both attributes together, I mean continuity and division? Now, does its continuity precede its division, or does its division precede its continuity? Or did it have both states together from the beginning at its creation, as we have described? And what do you say about the five bodily senses: Are [they] continuous, one part bound in the body with another part, or are they divided and separated, and [the body is] not bound to them? Or do they have things in common?

***

Now, does continuity precede division in the senses of the body, or does division anticipate continuity? For if the soul and the body and the senses are creatures, created things [which are] continuous and divided simultaneously without continuity anticipating division, and division [preceding] continuity, then [this] is established as fact as we have described [it, namely] that God, may He be praised! is three *hypostaseis* bound through the coincidence of their *ousia*, and separated through the state of existence of the being of each one of them, without their continuity preceding division and division [preceding] continuity.

***

Now, if they say: "What prompts you to describe God, May He be praised! as three *hypostaseis* rather than ten or twelve, or fewer than this or more?," it should be said to them: Truly, we do not describe Him as three *hypostaseis* instead of one *ousia*. These three *hypostaseis* are one *ousia* in all aspects. It is not possible to find an equivalent or a likeness for this.

As for when you say: "What prompts you to describe three *hypostaseis* without adding or subtracting?," we say that that which prompts us to describe [God] by this attribute is the existence of the *hypostaseis* themselves. Because they, without ceasing to be three, are one *ousia*. As we have already explained, God possesses knowledge and spirit, and the knowledge of God and His spirit are permanent and perpetual, not ceasing. For it is not permitted in a description of God, May He be glorified! that He be described in His eternity without knowledge or spirit.

***

All people should see how God is described in every religion. When a religion finds that it describes God by the attribute "nothing is like Him," then it [truly] worships of Him and knows Him. And if a religion discovers [that] it describes God with anthropomorphism and comparison with creatures, then ignorance of Him is its perpetual goal. Each of those professing the unity of God, with the exception of the Christians, do not hesitate to describe Him as one, single, and numberable.

***

. . . When it is found that He is three *hypostaseis* and one *ousia*, then His description is above every comparison and likeness [with creatures], because it is not possible that a single *ousia* [having] three *hypostaseis*, which is identical in all of its essences, exists in creation.

This description of God is true, without adding or subtracting, for His description is perfect in two ways. [It is perfect] with regard to the number [one], because [the *hypostaseis*] are identical in every way with what describes their essences, and [they are perfect] with regard to the [number] three, because it isolates the substantial being of each one of them. [This description is also true] because of the perfection of the species of number, for the species of number are two: The even [numbers] are one and the odd [numbers] are one. And the two exist in [the number] three. Now, more than three are a repetition in the number, and fewer than [three] are a decrease in it, and no person having good judgement accepts this in a description of God.

***

Now it is necessary for us to notice in the teaching about analogy that "God" is not counted as a single one, in keeping with the witnesses of the [sacred] books, cautioning the one who differs from us, and strengthening with support the one who follows us, even if the ones who differ from us on it declare it to be false when they claim we have altered [the sacred books] by adding to them and taking away from them.

The intimate friend of God, Moses, said about God that at the creation of Adam, [He said]: "Let Us fashion a human being in Our image and Our likeness." He did not say: "I shall fashion [a human being] in My image and My likeness."

***

You recall that in your book, . . . similar to what we have referred to from the sayings of Moses and Daniel, is written in accounts concerning God: "We said," "We created," "We commanded," "We inspired," "We destroyed," and "We annihilated," along with many others comparable to these. Does one who thinks doubt that these words are the speech of several and not the speech of one single [individual]?

If they say: "The Arabs permit this [type] of speech," it should be said to them: If it were the Arabs alone who had invented it, then they could refer to it [as an argument]. However, since the Hebrews, the Greeks, and the Syrians, and other languages anticipate the Arabs in this [type of] speech, what they describe as permitted for the Arabs is not evidence for this.

***

If they say: "When [God] says: 'We sent' and 'We commanded' and 'We revealed,' this is a reverence to God and to honor Him and show respect," it should be said to them: By my life! If this were not said of what is not deserving of glorification, then your teaching would be permissible. However, if one who is mean and base is greatly exalted by it, your teaching that this is a glorification for Him is not proven. So you should know that God is one and three when He speaks in both [types] of utterances: "I commanded" and "We commanded" and "I created" and "We created" and "I revealed" and "We revealed." For "I commanded," "I revealed" and "I created" indicate that His *ousia* is one, and "We commanded," "We revealed" and "We created" indicate three *hypostaseis*.

The clarification of this is from the teaching of Moses the Prophet.

He reports in the Torah concerning Abraham, the Friend of God, saying: "God appeared to Abraham [while] he was before the door of his tent in the place of such and such. As the daylight became hot, Abraham sat before the door of his tent. He lifted his eyes, and beheld three men standing before him. So he stood, facing them, and bowed to them, and said: 'Lord, if you regard me with merciful eyes, then do not pass by your servant.'"

Do you not see that those who Abraham saw with his own eyes were three in number, because he said "three men," yet he called them one Lord, humbling himself before Him, and asking Him to stay with him? Now the number three is a *mysterion* for the three *hypostaseis*. And he called them "Lord," not "Lords." [This is] a *mysterion* for one *ousia*. So in three can be one, just as we have described. Then Moses also reports: "Hear, O Israel, your God is one Lord." This means that God, Who is described by three *hypostaseis*, is one Lord.

***

Now, if they deny this teaching, and reject it, saying: "The prophets did not say this, rather, you have altered the words from their places, and you have made [the prophets] say what is false and a lie," it should be said to them: If these books were only in our possession, and not [also] in the hands of our enemies the Jews, then, by my life! one could accept your teaching that we have changed [them] and substituted [words for other words]. However, if the books are also in the hands of the Jews, no one can accept your teaching, unless it were found that the books that we possess differ: [But] what is in the hands of the Jews is in harmony with what we possess.

If they say: "Those who are responsible for the alteration [of the books] are the Jews, who are attempting to deceive you with this," we should say to them: If the matter were as you have described, then there ought to be in their possession genuine [copies which have] not been altered. Because the one who seeks the destruction of another does not seek his own destruction. Now, we find what they possess and what we possess to be one [and the same], with no difference in it, just as we have pointed out. [Consequently,] no one can accept what you have reported about alteration.

***

Now, if they say: "Is the name 'God,' according to you, the name of the *ousia* [in general]? Then you ought not describe each one of [the *hypostaseis*] as God, instead of all three of them [together as God], since, according to you, they are [collectively] the *ousia*." It should be said to them: Certainly, if the name "God" is the name of an *ousia*, that is, the name of all three of them, then each one of them is entitled to be called by the name of the whole.

For [none of them] is different in its being from the being of another of the *hypostaseis*, together with which it is the *ousia* in general, just as the name of "gold" in general is for all gold, and for a piece of gold. It is perfect, not [just] a part of what is golden. Now, when one of the *hypostaseis* is mentioned, it is permitted that it be described as "God," and "Lord," and "*ousia*," and other names for the *ousia* like this, but [it is] not [permitted to describe the individual *hypostasis*] by the plurality of the collective. And if two [*hypostaseis*] are brought into relation to the one, that is, the Son and the Spirit to the Father, then they are described as "one God."

Now if they say: "If the Father is the cause of the Son and the Spirit, as you have described, then it ought to be the case that the Father [exists] before the one of which He is the cause. And if the Father does not [exist] before the Son and the Spirit, and they exist eternally together, then one of [the *hypostaseis*] is not [more] worthy than the others of being the cause of [the others]. And your teaching that one is the cause of two is false."

It should be said to them: By my life! Some causes, such as you have described, [exist] before those [things] for which they are the cause. However, this is not as you have described with all causes. You see the sun, and it is the cause of its rays and its heat. In the same way fire is the cause of its light and its heat. And it is never lacking its light and its heat. The teaching about the Son and the Spirit from the Father is the same as this: [They are] two [things which are] eternal from [something] eternal, although the Father does not anticipate them.

The Second Risalah on the Incarnation
(ca. 815–822; after The First Risalah)

Abu Ra'itah al-Takriti (ca. late-eighth century–ca. 830)
Language: Arabic
Source: Sandra Toenies Keating, *Defending the "People of Truth" in the Early Islamic Period: The Christian Apologies of Abu Ra'itah* (Leiden, Neth.: Brill, 2006), 222–97.

The second risalah builds on the arguments Abu Ra'itah lays out in his previous work. In fact, the text is written to the same audience and serves a similar purpose. In this treatise, however, Abu Ra'itah turns his attention to the doctrine of the incarnation, making use of a series of analogies and scriptural proofs.

It is also in this treatise that readers see more extensive use of qur'anic phrases in Abu Ra'itah's effort to articulate Christian doctrine in an Islamic context. For readers who found themselves in daily contact with Muslims, Abu Ra'itah's work—based on common Muslim objections to Christian doctrine—provided them with a means and the confidence by which to explain their faith.

***

If they say: "Are you claiming that God, His remembrance is exalted! dwells in this body?," it should be said to them: Of course! We describe Him as dwelling in the body in the manner of [His] incarnation in it, not the "dwelling" that is sent out [from God], like His dwelling in creatures other than Himself.

If they say: "If He dwells in the body, as you have described, then the body confines Him, and what is confined is limited, and what is limited is created. Is God therefore a creature, according to your claims?," it should be said to them: Certainly, what you have described must be necessary for God. Your syllogism has accurate and true premises, just as when one maintains that the human being is an *ousia*, and demonstrates this, saying that the human being is living, and what is living is an *ousia*. The syllogism returns to its first part, so he says: "The human being is without a doubt an *ousia*." The syllogism is formulated from true and accurate premises.

However, if his syllogism is formulated from false premises that should be rejected and denied, certainly it is not possible that the conclusion of the syllogism will be accurate. As when one states, "The human being is eternal, eternity has no beginning, the human being is, therefore, God," his syllogism is formulated from many premises, the first of which is false. For if the beginning of the syllogism is formulated invalidly, then the conclusion will not result in the truth, even if the premises linked to it are accurate and true. This is the same as what you have argued, [when you say] that the body confines the Word, and you build the syllogism on a premise that should be rejected, adding further accurate and acceptable premises. Then you reach the conclusion [you desire] with what you set out, although the conclusion is not necessarily what you have described.

If they say: "How are we building our syllogism on a premise that should be rejected, as you have described? Have you not made it necessary that the Word [of God] dwells in the body? Then it must be one of two things: Either the body is encompassed by [the Word] which has come into it, or the Word grasps it, then [the body] is devoid of [the Word], just as [all of] the rest of bodies," it should be said to them: If we have made it necessary that the Word dwells in the body, we have [also] denied that it dwells in it in a similar [manner] to its dwelling in the rest of bodies. We have only described its dwelling in the body as a dwelling of "incarnation" in it, not like a dwelling [of the Holy Spirit] sent out [by God].

Yet, it is necessary that you ask us: According to your affirmation of the dwelling of the Word in the body, does [the body] encompass it, or not? Now, if we say it encompasses it, you are permitted to pursue the syllogism, [saying]: In what does this result? And if we deny this, you must pay attention to what is necessary for us [to make the argument]. For we are obligated to set out for you sound evidence, that should not be rejected nor denied.

If they say: "Verily, can something dwell in something [else] without being encompassed by it?," it should be said to them: Either [it is something] in corporeal things, and then it is not possible that one dwells in another, without being encompassed by it, or [it is something] which does not have a body, and it is not possible for the body to encompass it when it dwells in it. Rather, the body is encompassed by it, as is the case of the light embodied in the disc of the sun, just as fire is embodied in coal and so, [too,] the soul is incarnated in the body. For the disc of the sun is encompassed by its light, not [the light by the sun]; and the coal is encompassed by the fire burning in it, [the fire] is not [encompassed] by the coal; and the body is encompassed by the soul, not [the soul] by [the body].

The sun and its light, and the coal and its fire, and the soul and its body are a *mysterion* for the incarnation of the Word of God in the body. For just as each one of these three things mentioned is embodied in what embodies it, without change in its state or alteration in its *ousia*, and without the thing with which it is embodied being two, but rather that it is in truth one, just so is it in the teaching on the Word of God: [It is an] [i]ncarnation [of the Word in] a body possessing a soul, through Mary, the immaculate, without change in its state nor alteration in its *ousia*, without being limited by the body; rather, the body is limited by [the Word]. And [the Word] and the body are one in a real and eternal union, without difference [like that which] occurs in number, and they are not drawn to become two. Yet, a substantial distinction is inherent in [the body] and enduring in it, just like the substantial distinction between the sun and the fire and the soul, and those [things] which are embodied in them.

Now if they say: "Why do you deny that the body contains and limits the Word, yet you make it necessary that [the Word] is in it, just as it is in other corporeal things and bodies? It must be one of two things: Either all of the things that it is in have a body, or that body you have described, which [the Word took] to itself to became incarnated in, is not a body, since [the Word] is in [the body] without limit, as it is in other things," it should be said to them: Why should this descending [of the Word] into the body happen in the same way as its descending into everything else, for it is incarnated in [the body] and is united with it, and is in [other] things without being incarnated in them nor united with them? If we had described [the Word] so in its body, by my life! then you are right. But since our descriptions of [the Word] in its body and in [other] things are different, it is necessary for you to examine what we have described.

Similarly, the light of the sun is described in its disc and in the air and on the earth and on a house and other things with different relations and in many ways, because [the light] is bound up in [the sun's] disc and it is incarnated in it, and the air encloses it, uniting with it, without there being a composite or persisting union, and on the earth and house it is the same. [It is also] like [the relationship of] the sight of the eye of the viewer to the things [it sees]: The seeing is associated with the eye and with the things seen by it, yet [the sight] does not take possession over what it is associated with, because [the sight] is incarnated and bound up with its eye, without being united or a composite with the things, both those near and far. And it is like the intellect in the soul, through which it is rational, and other [things] that do not need to be described [here] in order restrict [ourselves] to what precedes us.

It is the same with the teaching about the Word of God, may He be praised! [The Word] is described in its [own] body and in things: in its body as a united composite, lasting and eternal, and in things as one that has no limit and no end, without being bound up with them or embodied in them. Because it is not possible of an attribute of God, may He be praised! that He be described as [being] in one place to the exclusion of another place, since He is in everything, without limit, exalted over everything, without end, there is nothing, praise to Him! in which He is embodied or with which He is a composite, except that pure body [of Christ], as we have described.

Now if they say: "Is there a separation or differentiation between the body in which He became incarnated, and the rest of bodies, since you describe it as created?," it should be said to them: From the perspective of the creation, no; [from the perspective] of the union and honor and esteem, there is a great [difference] between them and that [body] in which He became incarnated and with which He united Himself. For He adorned it with His [own] ornamentation, He clothed it with His light and the garment of His rank, enclosing it in the rays of His brightness, and filled it with His holiness, so that it became living, pure and holy, like the coal, described as burning, becomes luminous and light-giving, and anything else with which one describes fire, without the coal being two [different things]. Rather, [the coal] is one from two: from immaterial fire and a perceptible corporeal body, without the fire changing its *ousia*, or the corporeal thing [changing] its nature.

***

[After asserting that sin marred creation, the author anticipates a rebuttal and writes:] Now, if they say: "Did He not have the power to deliver them without becoming a human being?," it should be said to them: Certainly, may He be praised! He is powerful over what He wills. However, He did not will that their salvation and deliverance would be an act from Him alone without them, in order not to deprive them of the reward from following Him, because the reward and recompense comes to [the ones who do] the work [earning] the reward, not the work of others on their behalf. And what would have caused Him, may He be praised! not to become human to save those whom His goodness has caused Him to create?

***

If they say: "Would it not have been better, if He had sent someone else, either an angel or someone from among the holy people, for the salvation and deliverance of the world, than to have carried it out Himself?," it should be said to them: It would not have been better if

He had entrusted it to someone other than Himself, either an angel or someone else. For just as it is necessary for Adam and his descendents to worship [God] because He created them, so it would be necessary [for them] to worship the One who had been entrusted with their deliverance and salvation. Because their deliverance is the renewal of their creation, and it is impossible that someone other than the One who was entrusted with producing them renew their creation.

To be sure, He sent [to the people] some, such as Noah, Abraham, Moses, and other prophets and messengers, but each one of them was a warner to his people in his own time. But all of [the people] did not follow [the prophet], they only followed him a little for a short time, then they returned to what they were before, being overpowered by error. Also, these messengers were afflicted by weakness [themselves], because they were creatures, not outside of the destruction [of sin], although it was not master over them, as it mastered the [rest] of the people. When one of them was killed or died, he was not worthier [than the others] of the ability to [be resurrected and to] return, and this led their tribe to abandon them and to scorn their commands when they did not have the power to raise themselves up after their deaths.

Because of this and similar things, which we do not describe [here, God], may He be praised! did not send another to deliver and save the world. His compassion and mercy caused Him, Whose praise is exalted! [to effect] the [i]ncarnation of the Word, which can be described [thus]: It is begotten from the Father without beginning, Perfect from a Perfect, true God from true God. And the reason He describes Himself as "son" is in the identity of His being with the being of the One from Whom He was begotten in all relations of His being, in the same way the being of each one of [the relations] is identical with the being of His Father, although what is necessary for created fathers and sons is not necessary for Him.

[The Word] became a human being without change in its *ousia*, and delivered humanity and saved it from error through the proclamation of faith and [good] works. And this was shown to be true to [humanity] when [the Word] raised itself with the body into eternity, after its body had been killed. This is the reason why [people] desire [the Word] and make [His] glorification the highest object [of worship] and feel themselves compelled to His service, because they recognize the difference between His state and the state of all other creatures.

If they say: "Your understanding is astonishing, how it bears this teaching and believes in a God Who dies and is killed! Tell us about someone who dies: Is it possible that he is alive, and about [someone] who is not living: Is it possible that he is the God Who rules [all of creation]? When you make it necessary that He died, then He ceased [to exist], and when He ceased [to exist], then the rule and government [of creation] ceased, and when government ceased, then the world remained without a Ruler," it should be said . . . The teaching about the Messiah, may He be praised! is like this: He was killed, died in His body, and is living, not killed in His divinity, and He is one, not two.

The Apology of al-Kindi
(unknown; proposed ninth century)

'Abd al-Masih b. Ishaq al-Kindi (ca. late-eighth century–early ninth century)
Language: Arabic (Karshuni)
Source: N. A. Newman, ed., *The Early Christian-Muslim Dialogue* (Hatfield, PA: Interdisciplinary Biblical Research Institute, 1993), 381-545. This is an edited and slightly revised version of the unpublished translation by Anton Tien.

Nothing is known about al-Kindi beyond conjecture. We do not know his place of birth or his exact Christian confession. We cannot even be sure that his name is anything more than a pseudonym. His name means "son of the Messiah, son of Isaac," and his family name (nisbah) indicates his connection to the Christian tribe of Kinda. In the apologetic text associated with his name, al-Kindi's interlocutor is Isma'il al-Hashimi, or Ishmael from the Banu Hashim, the prophet Muhammad's tribe. Thus, the two names could be a rhetorical invention dramatizing a debate between the descendants of Sarah and the descendants of Hagar.

The treatise is structured as an exchange of letters between al-Hashimi and al-Kindi, each one inviting the other to convert based upon what is presumed to be a superior defense of his religion. Al-Kindi goes to great lengths to defend Christian doctrine but also deploys aggressive polemic in attacks upon Muhammad, the Qur'an, and Muslim beliefs and practices.

Significantly, The Apology of al-Kindi *is arguably the most well-known text of its kind written by an Arabic-speaking Christian. The text enjoys wide manuscript witness in both Arabic and Latin translations. It was even part of the monumental translation project of Islamic source material commissioned by Peter the Venerable in the twelfth century. As such, it was one of the main sources of information about Islam for many Christians in the medieval period.*

***

Now in regard to this question which you raise as to the religion you profess, "the orthodox faith" as you are pleased to call it; you protest that you are of the faith of our father Abraham, and affirm that he was an orthodox Muslim. . . . And, first of all, you tell me that you have read the scriptures and studied the sacred canon, particularly the Law, as revealed to Moses by God Most High, who imparted to him those mysteries which are contained in the first book, Genesis. You know then that Abraham dwelt with his father in Haran . . . worshipping the idol called al-'Uzza, known in Haran as the moon god, according to the custom of the people there. . . . This idol was worshipped with Abraham along with his father and forefathers and the people of the land. Yet you, an orthodox believer, claim that he was orthodox in so doing. . . . That is to say, [Abraham] abandoned an "orthodoxy" which meant the worship of idols, and became a worshipper of the one God and a true believer. For we find what you call "orthodoxy" is described by the Word of God as idolatry.

The doctrine of the unity of God was bequeathed by Abraham as a precious legacy to Isaac, the child of promise.

***

[God] proclaims the unity, and then proceeds to repeat the glorious name three times [in Exod. 3:11-15]. Do you suppose there are three gods? Or one three times affirmed? If we should say there are three gods, we should be polytheists using . . . misleading language; whereas if we say there is one God thrice affirmed, we do justice to the truth as it is written. . . . And what is it if not the one God in three persons? How can the point be proved more plainly? It is clearly as daylight to anyone who is not determined to resist the truth and eager to deceive himself, who is not blind and deaf. God enshrined this mystery in the scriptures as written by the prophets, which are still, God be gracious to you, in the hands of those who read the Law. Yet what was the result? It was not understood till Christ our Lord came, Master of all mysteries, and discovered it to us.

***

. . . I must ask you, in regard to this One, whose unity you now summon me to acknowledge, how do you understand He is one and in how many senses may it be said of one that He is one? . . . Do you not know that one cannot be said to be one except in one of three senses, either generically, specifically or numerically? . . . If you say He is generically one, then, as one genus, He includes various species; for the category of generic unity is that which includes an indefinite number of various species. But such reasoning is inapplicable to God, most High. If you say He is specifically one, then He is the one species which includes various individuals; for the category of the species includes within it a plurality of individuals. But, if you say He is numerically one, you contradict your own affirmation that He is one, sole, eternal. . . . And how can you reasonably accept a definition of the Deity which gives Him no preference over the rest of His creatures? I should like to know why, if you are going to describe

Him numerically, you do not proceed to divide Him and subtract from Him as well. Do you not see . . . that the single unit is only part of Number as a whole?

***

If, on the other hand, you suggest that He is one in essence, we must further interrogate you. In your judgment does specific unity exclude numeric unity; or do you hold that the specifically one is numerically one as well, in as much as He is all-inclusive? If you say that they exclude each other, we must remind you that in the judgment of all who are versed in the laws of language and the rules of logic, the category of specific unity is regarded as including various individuals, whereas, taken one by one, each stands for itself. Do you then affirm that God is one in essence as including various persons, or do you affirm Him a single personality?

***

. . . We describe Him as One, perfect in essence, threefold in His personality. This definition of God is only complete when both aspects are included. In regard to essence, we affirm His unity . . . above all His creatures, over all things sensuous and non-sensuous. No one resembles Him, nor is He involved in other than His own, whether simple or complex. He is the Father of all existence in virtue of His essence, without mingling, merging or composition. So then, as to His number, because He is the Universal, including all the powers of Number, for His number cannot be reckoned. And since numbers are of two kinds, odd and even, both kinds enter into each of the three Persons. And whichever way we describe God, as one or three, we do not detract from what is due to His perfection in any way, as indeed is fitting. But we make it plain that when we predicate the unity of God, it is not in your sense of the phrase.

***

Of course when you protest that God never took Him a wife, gat a son, or had a peer, you say what is absolutely true. [For] we do not say that God has a wife, or has gotten a son; we do not impute to the Deity such puerilities and vanities, predicating of God what is true of man. You credit us with these gross anthropomorphisms on the authority of the Jews, who sought to deceive you in this way, patching up idle tales which they tell at the corners of the streets and in the market places. . . . I do not wish to give currency to a story by contradicting it. I will not trace it back to its source in the cunning of Wahb son of Manba, 'Abdullah son of Salam, and Ka'b, the notorious Jewish doctor, cunning and crafty fellows every one of them. These men insinuated these and other blasphemies of the same sort against us and against you.

***

[Muhammad] grew up till he entered the service of Khadija as a camel driver. . . . He married Khadija. Backed by her fortune he conceived the idea of claiming power and headship over his tribesmen, but they were not well disposed to him, nor did they follow him except a little handful of men whom he swept off their feet by his artifices. . . . And when he despaired of what he really desired, then he claimed to be a prophet and an apostle.

You know the stories that have reached us as to the crimes committed by this fellow. . . . If he went out against a tribe and found them weak and defenceless, he drove away their trains, took their merchandise and killed as many as he could of their people. If he found them in considerable numbers or entrenched in a strong position, they very soon saw the last of him; he turned and fled. . . . And certainly I wonder at the baseness of his conduct, the impudence and barbarity of the man. . . .

Let me linger over the battle of Uhud with its memorable incidents. The Prophet's front tooth, right side lower jaw, was broken, his lip slit, his cheek and forehead gashed. . . . Where was the angel to help and protect him, the friend and messenger of God? Earlier prophets were protected.

. . . He was a man who had no thought or caring save for beautiful women whom he might marry, or men who he might plunder, shedding their blood, taking their property and marrying their wives. He himself says that God gave him two passions: one for perfume and one for women. Are we to hold him as a prophet because God gave him the strength in loin to deal with as many women as forty ordinary men? By my life, this is a proof of the prophetic character quite peculiar to himself.

***

. . . Let us consider next those credentials of a true prophet . . . and then consider those of your master. . . . To begin, the word "prophet" means "one who prophesies" . . . Tell us, when did [Muhammad] ever prophesy?

But you know he came not by this gate to his goal. He never claimed to have this faculty of foreknowledge. . . . He has taught us nothing either of the past or of the future, while the signs and wonders by which a true prophet is verified were denied him.

. . . Let us inquire if he really produced any signs. . . . You know, we all know that your master disowns all claims to be a worker of miracles, simply because he had no such power. . . . Rather, he was sent with the sword, enforcing his pretensions and those who did not confess that he was a prophet were slain or paid a heavy fine.

***

[The Qur'an] you hold in your hands and the proof that it is divinely inspired is that it contains old-world stories about Moses, the prophets and our Lord the Christ. You urge that your master was an illiterate person, not in any way conversant in such matters, and you ask how could he have composed such a book if he had not been inspired? . . . Well then, there was a certain Christian monk named Sergius who had perpetrated some offence for which his companions disowned him and excommunicated him, refusing him as was their wont, access to their churches and intercourse with themselves. . . . [Sergius] travelled to the country of Tehama, and reached Mecca. There he found a prosperous city divided between two religious sects. The majority were of the Jewish faith, the rest were idolaters. So kindly and skillfully did he handle your master that he quite won his heart. Among his new friends he was known as Nestorius, hoping by this change of name to strengthen the Nestorian heresy which he had embraced. He continued imparting instruction to your master, in repeated conferences he insinuated point after point of the new doctrine, till at length his pupil ceased to worship idols. So he drew him to confess the religion of Nestorius. . . . This is the explanation of the fact that Muhammad mentions the Messiah and the Christian faith in the Qur'an . . . Muhammad had been coached by Nestorius the Christian.

***

If you say there is nothing like the Qur'an in point of style and ornamentation, we reply that the style of our great poets is genuinely poetical, their rhythm is so perfect that, however difficult and subtle the thought, it is never broken at any point. . . . The Qur'an on the other hand, is broken in its style, hybrid in its diction and, while high-sounding, often destitute of meaning. If you protest that it has very good meaning, we ask you what far-fetched meaning you have found? Let us have it; expound it to us, gladly will we learn of you. . . . What have you to tell us that we do not already know, which we have not already read in some old book from which you are content to borrow?

3

Refuting Christianity

Muslim Assessments of Christian Doctrine and
Practice (Ninth to Tenth Centuries)

The Refutation of the Three Christian Sects
(ca. mid-ninth century)

Abu 'Isa al-Warraq (ca. late eighth-century–ca. 864)
Language: Arabic
Source: David Thomas, *Anti-Christian Polemic in Early Islam*
(Cambridge: Cambridge University Press, 1992); Thomas, *Early Christian Polemic against Christianity* (Cambridge: Cambridge University Press, 2002).

Few details are known about the life of al-Warraq. Likely a monotheist to his death, he converted from Mu'tazili Islam to some stream of Shi'ism but was nevertheless accused by critics of atheism (specifically Manicheism) and dualism. With this in mind, he is often described as a free thinker. Indeed, he is frequently critical in his writings of various beliefs and sects, oftentimes in an objective manner that left many of his readers uncertain of his personal religious allegiances.

None of al-Warraq's works survive in their original forms. Instead, we know them only by their titles or in fragments as they are referenced in other works. Thankfully, for this study at least, his refutations of Christianity are transmitted in a form that gives us a strong idea of what they were originally. Pre-eminent among these is al-Warraq's Refutation of the Three Christian Sects, *which Yahya b. 'Adi, a tenth-century Christian author, quotes at great length. This text is one of the longest and most thorough Muslim attacks of Christianity to emerge from the medieval period. As such, it exerted much influence on later anti-Christian polemic.*

In the Refutation, *al-Warraq focuses on the incarnation and the Trinity and exhibits detailed knowledge of how Eastern Christian traditions articulated the doctrines. Relying on reason and logic, he also mounts piercing and sustained attacks against these two central Christian doctrines. Works like al-Warraq's help to show that Christians had encountered a new theological opponent in Islam, and the arguments they used in support of their beliefs did not necessarily stand up to fresh (Muslim) criticism.*

***

One of [the Nestorians, Jacobites, and Melkites] has given a defence of the Trinity and of his assertion that the substance is one with reasoning of a different kind. He claims that he can affirm it is one substance because of its transcendence above creation and all it has made, its dissimilarity from them in attributes, and because it is not a blend of two substances or a mixture of two classes. He affirms that it is three in number because three, he claims, combines the two types of number, even and odd. He says: That which combines the two types of number is more perfect than that which does not and is itself one of them, and because one type of number falls short of the perfection of number. So he ascribes perfection to it, he claims, and does not ascribe deficiency or imperfection. In this way he claims that it is one in substance and three in number. The author of this proof is quite besotted with it and insistent about it.

Say to those who offer this reasoning as a defence: Tell us about the Father alone. Does he combine the two types of number? If they say: Yes, then they claim that the Father alone is three hypostases, and the same applies to the Son and the Spirit; each will be in itself three hypostases so that the hypostases of the substance will be nine. This is opposed to their teaching. The subsequent question about each of the nine will be like that about each of the three hypostases, until its proponent exceeds all limitation of number.

If they claim that the Father alone does not combine the two types of number say to them: Then you have reduced him below the level of perfection and attributed deficiency to him in himself, since the perfect, as you say, is that which combines the two types of number. The same question will concern the Son and the Spirit. And if every one of these three hypostases is reduced below the level of perfection because it does not combine the two types of number, then you have attributed to them deficiency and imperfection and removed them from the bounds of perfection and divinity.

Next say to them: Can one who is short of perfection be divine? And if they reply: Yes, they will be unable to deny divinity to any deficient thing whoever or whatever it may be, since deficiency will not be a bar to divinity and lordship. If they say: The divinity is in no way deficient or imperfect, say to them: Then according to you the Father is not perfect in number since he does not combine the two types, and is thus not divine, and the same applies to the Son and the Spirit. And if each of these three is excluded from divinity because of his deficiency and imperfection then they are all excluded from divinity and lordship. But if the Father, Son and Spirit are excluded from divinity then the Divinity must be other than them. And if the Divinity is other than them then the eternal is other than them and they must be contingent and subject. Thus we see that the reasoning by which you attempt to show the validity of the doctrine of the Trinity instead proves its invalidity, and your teaching about the hypostases is also destroyed by it. . . . "All you Trinitarians adhere to the details, but you abandon the principles; you uphold metaphors and figures, but negate your principles and the truth."

This argument, or the greater part of it, has been set out previously in this book, and it applies here as well as there.

***

As for the teaching of those from these groups who say: The uniting was the mixing of the Word with the body and its mingling with it, this is a teaching which is clearly weak and wrong from many aspects. One is that the most balanced mixing and mingling with the body require that what mixes and mingles with it should have the same surface size as this body and that the parts of the two should be adjacent to one another. This imposes a limit, an end and a reduction in the size of the Word, as well as dividing and partitioning. And in their view the Word is totally unlike such descriptions.

If this was possible for the Word, which for them is one of the hypostases of the eternal substance, it would be possible for the two other hypostases, so that the size of the substance in its entirety would be the size of three bodies like the body of the Messiah; its area would be exactly the area of that, and the number of its parts would be like that of these three bodies without any difference. In addition to the partitioning and dividing, the limiting and the restricting imposed by this, there is the small-mindedness of the one who gauges and judges that this is right for a Divinity and demands his Divinity to be measured, even if he were to increase the size and capacity immensely. And this is one point.

Another point is that the mixing and mingling which can be understood are actually only of physical bodies which have composite parts. So if one mixes with another, the parts of each of the two bodies spread through the parts of the other with which it is mixing. But according to them the Word is not a physical body. For them it is a simple substance which cannot be enclosed in locations or contained in bodies, and it does not have composite parts. Mixing occurs when the parts of each of the two things mixing together spread through its companion, as we have just said, to produce the most intimate adjacency and closest proximity, and it is the same with mingling. And if the Word does not have composite parts which could spread through the body so that its parts might come into adjacency with those of the body, as we have described, then mixing and mingling are not possible for it.

If they say: But this mixing and mingling were different from mixing that is understandable and mingling that is familiar among us, we say: Then it was possible for the Word to be in contact with physical bodies and be separate from them differently from the contact and separation which are understandable. In the same way its being contained by physical bodies was different from the familiar containing, and likewise it moved and was at rest, was happy and suffered differently from what can be understood about them among us. This is too huge and enormous for us to bring together in a book.

Likewise, those who claim that the Word took this body as a habitation and dwelling, and those who say: It put on the body like a garment, are forced to accept this. And say to them: If this occurred in the way understood of physical bodies then you have made the Word into a restricted, mobile physical body which can move from a position or occupy it, can be close to its other two hypostases at times and be distant from them at others. If this occurs differently from what is understood about physical bodies, then the Word can come into contact and be separate, be moving and at rest, be close to and be distant from the other two hypostases, be happy and suffering, in ways different from what can be understood about physical bodies.

As for those of them who claim: It inhered in him and controlled affairs through him and by means of him, we ask them about their statement, "It inhered in him," just as we have asked the one who says, "It mixed with him," or who says, "It took him as a habitation and dwelling," or who says, "It put him on like a garment." The question against them on this is one: If it occurred in the way that is understood concerning the inhering of physical bodies in physical bodies, then they have affirmed that it was a small, contained physical body which inhered in the flesh, bone, sinew, veins in the blood vessels and passages of food and drink, and where these are found.

We question them about their statement, "It controlled affairs through him and by means of him," what they mean by it. Do they mean that it made him a tool and instrument for its control, as it is said, "So and so cut with the sword, chopped with the axe, wrote with the pen" and similar? But in this it had no superiority over the majority of creatures, and it is also different from their teaching about the uniting and their claim that one came from two. This is because the man and pen do not have to be one thing when he is writing with it, and similarly the sword, axe and other tools, when the user is using them, they do not have to become one thing with him. Nor does he become united with them by using them or taking them as tools and instruments, whatever the uniting might be. It is also just like they say, "He revived the earth with a downpour," "He drove the clouds with the wind," "He made the seed grow with the rain," and similar. If they think in this way, there is no superiority to the human in the Messiah over these created things which we have named. For the Divinity, may he be blessed and exalted, does not have to be united with the wind in order to drive the clouds with it, or with the rain in order to make seeds appear with it, or with the downpour in order to revive the earth with it, nor for any control that he exercises in this way.

Likewise, they should be questioned about their statement, "He controlled through him," what sense it has for them. Do they mean that he caused signs, proofs and wonders to appear through him? But he performed this for the prophets before him, God's blessing be upon them, and the signs of some of them were more excellent and miraculous than many of the signs which appeared through him, peace be upon him and upon them all. So if the uniting was this, then the Divinity united with prophets without number and controlled through them. And if they mean that he controlled through him in the sense that he ordered him to control his creation, then when was he ordered to do this? And over what part of God's creation, the heaven or the earth, animals or plants, or anything else was the Messiah given authority, unless they are thinking of what he created from clay like the shape of a bird, then he breathed into it and it flew with God's help? But this conforms to extraordinary signs, not to control over creation. If they go beyond this and similar signs of the messengers, on whom be peace, then they can only be claiming a thing which is secret and something which is hidden, though this is something which anyone can claim. However, when he orders someone to control a thing God, blessed and exalted, does not have to be united with him, nor does the order require him to have worship from creatures or to be Lord of the worlds.

And as for the teaching of those of them who say, "It appeared from him to creation not by means of indwelling or mingling," we will ask them about the meaning of their statement "It appeared," what this is. Is it that the Word showed itself to the creation through this body and was disclosed to them in it after being concealed, and they saw it and touched it? But these are attributes of restricted physical bodies which can be contained, enclosed and measured. Or is it that it appeared in him as control, which indicated the wisdom and power of the controller? But there is no single physical body in the creation without God's control in it indicating his wisdom and power, even if the scope of this control and indications seem to be superior. And if this and the like is the meaning of "It appeared" and of "It united," according to this view there is no physical body of any of the prophets and other people, or indeed of other animals or plants, or of dead and inanimate beings, that the Word has not united with or appeared from it to creation. This is why it contains fallacy and faultiness all through it.

As for the statement of the one who says, "It appeared in him as the imprint of a seal appears in pressed clay," we say to them: Do we see you daring to compare it with restricted physical bodies? Then we will permit you this comparison. Do you claim that the Word was manifest in the body of the Messiah as something to be beheld in him, like the appearance of the imprint of a seal in imprinted clay, obvious in the way that this becomes obvious to the eyes? If they say: Yes, we say: So everyone who saw the Messiah beheld the Word apparent in his body, like their beholding of the imprint of the seal in impressed clay. There are two points in this. The first is the self-important tone of the one who says this, his seriousness about it and the claim about what people saw but was not there. And the second is that by this they require the Eternal to be seen and sensed, although their teachings do not contain this. And if they claim that the Word was not manifest in the body of the Messiah, to be beheld in him like the appearance of the seal in the clay, we say: You have made your comparison collapse, you have destroyed your proof, and you have made contradictory judgements about the two, because you have claimed they are equal, though it is not possible for anyone to say "This appears as that does" about two things, one of which is hidden and not apparent and the other apparent to the sight and eyes, tangible and not at all hidden.

The same applies to the one who claims that the Word appeared in the bodily form like the image of a man appears in a polished, clean mirror. And this is because there is no one in the world with perfect eyesight without defect or imperfection, who could look into a polished mirror in which is a clear image and not see it. Anyone with him who fixes his gaze upon it will see the same, as long as he has the same judgement and attitude. The Word was not visible in the body of the Messiah, nor could it be beheld. Between the outside and inside of his body, may God bless him, and the outside of the bodies of humans like him and equal to him there was no difference, in that it was not perceptible in him or in them, nor visible in his physical body nor in theirs. And if he and those equal to him could be like this in sense and sight, and in a test and inspection on this matter of him and them—may God bless him and all prophets and messengers of God—eyesight could not make any distinction between them, even though in his body and not in theirs the Divinity was manifest like the appearance of the imprint of the seal in the clay and the appearance of the image in the mirror, then it would be possible for us to examine with our eyes two pieces of clay, one of them impressed and the other clear, and for us to look at them with one glimpse, and see that they were in the same condition. Similarly, we could inspect two mirrors, one with the image of a human apparent and the other with no image, and yet see nothing in either. But this smacks of ignorance; our eyes belie it and what is evident rejects it.

If they say: The image of the human can be beheld and similarly the imprint of the seal can be seen and beheld, but the Word cannot be seen or beheld, we say: Then why do you compare what can be beheld with what cannot be beheld clearly, what can be beheld when it appears and what cannot be beheld at all? And what is the reality of the appearance which is comparable to the appearance of the imprint of the seal and the appearance of the image in the mirror, if you refuse to say that it is an appearance that can be understood? If they say: His appearance was in his acts or in signs about him, this is not similar to the appearance of the imprint of the seal in the clay or to the appearance of the image in the mirror. The appearance of the imprint and of the image in the clay and in the mirror is an appearance to the eyes and the senses, not the appearance of an action upon the imprint and the image, nor the appearance of an indication about them. To behold them in the mirror and the clay renders any requirement of proof about them unnecessary.

Further and in addition is that if the appearance of the Word in the body was only its appearance in its actions or in signs about it, then it is visible in all bodies, since according to you there are one of its actions and signs about it in every body. If they say: But the acts and signs which appeared in the body of the Messiah are not present in every body and have not appeared in every individual, we will return to their references to what they claim appeared in the prophets who preceded the Messiah, and to the account they give of the signs, proofs and wonders which appeared in them and to them and through them. And we say to them as well: Your separation between what appeared in the body of the Messiah and what appeared in the body of others is not a denial of appearance by you, but only a distinction between two appearances, in which you favour one over the other. From another angle, if the appearance of the Word is only by control, it appears in every body by control. But when they reach this point in the argument they have discarded their first comparison of the appearance of the imprint and of the image.

And say to them: Have you been comparing the appearance of the Word with that of the imprint in the clay and that of the image in the mirror because the two appearances are similar to one another and are alike, or have you been comparing two opposite appearances which are not similar? If they insist upon similarity and accord, they are comparing the eternal with the temporal in self and act. And if they claim that the appearances are not similar to one another, and that the appearance of each does not resemble the appearance of the other, they contradict their teaching and their first comparison. If they say: The two are similar in one respect and different in another, we say: Are they different from each other in the respect in which they are similar to each other? If they say: Yes, they contradict themselves. And if they say: No, we say: Then in this respect the Word is not eternal, and its appearance in this respect is not the appearance of something eternal, because if it were eternal in this respect then it would be different from the temporal with which you compare it in the respect in which you are comparing the two. Likewise, if its appearance in this respect was the appearance of an eternal thing and the appearance with which you compare it was of a temporal thing, they would be different in the respect in which you are comparing the two.

From another angle, if you insist that the comparison between them and between their appearances was actual in any respect, then you have no alternative but to transfer the Word to temporality in this respect since temporality includes the temporal in all its respects and it cannot escape from temporality in any respect. Or they could transfer the temporal to eternity in this respect, since the Word cannot be characterised by temporality in any respect. The discussion about their appearances and about their acts or not is similar to this. But if they can make them the same in the respect in which they are different, then there could be a difference between them or two other separate things in the respect in which they are alike.

***

. . . Say to [the Nestorians, Jacobites, and Melkites]: Who created the humanity of the Messiah, the Messiah or another?

If they say: The Messiah, we say: Then the Messiah was before humankind and before the entire creation. This destroys their teaching that the Messiah was divine and human, two substances, possessing two substances, and a substance from two substances, because the eternal one before creation was not divine and human, or two substances, or the possessor of two substances, or a substance from two substances.

If they claim that the one who created the humanity of the Messiah was other than the Messiah, they acknowledge that the Creator is other than the Messiah, and they make the Messiah temporal.

Say to them: Tell us, could he, in your view, have had intercourse with a woman so that a child was born to him, and have become father to a man just as he was son to a man? If they say: This is not possible, we say: Then what is the difference between being born and not having a child, and why could he be son of a man but not father to a man?

If they say: This was possible, we say: If he had a child, then his child would be divine and Messiah. So they would then implicate the Divinity in reproduction and allow there to be a Divinity who was son of the Divinity for ever, as long as they reproduced, and similarly Messiah son of Messiah for ever. So the Messiah would be Messiah by uniting at one time and at another by generation. This is extreme confusion. If they say: His son would not have been divine or Messiah, we say: What is the distinction between this and the child of a human not being human or the offspring of an animal not being an animal? And if in your view a child of the Divinity need not have been a Divinity, and a child of the Messiah not Messiah, then why do you deny that a child of the Messiah would not have been human? If the child of the Divinity need not have been a Divinity, then why do you deny that the Word, which according to you is generated from the Divinity, is not the Divinity? All this is confusion from those who say it, and who pass it on.

Say to them: In your view, if the Messiah had had intercourse with a woman and had a child born, would not this child have been, in your view, the son of the Son of God, may God be exalted and praised, and would not the eternal Divinity, in your view, have been the grandfather of the Messiah's child, and Mary, the Messiah's mother, the grandmother of the Messiah's child, since he had a child? If they say: No, they abandon what is reasonable and make the Father not a grandfather, and are forced to make the mother not a grandmother, which smacks of ignorance. If they acknowledge that the Divinity, praised and exalted may he be, was grandfather to the Messiah's child, they place the human between the eternal and the temporal and are forced to accept reproduction, even though they loathe it.

Refutation of the Christians
(ca. mid-ninth century)

Abu 'Uthman 'Amr b. Bahr al-Jahiz (ca. 776–869)
Language: Arabic
Source: Joshua Finkel, "A Risala of Al-Jahiz," *Journal of the American Oriental Society* 47 (1927): 311–34.

Al-Jahiz was born in Basrah in present-day Iraq. An accomplished writer, he completed nearly two hundred works on a wide-range of topics. These include texts devoted to political concerns as well as religious treatises.

Of particular interest in al-Jahiz's Refutation of the Christians *is the focus he gives to the social status of non-Muslims under 'Abbasid rule. He routinely laments Christians' upward mobility and the ways in which they toy with Muslims of lesser intellectual ability when they engage them in theological debate. He also takes Christians to task for what he concludes are confused and perplexing beliefs. It is thought that his text may have supported later efforts to curb Christian social mobility by drawing attention to their problematic religious beliefs and allegedly unmerited social status. Nearly all of the writers that appear in the present chapter of this book either make use of al-Jahiz's* Refutation *or are at least aware of it.*

***

Another circumstance [which caused Christians to be more liked than Magians or Jews], which is the most potent cause, is the wrong interpretation given by the masses to the [qur'anic] verses: "Thou wilt surely find that the strongest in enmity against those who believe are the Jews and the idolaters; and thou wilt find the nearest in love to those who believe to be those who say, 'We are Christians,' that is because there are amongst them priests and monks and because they are not proud."

. . . The wrong interpretation of the above verses supplanted that of the learned, and the Christians craftily used it to seduce the common and the vulgar. In the very verses lies the proof that here God is not referring to the Christians we are acquainted with nor to their associates the [Melkites] and Jacobites, but rather to the type of [the monk] Bahira, and the kind of monks whom Salman used to serve. There is a vast difference when we consider the phrase "Who say we are Christians" (as an insinuation) that these monks misnamed themselves or [that it is] a real term to be taken like the word "Jews" (which refers to the Jews who plotted against [Muhammad] in Medina).

***

. . . What filled the hearts of the Arabs with affection for the Christians were the ties of blood and our regard for royalty.

. . . But if our masses knew that the Christians (Arabs) and

Byzantines are not men of science and rhetoric, and are not people of deep reflection, and possess nothing except the handiworks of iron and wood and the crafts of painting and silk-weaving, they would remove them from the roll of men of culture, and would strike their names off the list of philosophers and scientists.

***

And the Christian faith—may God have mercy on you—resembles [Manicheism], and in some of its aspects it is akin to atheism. It is the cause of all perplexity and confusion. Indeed no other people has furnished so many hypocrites and waverers as the Christians. This results, naturally, when weak minds attempt to fathom deep problems. Is it not a fact that the majority of those who were executed for parading as [Muslims], while hypocrites at heart, were men whose fathers and mothers were Christians? Even the people who are under suspicion [today] have come mostly from their ranks.

Another cause for the admiration accorded by the masses to the Christians is the fact that they are secretaries and servants to kings, physicians to nobles, perfumers, and money changers, whereas the Jews are found to be but dyers, tanners, cuppers, butchers, and cobblers. Our people observing thus the occupations of the Jews and the Christians concluded that the religion of the Jews must compare as unfavorably as do their professions, and that their unbelief must be the foulest of all, since they are the filthiest of all nations. Why the Christians, ugly as they are, are physically less repulsive than the Jews may be explained by the fact that the Jews, by not intermarrying, have intensified the offensiveness of their features. Exotic elements have not mingled with them; neither have males of alien races had intercourse with their women, nor have their men cohabited with females of a foreign stock. The Jewish race therefore has been denied high mental qualities, sound physique, and superior lactation. The same results obtain when horses, camels, donkeys, and pigeons are inbred.

And we—may God be gracious to you—do not deny that the Christians are rich, and that they wield the sceptre, that their appearance is cleaner, and their professions more refined. We do, however, differ with the majority of the people as to which of the two, the Jew or the Christian, is more controversial in word and deceitful in manner, though both be low-born and impure of blood. As for the manifestations of the high social rank of the Christians, we know that they ride highly bred horses and dromedary camels, play polo, . . . wear fashionable silk garments, and have attendants to serve them. They call themselves Hasan, Husayn, 'Abbas, Fadl, and 'Ali, and employ also their forenames. There remains but that they call themselves [Muhammad], and employ the forename Abu l-[Qasim]. For this very fact they were liked by the [Muslims]! Moreover, many of the Christians failed to wear their belts, while others hid their girdles beneath their outer garments. Many of their nobles refrained, out of sheer pride, from paying tribute. They returned to [Muslims] insult for insult and blow for blow. Why indeed should the Christians not do so and even more, when our judges, or, at least, the majority of them, consider the blood of a patriarch or bishop as equivalent to the blood of Ja'far, 'Ali, 'Abbas, and Hamza? They also believe that a Christian when he slanders the mother of the prophet with the accusation of adultery should incur only a slight punishment or a reprimand, defending their decision on the ground that the mother of the prophet was not [Muslim]. Good Lord, what a queer judgment, and how utterly untenable! Was it not the decree of the prophet that the Christian should not sit on an equal level with the [Muslim]? Did he not say: "If they insult you, strike them; and if they strike you, kill them?" But the Christians, calumniating his mother with adultery, suffer at the hands of his believers only a slight punishment, for our judges think that forging a lie against the prophet does not constitute a breach of covenant. But they forget that it is with regard to the Christians, against whom the prophet decreed that they deliver the tribute in a spirit of gratitude, considering the very receipt of it on our part as a gracious act, for thus we grant them the privilege of being tolerated, and give them a guarantee of personal safety. God verily doomed them to abjectness and destitution.

***

Moreover . . . (in the polemics with us) they choose contradictory statements in [Muslim] traditions (as the targets for their attacks). (They select for disputations) the equivocal verses in the [Qur'an], and (hold us responsible for) Hadiths [i.e., traditions of Muhammad], the chains of guarantors of which are defective. Then they enter into private conversation with our weak-minded, and question them concerning the texts which they have chosen to assail. They finally insert into the debate the arguments that they have learned from the atheists and accursed Manichaeans. And notwithstanding such malicious discourse they often appear innocent before our men of influence and people of learning; and thus they succeed in throwing dust in the eyes of the staunch believers and in bewildering the minds of those who are weak in faith. And how unfortunate that every [Muslim] looks upon himself as a theologian, and thinks that everyone is fit to lead a discussion with an atheist!

Moreover, were it not for the Christian theologians, their physicians and astronomers, the books of the Mananiyya, Daysaniyya, and Markuniyya . . . sects would never reach our young people and the rich. They would be familiar with naught save the book of God, and the Sunna of His prophet, and the heretical writings would remain with their original owners, passing only as heirlooms to the next of kin. Indeed, for all our grief over the seduction of our youth and unintelligent we have primarily the Christians to blame. And when one hears their notions about forgiveness, and wanderings in quest of God, their censure for partaking of meats, and their predilection for grain products; when one hears them preaching abstinence from marriage and from the begetting of offspring; when one observes them worshipping the Church leaders, and praising the bishops for practicing celibacy, one is convinced that there is a resemblance between Christianity and [Manicheism], and that the former leans toward the teachings of the latter.

And how marvellous is this! We know that the Christian bishops as well as all inmates of monasteries, whether Jacobites or Nestorians, in fact monks of every description, both male and female, one and all practice celibacy. When we next consider how great is the number of the monks, and that most of the clergy adhere to their practices, and when we finally take into account the numerous wars of the Christians, their sterile men and women, their prohibition against divorce, polygamy, and concubinage—(is it not queer) that, in spite of all this, they have filled the earth, and exceeded all others in numbers and fecundity? Alas! This circumstance has increased our misfortunes, and made our trials stupendous! Another cause for the growth and expansion of Christianity is the fact that the Christians draw converts from other religions and give none in return (while the reverse should be true), for it is the younger religion that is expected to profit from conversion.

***

And the Christian, though cleaner in dress, though engaged in more refined professions, and physically less repulsive, yet inwardly is baser, filthier, and fouler; for he does not practice circumcision, does not cleanse himself from pollution, and in addition eats the flesh of swine. His wife, too, is unclean. She does not purify herself from the defilement of menses and childbirth; her husband cohabits with her in her courses, and, in addition to all this, she too is uncircumcised. In spite of their evil natures and overruling lusts, their faith offers no restraints against passion such as eternal hell-fire in the world to come or punishment by religious authority in the world we live in. How indeed can one evade what harms him, and pursue what profits him if such be his faith? Can such as we have described set the world aright? Can anyone be more fit to stir up evil and corruption?

Even if one were to exert all his zeal, and summon all his intellectual resources with a view to learn the Christian teachings about Jesus, he would still fail to comprehend the nature of Christianity, especially its doctrine concerning the Divinity. How in the world can one succeed in grasping this doctrine, for were you to question concerning it two Nestorians, individually, sons of the same father and mother, the answer of one brother would be the reverse of that of the other. This holds true also of all [Melkites] and Jacobites. As a result, we cannot comprehend the essence of Christianity to the extent that we know the other faiths. Moreover, they contend that the method of analogy should not be applied to religion, nor should the validity of faith be maintained by overcoming objections, nor should the verity of a dogma be made subject to the test of intellectual scrutiny. Faith must be based on the unqualified submission to the authority of the book, and on following blindly the traditions of old. And, by my life, any man who would profess a faith like Christianity would of necessity have to offer blind submission as an excuse! The Christians also believe that the Magians, Sabians, and Manichaeans, who oppose Christianity, are to be pardoned as long as they do not aim at falsehood, and do not contend stubbornly against the true belief, but when they come to speak of the Jews they brand them as obstinate rebels, not merely as people walking in error and confusion.

Book of Religion and Empire (ca. 855)

Abu l-Hasan 'Ali b. Sahl Rabban al-Tabari (ca. 780–ca. 860)
Language: Arabic
Source: Alphonse Mingana, *The Book of Religion and Empire: A Semi-Official Defence and Exposition of Islam Written by Order at the Court and With the Assistance of the Caliph Mutawakkil (A.D. 847–861)* (Manchester, UK: The University Press, 1922).

Al-Tabari was born into a Christian family of some means and was employed by caliphs. Quite late in life, perhaps at seventy years old, al-Tabari converted to Islam and wrote a refutation of Christianity in support of his conversion.

Not long after his conversion and after refuting his former faith in print, al-Tabari wrote his Book of Religion and Empire. *It is an extensive defense of the prophethood of Muhammad that includes lengthy proofs of his appearance in passages of the Bible, both Old and New Testaments. With this in mind, al-Tabari's text addresses a common theme in Christian-Muslim theological treatises: the nature of Muhammad's role as prophet and the ways in which his role was substantiated.*

***

They have hidden [Muhammad's] name and changed his portrait found in the Books of their prophets—peace be with them. I shall demonstrate this, disclose its secret, and withdraw the veil from it, in order that the reader may see it clearly and increase his conviction and his joy in the religion of Islam.

***

I have found that people who have contradicted Islam, have done so for four reasons: *firstly*, because of doubts about the history of the Prophet—may God bless and save him; *secondly*, because of disdain and egregious insolence; *thirdly*, because of tradition and custom; *fourthly*, because of folly and stupidity. By my life, had they discerned and grasped the truth of that history, they would not have rejected it.

***

If we ask especially the Christians why they disbelieve in the Prophet—peace be with him—they would say because of three reasons: *first*, because we do not see that a prophet has prophesied about him prior to his coming; *second*, because we do not find in the [Qur'an] the mention of a miracle or a prophecy ascribed to the man who produced it; *third*, because the Christ has told us that no prophet will rise after Him. These are their strongest objections, and I will refute them, by the help of God. If I am able to prove that the contrary of what they assert is true, and that for our belief in prophets there is no such necessary condition as they mention, they will have no more excuse before God and their conscience, and those who adduce such pleas and cling to them are in the path of unbelief and perdition.

The answer to their saying that no prophet has prophesied about the Prophet, and that the prophetic office of the prophets is not true and acceptable except when it is preceded by other prophecies, because he who believes in a prophet who has no previous prophecy about him would be in error and unbelief, is this: let them tell us who prophesied about the prophet Moses himself—may God bless him—or about David, or about Isaiah, or about Jeremiah, who are considered by them as the greatest of the prophets—peace be with them; and since there is no previous prophecy about them he who believes in them would, therefore, contradict truth for falsehood, and thus incur the wrath of the Lord of the worlds. The answer to their saying that in the [Qur'an] there is no mention of a miracle wrought by the Prophet—may God bless and save him—and that he who has no record in his book of a sign or a miracle has no reason to be acknowledged, is this: let them show us the miracle wrought by David and recorded in his Psalter; if they do not find it for us, why and for what reason have they called him a prophet, while no prophet has previously prophesied about him, and there is no record of a miracle in his Book?

From what I have explained it has become evident that, in the process of the verification of the history of prophets, there is no need of a previous prophecy about them, nor of a mention in their books of their miracles or the outward signs of their claims. There are indeed prophets who, as stated above, have in their Books the record of a miracle and a manifest prophecy, but about whom no previous prophet has prophesied; and no one has for that denied their claim; such is the case of Moses, Daniel, Isaiah, and the like—peace be with them. There are also prophets on whom God has bestowed all these prerogatives; such is the case of the Christ—peace be with Him—who has wrought wonderful miracles, foretold hidden and unknown things, and has previous prophecies about Him prior to His appearance. There are prophets who have miracles recorded in their Books, but who did not prophesy; such is the case of Elisha, who gave life to two dead men, but has no direct prophecy. Some prophets, such as Ezekiel and Hosea and others, did not work any miracle, and they prophesied; but their prophecy having been realized long after their death, people who saw them and acknowledged them had no reason for their belief in them, in the absence of a miracle shown by them to their contemporaries. There are some prophets who have in their Books neither miracle nor prophecy, nor convincing stories, and are counted among the prophets; such is the case of Malachi, Haggai, and Nahum, whose Books of prophecies does not exceed three or four pages, for each one of them; such is, also, the case of Miriam the prophetess, Moses's sister, and of Hannah the prophetess, who have neither Book, nor prophecy, nor miracle, nor sign, and they have counted them among the prophets. O my cousins, why and for what reason have you called these prophets?

This being the condition of the Christians, why do they disbelieve in the prophetic office of the Prophet—peace be with him—who actually possesses the above mentioned prerogatives, some of which are perpetuated in the [Qur'an], and some in the Tradition, which is of equal value to the [Qur'an] with the sole difference that those which are contained in the [Qur'an] afford stronger and clearer argument, and more cogent prophecy. How can they reject them with the explanation that I shall give of the prophecies of the pious prophets about him, and with the allusions of the majority of them to his prophetic office, and to his time—may the peace and the blessings of God be with all of them. If you say that you have rejected and avoided the Prophet—may God bless and save him—because there is no prophet after the Christ, I will make it clear from your own Books that the man who whispered this into your ears and made it flow from your tongues was not an adviser but a deceiver to you, not reliable but suspect.

To this effect, it is written in the eleventh chapter of the Book of the Acts, which contains the Epistles of the Apostles, that "In those days, prophets came from Jerusalem, and one of them, called Agabus, stood up and prophesied to them that in those countries there will be famine and great dearth." It is said in this same chapter, that "In the church of Antioch, there were prophets and teachers, as Barnabas, and Simon, and Lucius of the town of Cyrene and Manael and Saul." All these five prophets, according to what is recorded, were in Antioch. Some of the women prophetesses are also mentioned. It is said in the nineteenth chapter of this book that "Philip the interpreter had four daughters prophetesses."

. . . The Christians are therefore short of evidence for their claim, and their saying is incoherent, and their arguments have been refuted and overthrown; it has become evident that after the Christ there were people whom they have called Apostles and Prophets; such is the case of Paul himself.

I shall now, by the help and assistance of God, explain the ten prerogatives which I have set forth. I shall present in each chapter what is perpetuated in the [Qur'an], as a reproach against those who pretend that there is no mention of a miracle in it. I wish the reader of this book to realize its merit and the excellence of its value, and to know that those born in the religion of Islam and firmly attached to it, who have profusely dealt with this subject, did not reach what I have attained; he who has a doubt in his breast, let him compare my book, the prophecies, the convincing and peremptory proofs which it contains, the riddles and the intricacies of the adversaries which I have carefully examined, with all that other writers have written, since the appearance of Islam down to our own time. This is due to the help and assistance of God, and to the blessings of the Commander of the Faithful—may God strengthen him—and to the obligations which God imposes through him on his friends and freedmen. It is he—may God prolong his life—who called me to this work, guided me in it, and convinced me that on account of it I shall be entitled to a great reward from God and a good memory from man. Before I became Muslim I was neglectful, led astray, unaware of the right direction, and groping my way far from what later was disclosed to me. Thanks and blessings be to God who has lifted up the veil from my sight, opened the locks for me, and saved me from the darkness of error!

The Middle Way among the Teachings (ca. 893)

Al-Nashi' al-Akbar (ca. ninth century–906)
Language: Arabic
Source: David Thomas, *Christian Doctrines in Islamic Theology* (Leiden, Neth.: Brill, 2008), 35–77.

Little is known about al-Nashi' al-Akbar except that he was born in Baghdad and moved to Egypt where he worked as an official in the government and eventually died.

One of his written works, which survives only as a series of quotations in later works, carries with it the likely title of On the Teachings *or* The Middle Way among the Teachings *and concerns itself with descriptions of religious and philosophical beliefs. The bits focused on Christianity consist of descriptions of different Christian groups and their theological variations. Al-Nashi' al-Akbar also takes time to refute the Christian doctrines of the Trinity and incarnation. Without a complete version of his work, it is difficult to assess the original intention behind it, but it remains clear from what does survive that debate between Christians and Muslims of the ninth century was not uncommon and that both groups employed similar argumentative strategies with one another.*

***

'Abdallah said: The Christians have differences, with Unitarians and Trinitarians among them.

The Trinitarians: People among them claim that the Creator is three hypostases and one substance, Father, Son and Holy Spirit, with the substance being the hypostases in a general way. They claim that of these the Father is the cause of the Son and Spirit, without preceding them in essence, but rather they are equal with him. They call the Son the Creator's Knowledge and the Spirit his Life.

This is what the community agree [sic] on, except for those we are about to mention.

Then they differ. The community say [sic] that the Son is the Word, and that he inhered within a complete and perfect man created from the seed of the Virgin Mary without intercourse. They claim that the inhering of the Word in this man was by volition alone, not by substance, composition, mixing, mingling or removal from one location to another, because each of the three existences is without limit and movement is inappropriate for it. They claim that this man was only called Son because of the locating of the Son who inhered within him, just as iron is called fire if fire inheres within it.

They say: This term "Christ" is a name which applies to the two substances together and the two individuals together, not to one of them, and the two individuals were one actuality in the Christ nature. They claim that the action of both and the volition of both were one. And they direct all that is said about Christ along three ways.

One is that they claim there are characteristics that apply to the human and not to God, such as being born, eating, drinking, crucifixion, death, burial and ascension to heaven. So they say: All these are characteristics of the human; and if they are asked whether Christ died, was crucified and buried, ate and drank, they say: Yes, in his human aspect.

They say: The second apply [sic] to God, great and mighty, such as our statement, "The eternal who does not die." And if they are asked: Is not Christ who died the one who did not die, and the one who was crucified the one who was not crucified, and the one who came into being after he did not exist the one who was nevertheless eternal?, they will say: Yes, in his human aspect and his divine aspect respectively.

The third they claim are of God, great and mighty, and of the human together, such as performing miracles, raising the dead and walking on the water. So they claim that these were feats of God through the human, like fire through iron.

They acknowledge all the ancient prophets, the Torah and the

Gospel, the old and new books, the book of the Apostle Paul, the accounts of the Apostles, reward and punishment, and the resurrection of bodies, and they teach about justice and capacity before the act, with the exception of those people we are about to mention.

***

The Unitarians: there are seven groups of them. Among them were the Arians, the followers of Arius. They taught about divine unity and denial of the Trinity and hypostases, claiming that Christ and the Holy Spirit are two created servants, except that God, great is his praise, empowered them to create and oversee the world. So it is they who were its creators and overseers, and the ones who sent the prophets.

'Abdallah said: The Christian Trinitarians are of two sorts, people who argue according to rational criteria, and people who take refuge in the literal meaning of the Gospel and in imitation of their predecessors.

As for those who take refuge in the literal meaning of the Gospel, they hold only to the teachings narrated in the Gospel from Christ, who said: "Consecrate people in the name of the Father and the Son and the Holy Spirit." Here there is no clear indication that they are eternal or temporal or that they are one substance or otherwise, nor in the Gospel is there any utterance which suggests substance or hypostases. Such utterances are philosophical, Greek . . . passed down to the people, and they employed them in their discussions.

Nor can any of those who take refuge in the words of the Gospel possibly establish on it a proof that Jesus and no others was Son of God. For Jesus is recorded in the Gospel as saying, "I am going to my Father and your Father, to my Lord and your Lord," associating himself jointly with them in both instances; and in the Torah Israel is named "first-born son." So this does not allow the possibility of establishing a proof on it according to its literal meaning because of its probable senses.

They cannot claim that Jesus is Son of God arising from what the prophet informed them about this, because they have nothing more than the utterances of the Gospel to use in contention—those who favour imitation might have been able to command the concurrence of the followers of religion on this. And no single one of the people has a proof from a book or information about any detail that he is God's son, either that he united with him substantially, hypostatically, by volition or in any other way. This is too extreme for them to claim any information about it.

If we come to rational argument, we do not find any sense at all in their teaching that the human became eternal and the eternal became human, for if the two were stable in their essences and unchangeable, then this could not become that in any respect. And if they were not stable in their essences they could have changed, though it is rationally fallacious for the eternal Creator to change and become temporal, not existing and then existing, and for the temporal that is subject to time to change and become eternal, never being temporal. The ignorance of the people is shown by the fact that they refuse to say, "The Creator mingled with the temporal," or "He mixed with it," or "He came into contact with it," or "He sent him down with it," although they say "He united with it and he became it." As they see it, the essence of the Creator is not susceptible to mixing with concrete bodies, touching physical bodies or mingling with things that are susceptible to mingling, although he is even more remote from uniting with a thing.

If those who claim that the Creator—mightier than they say—died, was crucified and was buried cannot prove by this teaching that the Creator was affected by what affected the one to whom this sort of thing was done, there is no reason to take the teaching definitively. And if they can prove this, then it is beyond doubt that one who has died has become nothing and is obliterated, and this is not possible for the eternal One.

The one among them who makes a special case and says "in the aspect of his human nature," cannot avoid declaring by this teaching that the Creator himself must have died in one or other aspect. It is of no consequence to me whether this aspect was that of his human nature or not his human nature, for he himself was the one who died. Now we know that all those who die do not die in every aspect because they do not die in the sense of their colour vanishing or their body fading away: in many respects they do not die, but only die according to the aspect of which they are deprived. So no special case can be made for the aspects of a thing if it dies, for that it has died cannot be uncoupled from it. The alternative is that the teaching that the Creator died does not state that he died but another than him, so there is no content to what is said about him concerning death. Nothing can be clearer than this.

Those who say that Christ was two substances and hypostases in order to separate their arguments and say, "He died in his human aspect but did not die in his divine aspect," cannot escape by what they do from what bears upon their companions. For if Christ was both Creator and human, then it is the same whether they were two substances or composed as one substance when it is said that Christ died, for this necessitates both of them being affected by death whether they were supposed to be one or two.

This claim of the Christians—that of the three hypostases one is cause to its two companions and they are its effects and that they are all eternal—is like the claim of the fatalists among the philosophers that the Creator is the cause of the universe and the universe is his effect although neither is prior in essence. This is the most patent impossibility, because in practice things are surely marked out so that one possesses what another does not, and hence reason finds that they are distinguished by themselves or that one possesses what differentiates it from another. However, if it finds that they are uniform and not distinguished by themselves, and there are no items within them to distinguish them, nor any one among them that precedes its companions in essence, nature, degree, quantity or time, then it has no way of claiming that one of the two is cause and the other is effect. Nothing is clearer than what we have said.

You must have noticed that the people say, "Three uniform

hypostases, uniform in the substance with no distinction between them, uniform in eternity with no one of them preceding another, no difference in themselves nor in any feature they possess by which it differs from its two companions." Then they claim that the so-called Father is not Son or Spirit, and the so-called Spirit is not Father or Son, and the so-called Son is not Father or Spirit, and that the so-called cause of these other two is not an effect and the two so-called effects are not a cause, though they are not distinguished by themselves. So it is true that each of them is not like the other, but that they are not distinguished by any features within them is also true. There is nothing more patent than the fallacy of what they teach on this.

Refutation of the Christians (before 915–916)

Abu 'Ali al-Jubba'i (ca. 849/850–915/916)
Language: Arabic
Source: David Thomas, *Christian Doctrines in Islamic Theology* (Leiden, Neth.: Brill, 2008), 226–27, 250–61, 284–89, 296–99, 352–55.

Al-Jubba'i was a leader of Mu'tazila in Basrah. Among his students was Abu al-Hasan al-Ash'ari, who went on to spend much of his life refuting Mu'tazili thought. Al-Jubba'i was apparently a prodigious author, but none of his works survive. Instead, quotations from some of his works are included in treatises by other authors.

Al-Jubba'i's Refutation of the Christians, *which is referenced and quoted intermittently by 'Abd al-Jabbar (see below) in his* Summa on Divine Oneness and Justice, *consists of a description of the doctrine of the Trinity and aspects of the incarnation. Of particular interest is his interaction with the Christian argument in which the notion of Abraham as a friend of*

God is used to support Christ as the Son of God, an argument discussed by al-Jahiz.

Al-Jubba'i's descriptions of Christian theology, while they seem informed from a theological perspective, lack the complexity of other, earlier Muslim works that focused on Christian theology. Specifically, any discussion of how these Christian beliefs are articulated in context, by specific Christian traditions, is absent. This may be due to the fact that his work comes to us as fragmentary quotations. It may also be the case, however, that al-Jubba'i was less concerned with how Christians themselves might respond to his attacks than he was with how his Muslim readers would think of them, a feature also common to many Christian texts devoted to Islam.

In the selection that follows, both quotations from al-Jubba'i and al-Jabbar's descriptions of his arguments are included.

***

Our master Abu 'Ali [al-Jubba'i], may God have mercy on him, reported that among the beliefs of all the Christians, except for a small group of them, is that God almighty is the Creator of things, and the Creator is living and speaking. His Life is the Spirit, which they call the Holy Spirit, and his Word is Knowledge. Some of them say that Life is Power.

They claim that God and his Word and his Power are eternal, and that the Word is the Son and, according to them, is Christ, who appeared in the body which was on earth. And they differ over who is entitled to the name Christ. Some say that it was the Word and the physical body when one of them united with the other. Others claim that it was the Word apart from the body. And others claim that it was the temporal body, and that the Word became a temporal body when it entered Mary's womb and appeared to humankind.

They all claim that the Word is the Son, and that the One to whom the Word and the Spirit belong is the Father. And they claim that these three are one God and one Creator, and that they are of one substance.

This is the whole of what he reported.

***

As for the one who says, "If it is correct for Abraham to be friend, then why is it not correct for Jesus to be his Son, not in the true sense of sonship but in the sense of honour?" Our master Abu 'Ali, may God be merciful to him, said, "'Friend' in the true sense is correct for Abraham together with the almighty One, because friendship is derived from selecting and distinguishing. For it is only said that a man is a friend of another if he has distinguished him in ways he has not distinguished others. And since he, great and mighty, distinguished Abraham, peace be upon him, by revelation and honour to him with which he did not distinguish others in his time, it can rightly be said that he was friend of God. Indeed, he called him friend of God."

This analogy means that every single one of the prophets must be described as friend to him, because he distinguished every one of them by revelation and honour that marked him out from others. Thus, our Prophet, God's blessings be upon him, said, "If I were to take a friend, I would take Abu Bakr as friend, but your master is the friend of God." Thus, he called himself friend of God, great and mighty, and refused to take any of his community as friend because he gave all of them the announcement and communication. So he could not properly have distinguished one of them by this in the way that God the exalted distinguished him by charging him and not the other people of his time with apostleship, although he distinguished Abraham by this and it virtually became his title. This is not impossible for a name. Can you not see that the Qur'an has been given such a distinct designation, even though the meaning of it is also appropriate for things beside it, and Moses was distinguished as the one to whom God spoke, even though the exalted One had spoken to the angels.

This is preferable to giving "friend" the meaning of "love" or "need," because it is barely consistent with them; such is figurative in that the lover distinguishes his beloved in a way he does not distinguish others, and in that the one in need is dependent on the one he is in need of like the friend is dependent on the one who has taken him as friend. In this way it is not consistent with them, for it cannot be said about anyone whom he loves that he is his friend if he does not distinguish him with prophethood and other things with which he has not distinguished others.

If it is said, "Has not the poet said:

And if a friend should come to him on a day of demand,
He will say, What I have is not concealed or debarred,

and in this he characterises it as need? The grammarians have shown that 'friend' has the sense of 'need' when derived from 'want,' *khalla* with an 'a' on *kha'*, and has the sense of 'friendship' when derived from 'amity,' *khulla* with a 'u' on *kha'*, so which of these is right?" Say to him, We do not deny this usage in these two instances, but we only maintain that it is figurative. This is not because if it were literal it would detract from what we think about it, because Abraham should be described as friend of God, whether because his need was apparent in his devotion to God the blessed as was not made apparent from others of that time, or because the love of God almighty was made apparent to him as it was not made apparent to others, or because he favoured him in ways he did not favour others, and so the name became for him like a token. Such is not right in the case of sonship, because the reality of a son is that he is generated from a father, existing from his fluid, and this is impossible for God almighty. So it follows that Jesus cannot properly be described as Son of God, in the way that Abraham has been described as friend of God.

***

If it is said, "Since it is right in your view that God almighty says that Christ is his word and spirit, then why will you not allow him to say that he is his Son in the Gospel?," say to him, Our master Abu 'Ali said, "The intention in his describing Jesus as word of God is that people would be guided by him as they are guided by a word. And the meaning of our saying that he is the spirit of God is that people will be given life by him in their faith as they are given life by their spirits which are in their bodies." This is comprehensive, and it compares him with a word which is a sign, and the spirit upon which a living being among us depends. It is like a word through which is guidance being called light and healing, because truth is known through it just as the way is known through light, and because deliverance in religion is provided through it just like healing through a remedy. And if a word can be used metaphorically out of its context, it does not follow that another can be used metaphorically without evidence. And thus we do not say that Jesus was Son of God by analogy with our saying that he was a spirit and word of God. In a similar way it is said that Gabriel is a spirit, though it is not said that he is the son, and there is no difference between one of us who seeks to use the term "son" for him because we describe him as spirit, and our claim that he should be called God's father or brother by analogy with this. For general meanings are not literally appropriate to God, and neither are those instances in which a man is metaphorically called someone else's son, as we have mentioned above, appropriate to God almighty. So the claim that this is so collapses.

***

Our master Abu 'Ali, may God have mercy on him, compelled them to say that Christ was a worshipper of himself, if at the Uniting he and the Son became one thing. But a worshipper worshipping himself is impossible, because worship is like thanks, for just as he cannot thank himself so he must not worship himself. He compelled the one who said that the Uniting did not force the two to be one to say that Jesus worshipped a part of himself. And this is impossible, like the former.

He compelled them to acknowledge that with the Uniting the action of the divine nature was the action of the human nature. And as long as this is accepted, their two powers would have been one power, and what one was capable of so was the other. So, if the human nature was powerful of itself, like the divine nature, the two of them must have been similar, and likewise if the divine nature was powerful by power, like the human nature.

He compelled them to say that the other two hypostases could have united just as the hypostasis of the Word could, because the substance of both is one, so what was permissible for one of them was permissible for all of them.

He compelled them to say that the hypostases were different and separate from one another, in view of the fact that the Uniting was permissible for one of them and not for the other.

This compels them to say that the Son united with Mary as he united with Jesus, because Jesus was a part of her. In this respect, some of them interpreted the words of the exalted One, "When God said: 'Jesus, son of Mary, did you say to the people, "Take my mother and me as two gods beside God?,"'" as though the Almighty was saying this in the manner of a forced argument, because if Jesus was divine through being distinguished by being born without a male, Mary must have had the same status because she gave birth without sexual intercourse. However, our master Abu 'Ali, may God have mercy on him, took it literally, since there were among them those who held this teaching.

Divine Unity (before 944)

Abu Mansur al-Maturidi (ca. 870–944)
Language: Arabic
Source: David Thomas, *Christian Doctrines in Islamic Theology* (Leiden, Neth.: Brill, 2008), 96–117.

Al-Maturidi was born in Samarkand in present-day Uzbekistan. A prolific writer and theologian, he wrote several works refuting the theological teachings of his opponents.

Only two of al-Maturidi's works survive, one of them being his treatise on Divine Unity. This is a lengthy work and essentially a systematic theology. Within it, however, comes a refutation of Christianity. Here, al-Maturidi is especially concerned to address the notion of a divine Christ who is Son of God. It is clear from al-Maturidi's refutation that he is familiar with the variety of Christian thinking on the incarnation, but his arguments really only serve his greater concern of addressing and promoting the Islamic theology of strict, divine oneness (tawhid).

★★★

The Master [i.e., al-Maturidi], may God have mercy on him, said: The Christians are divided over Christ, for there are those among them who attribute two spirits to him, one of them temporal, the spirit of humanity which is like the spirits of people, and an eternal divine spirit, a part of God, and this came into the body. They say: There are no more than Father, Son and Holy Spirit.

Others make the spirit which was in Christ God and not a part, although a small group of them make in the body as it were a thing within a thing, and a small group control, without the body encompassing it.

Among them are those who say: A part from God almighty combined with it and also another part.

Ibn Shabib said: I heard one of their associates say that he was son by adoption and not son by begetting, just as the wives of Muhammad, peace be upon him, are called mothers, and as a man says to another, "My little son."

The Master, may God have mercy on him, said, Say to them: Since the spirit that was in him is eternal and is a portion, how did it become Son and the other portions did not? If it is said: Because it is lesser; he has to make all the portions of the universe sons to those that are bigger than them, and he has to make every portion from what remains the same, so that he will be entirely sons. Further, it is well-known that a son is younger than a father, so how can they both be eternal? And if the whole is regarded as being in the body, say to him: Which thing in it is the Son? And if he says: The whole; he has made the whole Son and Father, in this making the Father a son to himself.

If it is said: It was a part of him without there being any diminution in the wholeness of the original, like the part taken from the light; respond along the lines that if the part that was taken originated, as happens in the case of what is taken from the light, then his teaching about the eternity of the spirit, which is the Son, is disproved. And if he claims that it was communicated from God like that which is taken, the foregoing applies to him. Furthermore, how does he know that what is taken from the light will not disappear? If it is said: Such is our observation of it; say: Maybe God brought it into being, or it is like the fire in the stone which comes out. Whichever of these, it is temporal and the temporal is created, so how can it justifiably be Son?

He says: Because God manifested miracles from him; say: He manifested from Moses, so say that he was another son, though if you claim that this was through invocation and entreaty, the same applies to Jesus, in addition to which on the part of Jesus is that on the night of the arrest he said: "If your will is to take this bitter cup from any, then take it from me."

If it is said: Crying and entreaty on the part of Jesus were to instruct people; say: The same from Moses. Furthermore, both he and Moses used to pray and make entreaties towards Jerusalem; and once again, crying and entreaty are natural actions, neither can be prevented, so what is the meaning of "instructing"?

Next, if he merited this because of action, this must apply to Moses and others. So if it is said: He and no others merited this by reviving the dead; say: Ezekiel revived a man. And if he responds: Prolificness; say: The Jews say that Moses was more prolific than him. The jurist, may God have mercy on him, said: He caused a lifeless staff to become a living serpent on numerous occasions, so he is greater. And if as argument he refers to feeding many people with little food, respond that our Prophet produced in a vessel flour that had not been there. If it is said: He turned the water into wine; say: Elisha filled a number of vessels for a woman and turned it into oil. And if he refers to walking on the water as argument, they themselves acknowledge this of Joshua son of Nun, of Elijah and of Elisha. And if they adduce as evidence the ascension into heaven, they themselves acknowledge this of Elijah, and they say that he ascended into heaven in the sight of many people. And if as argument they refer to healing the blind, the leper and the like, bringing what is lifeless to life is greater than this, and they themselves acknowledge it of Elijah and Elisha.

In addition is what is against them in their own acknowledgement that the Jews crucified him and mocked him, for if the above is evidence of exaltation, this is evidence of diminution. And why did he not do what Elijah did, because when they came after him, he sent down on them fire which ate them up, God honouring him with this?

And if they go back to the manifestation of miracles as a guarantee of being distinctive, respond with the individuals I have mentioned, and further: Say that God is in heaven and earth since he manifests miracles in each thing in them. Thus, each thing has to be distinctive for the reason they make him distinctive.

***

Then he responded to the person who said: There is no greater mark of honour than his saying: "My little son." Say: Surely "Father" is greater [at] conferring esteem. If he should say: It necessarily entails priority; he disproves his point about conferring esteem, because it could not be meant in this sense. And since it is accepted that there were maybe others than him who were called by it, if it is said: In this is a conferring of equality with himself; say: A man may say to another, "My brother," and not mean it. Furthermore, although there may have been a mark of honour in his creation, maybe others were called by this, so that the disciples and prophets share in it.

"Friendship" and the like, that speaking of these as a mark of honour is justifiable, is answered. Say: Sonship is only justifiable within the same species, since it cannot justifiably be said to an ass or a dog; likewise, it is not justifiable in the first instance. In friendship there is an element of affection and affinity, and it occurs outside a species, as correctly applies to affinity, affection, custodianship and similar. So, while it is justifiable for God to have friends and loved ones from among creatures, the like is not acceptable with regard to sons. There is no strength other than with God.

The basis of this as we see it is that the distinction derives from two reasons. One of them is lordship, and God almighty, great is his praise, has made clear the impossibility of this in his eating, drinking, satisfying bodily needs in the privy, and his description as young and mature; his worshipping God almighty, entreating him and abasing himself; his calling creatures to the worship of God and to the affirmation of his unity, his announcement of Muhammad, may God bless him and give him peace, and his belief in the prophets. Furthermore, he, great is his praise, effected on him all the signs of temporality and marks of humanity that he effected throughout the universe. Similarly, he, may God bless him and give him peace, never claimed for himself anything other than human and prophetic status. So the teaching that he was divine is a teaching that has no meaning, not to speak of the fact that if it were applicable then it would be applicable for all people.

The wonder is that during his lifetime and period on earth they were not prepared to accord him the rank of prophethood, despite the proofs he provided. Then, after his ascension, or his death according to their ordinary people, they went further than according him humanity and prophethood, for they gave him the rank of lordship so that he might witness for them in humanity, physical substance and make-up. But all of this is deceit from beginning to end.

The second is that he should be his son, and this is a violation for many reasons. One of them is begetting, which is impossible and erroneous because the Lord is free from being affected by need, being overcome by yearning or being seized by loneliness, which are the reasons to seek to beget. It is also impossible for what exists through begetting to be different from the substance of the begetter, and God almighty is by his essence outside any resemblance to humanity, or the sense which this point implies. Also, as God has made clear, if he were to take pleasure it would not mean his taking the kind that we do.

Further, everyone who has a child endures sharing and surrender of his authority to him. But he who by his essence is Lord, King and powerful may not endure this. He makes no sense who says that a part from a thing is its son, and that he must be imperfect until he exists. The reference to signs does not necessitate this, because the way of recognising sonship in the observable sphere is not signs, apart from the fact that these were shared.

Further, he claims truthfulness in sincerity for himself regarding worship, and the signs require this and no more. Alternatively, he is connected with this in terms of excellence, though it is well-known in the observable sphere that this is not among the names that confer greatness, but being named "Christ" and "Messenger" is more splendid and significant in this respect.

Further, there have been miracles from God almighty to many creatures who have been distinguished by them, with nothing in them compelling the title of sonship. On top of this, in conversation sonship is only ever related to the young and feeble, not to those with strength and stature. It is the same with the matter of the effect that sons may have, that his honour should derive from this and his significance from his smallness, because this is a case of the significant in the small; and there is no strength except in God. Or that God was effectively his refuge and protection in every condition and crisis. In this respect every human is the same: it is like calling Eve the mother of her people, and the earth the mother of her people. In this respect he is effectively the refuge of creatures and the one on whom they can depend, although he should only be referred to in such ways when there is support. There is no strength except in God.

The Introduction (before 975)

Abu Bakr Muhammad b. al-Tayyib al-Baqillani (941/942–1013)

Language: Arabic

Source: David Thomas, *Christian Doctrines in Islamic Theology* (Leiden, Neth: Brill, 2008), 144–203.

Al-Baqillani was an Islamic jurist (qadi), teacher, and proponent of Ash'ari theology. As such, he was well-known in ruling courts of his day. In fact, some of his works come at the request of the ruling amir. This is certainly the case with The Introduction, *a work written for the amir's son, a student of al-Baqillani's.*

Within The Introduction *appears a lengthy refutation of Christianity. Like other works of this kind, al-Baqillani focuses on the Trinity and incarnation, though his remarks are much more extensive than others. At many points, al-Baqillani is keen to demonstrate the logical fallacies inherent in Christian doctrine, especially when they are propounded on the basis of Islamic theological patterns. Similarly, al-Baqillani questions the use of various theological metaphors that frequently appear in the context of Christian-Muslim debate. In this effort, al-Baqillani shows that not only is he familiar with much of the argumentation of the Christian communities active in the region but also with the earlier works of al-Warraq and al-Maturidi.*

***

Say to them: Why do you claim that God almighty is three hypostases, but do not claim that he is four or ten or more than this?

If they say: For the reason that it is established that the Creator, blessed be he, exists as substance; and it is established that he is living and knowing. So it necessarily follows that he is one substance and three hypostases, the existent One, Knowledge and Life. This is because a living, knowing being is not living or knowing until he is the possessor of life and knowledge. So it necessarily follows and is established that the hypostases are three; say to them: Why do you deny that the hypostases are four? For we say that the eternal One is existent, living, knowing and powerful, and one who is powerful must obviously have power. So it necessarily follows that the hypostases are four.

If they say: Power is life, so they are one hypostasis; say to them: So why do you deny that knowledge is life, so that the Creator, blessed be he, would then necessarily be two hypostases?

If they say: Knowledge can decrease and increase, disappear altogether and reappear, but definitely not life, so it necessarily follows that knowledge does not have the signification of life at all; say to them: But in the same way power can decrease and increase, can disappear altogether and reappear, but definitely not life. So it follows that power is other than life, with a different signification.

If they say: Knowledge can cease altogether in the condition of sleep and unconsciousness, though the person is living; say to them: In the same way power can cease altogether so that a person has no power to move his hand or tongue or a single one of his limbs, although he is still living in this condition. So it necessarily follows that power is other than life, and that the hypostases are four.

If they say: The attribute "knowing" can be used comparatively, as we say "knowing" and "more knowledgeable than him." But the impossibility of using the attribute "living" comparatively or of making one thing more living than another is evidence that knowledge is in no way life; say to them: So say that because of this very thing power is other than life, because we can talk comparatively about the attribute "powerful," and say "powerful" and "more powerful than him," and cannot say "living" and "more living than him." So it necessarily follows that power is other than life.

In the same way say to them: Why do you deny that the hypostases are five or ten? For we say: The Creator is existent, living, knowing and powerful, and we say: He is willing, everlasting, hearing, seeing and articulating. And the everlasting, seeing, articulating, willing One cannot be thus without the existence of everlastingness, will, hearing, sight and speech.

If they say: Everlastingness is him himself; say to them: Life and knowledge are both him himself, so say that he is one hypostasis.

If they say: Speech and will are actions of one who is articulating and willing; say to them: In the same way knowledge is among the actions of one who is knowing, so say that he is two hypostases.

If they say: Someone who cannot act may know by knowledge; say to them: Someone may will by will who cannot carry it out, and can articulate by speech who cannot perform it.

Similarly if they say: The Creator's, blessed be he, hearing and seeing are his knowledge itself, so it follows that they are not two hypostases other than knowledge; say to them: In the same way, the Creator's, blessed be he, knowledge is his life, so it necessarily follows that the almighty One is two hypostases. They have no answer to any of this.

If one of them says: The hypostatic nature of the Creator is established by there being an attribute that derives from his essence and is not attached to him by something other than himself. And his being existent and substance derives from himself, and his being living derives from himself and it is not attached to him by something other than himself, and his being knowing by himself derives from himself, and he has a hypostasis only by virtue of his being knowing by himself and not by anything other than himself; say to him: In the same way he is eternal by himself, and not every existent thing is a substance eternal by itself, so it necessarily follows that his being eternal is a fourth hypostasis.

In the same way he is a thing that is an existent by himself and is a substance by himself. So it follows that his being is a thing, existent and hypostasis, and his being is a substance and hypostasis. For not every existent is a substance. In the same way his being everlasting is an attribute that derives from himself, and is not attached to it by something other than him. And not every existent is everlasting. So it follows that his being everlasting is a fifth hypostasis.

They have no answer to this, and it means abandoning the Trinity.

***

Their explanations of the meaning of the Uniting vary.

Most of them say: The meaning of the Uniting is that the Word, who is the Son, inhered in the body of Christ. And most of them say: The Uniting was mingling and mixing. The Jacobites claim that the Word of God was transformed into flesh and blood through the Uniting.

The majority of them, the Jacobites and Nestorians, claim that the uniting of the Word with the human nature was a mingling and mixing like the mingling and mixing of water with wine and milk if it is poured into them and mixed with them.

People among them claim that the meaning of the Uniting of the Word with the human nature, which was the body, was its taking it as a location and substrate, and its directing things through it and its appearing through it and no other. They differ over the meaning of the appearance of the Word in the location, its putting it on, and the manifestation of direction through it. Most of them say: The meaning of this is that it inhered within it, mixed with it and mingled with it in the way that wine and milk mingle with water when they are mixed.

People among them say: The appearance of the Word in the body and its uniting with it was not in the sense of mingling and mixing, but in the way the form of a man appears in a mirror and polished, clean objects when he is in front of them, without the man's form inhering in the mirror; or like the appearance of an engraving on a seal or any stamp in wax or clay or any soft, impressionable body, without the engraving on the seal or imprint inhering in the wax or clay or earth or powder.

One of them says: I say that the Word united with the body of Christ in the sense that it inhered in it without touching, mixing or mingling, in the same way that I say God almighty dwells in the heaven and does not touch or mingle with it, and in the same way as I say that the reason is a substance which inheres in the soul, but even so is not mingled with the soul and is not touching it.

The Byzantines, the Melkites, say: The meaning of the Uniting of the Word with the body is that the two became one, the many became few, the Word and that with which it united became one, and that this one through uniting was two beforehand.

★★★

The Christians agree that the Uniting was a particular action by which the united being became united and Christ Christ. So say to them: Tell us about the Uniting with the human with whom the Word united; if it was an action, did it have an agent in your view or not?

If they say: It had no agent; say to them: Then why do you deny that all actions and events have no agent?—This is not their teaching.

If they say: The Uniting was an action of the agent who performed it and it united through it; say to them: Then who was its agent? Was it the substance which combines the hypostases and not the hypostases, or the three hypostases and not it? Or was it the three hypostases? Or was the agent of it one of the hypostases?

If they say: It was the common substance that combines the hypostases; say to them: Then the substance must be the one that united with the body and the universal substance, or the individual according to what you prefer. For, according to you, the one who united is the one that effected the Uniting and not those who did not effect it. And it also follows that he is the Divinity who is worthy of worship, for he is the effective being.

Similarly, if they say: The substance and the hypostases effected the Uniting; say to them: Then it follows that it was it and the three hypostases that united with the human, and there is no sense to your statement, "It was the Son alone who united, without the Father and Spirit or the common substance that combines the hypostases." This destroys your teaching that the Uniting was of the Son alone.

Similarly, if they say: The three hypostases alone without the substance effected the Uniting; say to them: Then it follows that the Spirit also united, unless the Son alone among the particularities of the substance united.

And if they say: The agent of the Uniting was the Son alone, and through his being singled out in effecting the Uniting he united without the Spirit; say to them: If it is possible for the Son to be singled out in effecting an event such as the Uniting without the Spirit and Father or the common substance, then why is it also not possible for the Spirit to be singled out by effecting an event and other events, and for each of the hypostases to be singled out by worlds and actions that the others did not effect, or for the substance that combines them to be singled out by an action that was not theirs? If this is so, it is possible for them to hinder one another and to be at variance.

And say to them: If the hypostases acted in the same way as the substance that combines them, then why should it combine them and they be particularities to it, rather than it being a particular to them and them combining it, so that it was one of the hypostases? They will not find a way to reject this.

Say to them: Tell us how the Word, which is the Son, united with the body of Christ without the Father and the Spirit, despite your teaching that it was not distinct from either of them or separated from them. And if this is acceptable, why do you deny that the water that is mixed with the wine and mingled with it can be drunk apart from the wine, or the wine drunk apart from the water, even though they are not separated or distinct from each other? If in your view this is impossible, and someone who drinks the wine mixed with the water must be drinking the wine and water if they are not separated or distinct from each other, then why do you deny that while the Son was united though was not separated from the Spirit and Father or distinct from them, the Father and Spirit were united just as the Son was united?

If they say: The Word only united with the universal human in the particular who was born of Mary; say to them: Then the Father and the Spirit must also have united with the universal in the individual who was born of Mary. We do not intend in this matter any discussion about the human with whom the Word united, and whether he was individual or universal, or whether it united with the universal in the individual who was born of Mary, but only discussion about how the Son could have become united with what he did unite, whether universal or individual, without the Father and Spirit, while not being distinct or separated from them. So answer this, if you can!

Then say to them: If the Word united with the universal human, then it can only have united with him in a location or not in a location. If it united with him not in a location, then between it and the body that was born and taken from Mary there is only what is between it and other bodies of people and other bodies. And Mary and the body taken from her have no distinctiveness, because the Son did not unite with it and nothing else. And the killing and crucifixion must have happened to the body alone, not to the Son or to Christ, because the body without the Son united to it was not Christ. So how could Christ be killed and crucified?

If the uniting of the Son with the universal was a uniting with it in any location, whether the body taken from Mary or any other body, then the universal would have to have been confined in this individual location, and the individual would have to have enclosed and contained the universal and been a location to it, even though the individual was from it. This is contrary to reason and its reverse, because if it were acceptable then it would be acceptable for the few to include the many and to exceed it, and for the smallest body to contain the greatest and enclose it. If we know by the basics of reason that this is wrong, we also know that it is impossible for the Son to unite with the universal, if there were such, in a small, individual location.

***

Say to them together: Tell us about the uniting of the Son with the body, did it continue to exist at the time his killing and crucifixion took place or not?

If they say: It continued to exist; say to them: So the one who died was Christ in two natures: divine nature, the Son, and human nature, the body. So it must follow that God's eternal Son died, just as he was killed and crucified, because to allow that he was killed and crucified is like allowing that he died. If at the killing the Son became lifeless, he cannot possibly have been divine at this time, because the Divinity is not lifeless or imperfect, and is not such for whom death is possible. If this were possible for him, death would be possible for the Father and Spirit—which is to abandon their teaching.

If they say: The Uniting ceased at the killing and crucifixion; say to them: So the Uniting must have been broken at the killing and crucifixion—which is to abandon their teaching.

It must also be the case that the one who was killed could not be Christ, because when the Uniting was broken and the being who was united with was separated from, the body was not Christ. For the body and what united with it was only Christ when the Uniting was certain and existent. If it was broken, the one who was killed and crucified and was affected by death and burial was human. So their teaching that Christ was killed and crucified is meaningless.

The Confirmation of the Proofs of Prophethood (995)

'Abd al-Jabbar (ca. 937–1025)
Language: Arabic
Source: Gabriel Said Reynolds and Samir Khalil Samir, *Critique of Christian Origins* (Provo, UT: Brigham Young University Press, 2010).

Al-Jabbar was a high-ranking qadi who at different times both enjoyed the favor of the ruling elite and endured their scorn. Thus, while he rose through the ranks as a qadi and theologian, he also made some enemies. He refused to officiate the funeral of one of these enemies. For this he was imprisoned. Before and even after his time in prison, al-Jabbar maintained a large following of students. In this context, he continued to write and teach until his death.

He is well-known for his prolific writings on matters of Islamic theology, in particular the Mu'tazila concerns of divine oneness and justice. His magnum opus, the Summa on Divine Oneness and Justice, *was devoted to these very topics. Less well-known, however, are his writings on Christianity. Of course, these appear in his* Summa, *but in another text,* The Confirmation of the Proofs of Prophethood, *al-Jabbar spends much time in a section called "Critique of Christian Origins" describing and critiquing in great detail the history of Christianity, Christian doctrine, use of Scripture, and various Christian practices.*

As the work's main title suggests, al-Jabbar is also keen to substantiate the prophethood of Muhammad. Part of his method for doing so is unique. Instead of great lists of miracles that might prove Muhammad's prophethood, al-Jabbar focuses on attacking his opponents. Thus, in tearing others down, he hopes to prop up Muhammad.

***

[Here is] [a]nother chapter, on [the claim] that these three sects of the Christians are the most determined in God's world to venerate Christ, to testify to him, and to love him. They claim that they are his faction and followers, that they are the people most obedient to him, that they follow his precedent, that they emulate him, and that they act according to his commandments.

Yet [Muhammad]—God's blessing and peace be upon him—said that Christ is a servant of God and His Messenger, that he brought the people what the prophets brought before him, such as Adam, Noah, Abraham, Ishmael, Isaac, Jacob, the tribes of Israel, Moses, Aaron, and other prophets—God's blessings be upon all of them—[namely] a call to worship God and to declare His oneness, that He alone is to be served, is uncreated, and is Lord. [Muhammad said] that the Christians lied about Him, changed His religion, and annulled His commandments, and that they imitated with their statement those who disbelieved before them, who took created things as gods and lords, supplicating to them and beseeching them, such as the philosophers and the Sabi'un of the people of Harran, by taking created things as gods and lords, invoking them and imploring them.

They believed in the sun, the moon, the planets, and the sky as we have presented. Likewise, the Egyptians said regarding Pharaoh what we have reported, and others [have adopted similar views]. Many people asserted the lordship of created things and created beings. The explanation of their affairs would take too long. Yet Christ—God's blessing and peace be upon him—is an enemy of these Christians. He washed his hands of them.

The people found the affair just as [Muhammad] said, as he clarified and detailed. How wonderful is this! An illiterate Arab man reports about a man who preceded him by about one thousand years, who had a different language, who came from a different land and a different people. Yet he knew about [Christ] and his various affairs.

[Muhammad]—God's blessing and peace be upon him—found communities among those that preceded him who claimed that they testify to this man and that they follow his model and manners. Now if he were one who fabricated lies he would not have had the audacity to do so in this case. Yet he did not trust that the people who preceded him in time and testified to this man were right about him or that they were Jesus' followers as they claimed. He would not have felt secure in bringing forth a lie, since he claimed that he was sincere, that he was a prophet, that he was carrying a message to all the peoples of the earth, and that his intellect was not astray. Look at how he took a stand in the face of grave matters and trying circumstances.

[Muhammad] related from his Lord—Mighty and Exalted—that the Christians do not follow anything that the prophets brought. He said, "Ask those to whom We sent Our Messengers before you. Did We make a god other than al-Rahman for them to worship?" [Muhammad] was bold about those things that intellectuals and overbearing rulers were doing before him, including their vices and dishonor. Then what he said became clear. If he had only these proofs, they would be adequate, satisfactory, and abundant.

***

Now someone might say: "By my life it is demonstrated that the Christians have said that Jesus, the son of Mary, is neither a prophet nor a Messenger of God nor a righteous servant, but rather that he is a god, Lord, Creator, and Provider, that God is the third of three, and that he was killed and crucified. Yet your master has said in your book, 'Did you say unto men, "Take me and my mother as two gods, apart from God"?' The Christians say, 'This is a lie. For although we said about [Christ] that he is a god, we did not say about his mother that she is a god.'"

One should reply to him: [God] did not report about [the Christians] that they say such a thing. For this is not a report that could be true or false. He only said, "Did you say unto men, 'Take me and my mother as two gods, apart from God'?" Even one who does not know Arabic well, or at all, would not consider this a report. This statement is in the form of a question and query. Yet this is not possible for God—exalted be His praise—[to query]. A person only questions and queries when he does not know what he has questioned and asked about. This is only a stipulation to bring out the answer from the one who is asked. This is like His address to Moses—God's blessing be upon him—"What is that in your right hand, O Moses?" when He—Mighty and Exalted—knew [the answer to] that better than Moses. [This is similar] to His address to the devil, "What prevented you from prostrating when I order you," or "when I ordered you," when He—Mighty and Exalted—knew what prevented him better than the devil did.

In this way He asked Christ, "Have you said this about yourself or about your mother, the one who begot you, who is the most intimate of people to you, and the one who most has a right over you, and is the most exalted to you?" [This He did] to demonstrate [Christ's]—peace be upon him—complete innocence. Thus that which the questioner supposed, that this is a report, is invalid. This answer is convincing and sufficient. . . .

Know that the masses of the Christians believe that God chose Mary for himself and his son, that He selected her as a man chooses a woman and took her as a concubine because of His yearning for her. Nazzam and Jahiz have related this. [Jahiz] reports, "They only declare this outright to one who has their trust." Ibn al-Ikhshid reports this about them in his *al-Ma'una,* saying, "This is what they indicate. Do you not see that they say, 'If He were not a Begetter He would be sterile, and sterility is a flaw'?" This is the opinion of all of them, which indicates physical intercourse. You will find this in his book *al-Ma'una* and in the book of Jahiz against the Christians. I think that Abu Ja'far al-Iskafi reports this in his book against the Christians as well. All who have mixed with the monks and sacristans of the churches, who have spent a long time with them and befriended them, know this from them.

***

One of the things that the Christians adduce as evidence, and this is the greatest of their specious arguments regarding their religion, the most exalted proof in which they take refuge, and a standard for the elite and the common people among them, is that they say, "Christianity is a difficult and strict religion. Yet great nations and kings have accepted it, with no compulsion, sword, coercion, or constraint. They would not have accepted it except for the signs and miracles which were brought forth through the monks and nuns who prayed for them."

One should reply to them: We have demonstrated, as is known, the Christians' substitution of the religion of Christ and their predilection for the Roman kings. We have clarified that and made it known. We have found only that the Christians became Romans; the Romans did not become Christians. The origin of your sects is the Romans. This is convincing and sufficient.

Even if we did not know this, how there was a plot from the beginning [of Christianity] to the end, it would not be difficult for us to show clearly the invalidity and flaw of this argument. God does not bring forth miracles through the people of this religion, nor does He do anything supernatural through any of them. How could this be, when only the prophets—peace be upon them—in their era, performed miracles?

Then one should reply to the Christians: You claim the validity of your religion on the basis of the number of people and the kings who have taken up your religion. Yet numbers are not a proof of the validity of religions. For the only proof, without exception, of the validity of religions is evidence and logical demonstration, whether the people of that religion are few or many. Christ and those who followed him were few, while the Romans, Jews, and companions of the king were greater in number. According to your analogy, this would prove that he did not perform miracles.

Then one should reply to them: You claim miracles and signs for your monks, nuns, and leaders in every era, which have not been cut off and have not ceased. Yet you have acknowledged this religion and have not seen a miracle or a sign. Thus it was with those before you who acknowledged it in the same way. This is enough for one who seeks the truth.

They meet together whenever they want to permit or forbid something and hold a synod (that is, a meeting to make decisions) to do so. If it was held long ago, they explain, "This thing was forbidden by that group only because of the appearance of a sign or a miracle." Do you not see that, according to them, the seats of the Katholikos and Metropolitan were once allowed to those who have a family and children? But then the Katholikos and leaders passed leadership on to their sons and bequeathed it to their offspring. The Christians met and forbade it to those who have family, children, or have been married. Thus this became their religious law. They met about it and acted according to it without any sign or miracle.

According to them, the marriage of two sisters to two brothers used to be licit. Then it happened that the enmity between two sisters, who were with two brothers, led to enmity between the two brothers. They met and forbade that. This became their religious law, by which they acted, even though they did not see a sign or a miracle.

According to them, marrying the daughter of one's brother used to be licit. Then this became a means by which some of them sought to promote themselves. They met and forbade that. This became their religious law without any sign or miracle.

Among these are things that they have done recently, in the Islamic world, in the 'Abbasid state, like that which the Metropolitan of Samarqand did. He forbade his people [to eat] fowl, for he claimed that the Holy Spirit descended in this sort of dove. They accepted this from him and made it a religious law.

If you mix with them, investigate them, [or] enter among them, if you get into the inner circle of the Katholikos and the monks, you would find there many instances of lies, ignorance, covetousness for this world, desire for leadership, hoarding, and prohibition. If one of them who had nothing becomes a monk, he becomes a burden to others. Not much time will pass before he has tremendous wealth. It may happen that he dies with tens of thousands [of dinars].

Then one should reply to them: You are many sects and between you there is a great conflict over the basis of religion. You say that the Melkites and Jacobites are misguided. Likewise the Nestorians do not accept the Melkites and the Jacobites. All of these sects claim that their monks, nuns, and leaders have miracles and signs, as do the Manicheans. According to their analogy, the truth is with one sect. The rest of them lie in their claims.

A wise man said, "You can know the lies of the people of these religions and articles [of belief], among which is Christianity, through the briefest contemplation. They claim that their great men perform signs and that these do not cease for them in any era, and that whoever accepted Christianity did so because of miracles. One should reply to them: You who have acknowledged it have seen neither a sign nor a miracle."

4

Strengthening Defenses, Refining Attacks

Christian-Muslim Theological Engagement in the
Western Mediterranean (Eleventh to Twelfth
Centuries)

Judgment regarding the Confessions, Inclinations, and Sects
(before 1064)

Ibn Hazm (994–1064)
Language: Arabic
Source: Olivia Remie Constable, ed., *Medieval Iberia* (Philadelphia:
University of Pennsylvania Press, 2012), 107–9.

A descendant of a Christian convert to Islam, Ibn Hazm was one of the
greatest Muslim figures to emerge from al-Andalus, the shifting territory
ruled by Muslims in the Iberian Peninsula. He received the finest education
of his day, and his writings demonstrate mastery in poetry, history,
philosophy, law, and theology. He was a controversial figure and at times
endured exile and imprisonment. He championed the Shafi'i legal school

and then became the leading figure of Zahiri jurisprudence, both fringe schools of thought.

In his writings, Ibn Hazm frequently attacks those who disagree with him. One of his most well-known works, Judgment regarding the Confessions, Inclinations, and Sects, *is a kind of systematic theology that not only articulates Ibn Hazm's perspective but attacks his opponents as well. In this effort, Ibn Hazm shows a deep familiarity with his opponents' various beliefs, which is especially true in his attacks upon Christianity. These attacks are deployed in two movements. In the first, Ibn Hazm builds off of his Muslim forebears in his criticism of the Trinity and incarnation as they are articulated by various Christian traditions. In the second, Ibn Hazm demonstrates his most original thinking, pushing the Muslim charge of corruption (tahrif) of the Gospels further than most other Muslim historians and theologians. Not only are Ibn Hazm's attacks piercing, but they also reveal an intimate familiarity with the New Testament texts.*

***

In this same chapter [of the Gospel of Matthew] the Messiah said to them, "Do you not suppose that I have come in order to introduce peace among the people of the land, but rather the sword; and I have arrived only in order to make division between a man and his spouse and his son, and between a daughter and her mother, and between a daughter-in-law and her mother-in-law, and in order that a man will consider the people of his household enemies" (Matt. 10:34-26).

And in the twelfth chapter of the Gospel of Luke the Messiah said to them, "I have arrived only in order to cast fire upon the earth, and my desire is only the spreading of it, and verily we will plunge all of [the earth] into it. And I am appointed for the completion of this. Do you think that I have come to make peace among the people of the earth? Nay, rather to make division among them. For five men will be divided in a single house, three against two and two against three, the father against the son and the son against the father, the daughter against the mother and the mother against the daughter, the mother-in-law against the daughter-in-law and the daughter-in-law against the mother-in-law" (Luke 12:49-53).

These are the two passages just as you see them.

And in the ninth chapter of the Gospel of Luke the Messiah (upon Him be peace) said to them, "I was not sent for the destruction of souls but rather for the welfare of them."

And in the tenth chapter of the Gospel of John the Messiah said, "I will not judge him who hears my words but does not keep them, for I did not come in order to judge the world and punish it, but rather in order to preserve the people of the world."

These [last] two passages contradict the two passages that preceded them, and each of the meanings [of the respective sets of passages] clearly refutes the other. For if it is said that [Jesus] meant only that He was not sent for the destruction of souls who believed in Him, then we say, [that Jesus] was speaking in general and did not single out [any particular group]. The proof of the falseness of this explanation of yours—that is, that He only meant that He was not sent for the destruction of the souls who believed in Him—is the text of this passage: In the ninth chapter of the Gospel of Luke . . . he says about the Messiah that "He sent before Him messengers and they made their way to Samaria in order to prepare for Him there, but they did not receive Him on account of His wending His way to Jerusalem; but when John and James saw this they said to Him, 'O our Lord, does it suit you if we call out so that fire will descend upon them from heaven and burn all of them just as Elias did?' But He turned to them and scolded them and said, 'The One Who possesses [your] spirits did not send the [Son] of Man for the destruction of souls, but for the salvation of them.' And then they made their way to another city."

. . . Ambiguity disappears, therefore, since it is certain that He did not mean by the souls which He was sent to save some of the souls to the exclusion of others, but rather He meant all the souls, those disbelieving in Him and those believing in Him, for just as you heard,

He said this only when His disciples wanted to destroy those who would not accept Him. So the lies of the first statement are manifest. And God forbid that the Messiah (on Him be peace!) should lie; rather the lying without doubt derives from the four iniquitous men who wrote these corrupted, altered gospels.

***

And in [Matt. 12] the Messiah said to them: "John [the Baptist] came to you and he did not eat or drink and you said, 'He is possessed.' Then the Son of Man came—He means Himself—and you said, 'This man is a glutton and imbiber of wine, a wanton friend of tax collectors and sinners'" (Matt. 11:18-19).

In this [passage] there is lying and contradiction [to the teaching] of the Christians. As for the lying, it occurs when he says here that "John did not eat or drink" so that it is said about him that "he is possessed" for that reason. In the first chapter of the Gospel of Mark [it says] that the food of John son of Zachariah (May peace be upon both of them) was locusts and wild honey (Mark 1:6). This is a contradiction; one of the two reports is a lie without doubt. As for the contradiction of the teaching of the Christians, [it occurs when this passage] relates that John did not eat and drink while the Messiah did eat and drink. Now without doubt whoever among mankind God (He is magnified and exalted!) makes able to do without food and drink He has distinguished, and He has raised his status above anyone who cannot do without food and drink. So John [the Baptist in that case] is more virtuous than the Messiah without doubt. . . .

A third narrative [is relevant here] and it is the acknowledgement of Jesus about Himself that He ate and drank, even though among [the Christians] He is considered a god. But how could this god eat and drink? What foolishness is greater than this? For if they say that "the human nature of Him is that which ate and drank," then we say, "and this is a lie on your part in any case, for if the Messiah is considered by you as both a divine nature and a human nature together, then He is two things; now if the human nature alone ate then only one of the combination of the two things ate and not the other."

So admit that in that case half the Messiah ate and half the Messiah drank. Otherwise you have lied anyway and your forefathers have lied in their saying "the Messiah ate," and you have attributed to the Messiah falsehood [as well] in His report about Himself that he ate, since only half of Him ate.

[All this shows that] the [Christian] community is altogether vile.

The Qadi Abu l-Walid al-Baji's Reply
to the Monk of France's Letter to the Muslims
(before 1081)

Abu l-Walid al-Baji (1013–1081)
Language: Arabic
Source: D. M. Dunlop, "A Christian Mission to Muslim Spain in the 11th Century," *Al-Andalus* 17 (1952): 259–310.

Al-Baji was a leading poet, historian, and qadi *in al-Andalus and an opponent of Ibn Hazm. He was well connected in Islamic courts in the peninsula and formed a special relationship to al-Muqtadir bi-llah, the Muslim king of Saragossa.*

It was for al-Muqtadir that al-Baji wrote a reply to a letter from a French monk in which the monk issued a call to convert after a brief explication of some of the finer points of Christian Christology and soteriology. The letter and al-Baji's reply come to us together and it remains quite possible that al-Baji wrote the entire correspondence himself. If this is the case, then the letter from the monk was used as a rhetorical invention on which al-Baji could build an articulation of superior Islamic belief.

***

This is the reply of the faqih [i.e., jurist], the qadi, the honoured (and) excellent Abu-l-Walid al-Baji, God's mercy and favour upon him, to the above letter.

In the name of God, the Merciful, the Compassionate. God bless Muhammad and his family and give him peace. Glory to God and blessing upon his Apostle.

***

We raise the like of you and heighten your value above (what is deserved by) the opening of your letter, where you say that Jesus—may God bless him and give him peace—is the son of God, who is Exalted. No, he is created man and a servant under authority, not exempt from the proofs of createdness, such as movement, rest, cessation, passing from place to place, changing from one state to another, eating food, and death, which is appointed for all men—things which are not right for an eternal God and impossible (to believe) for anyone of sound judgement. And if we admit that with these qualities and created states (Jesus)—may God bless him and give him peace—is an eternal God, then we must deny that the world or anything therein is caused and created, because there is in nothing of what we have mentioned, mankind, the world and what is therein of animals and inanimate objects, any proof of createdness other than what is in Jesus—may God bless him and give him peace. God, who is Exalted, created Jesus, on whom be peace, without a father, as he created Adam—may God bless him and give him peace—from the dust, and a mother bore Jesus. Adam had neither father nor mother. Since Adam is not a God, though he is (our) first father, but was created, much less is Jesus a God, being of the posterity and children of Adam, but [Jesus] is a servant under authority. This is plain to him who is ignorant of the meaning of createdness and has not distinguished the Creator from the created.

Whoever has considered any of the departments of knowledge and is aided by discernment and understanding finds the marks of createdness plainer and its proofs more valid than that they can be concealed or ambiguous, or that anyone with the least pretensions to knowledge can be doubtful in regard to them. There have appeared at the hands of all the Prophets, on whom be peace, clear signs and shining miracles, such as appeared at the hand of Jesus, on whom be peace, and more. If it is permitted to claim for Jesus, on whom be peace, because of instances of raising the dead and curing the blind and the lepers, that he is the son of God, who is Exalted, this can be claimed for Abraham, because of the instance of his escaping from the fire after he had been cast into it. (Jesus did not escape from a small number of persons who wished to crucify and kill him, according to what you say.) It can be claimed for Moses, on whom be peace, because of the instances of his turning the rod into a serpent, and dividing the sea. And the same claim can be made for Muhammad—may God bless him and give him peace—because of the instances of the splitting of the moon, the flowing of water from between his fingers, the declaration of praise by the pebbles in his hand and the calling out of the sheep to him, as well as other signs. But signs do not necessitate admitting what is absurd nor making absurd what is permissible (and) possible. Since our Lord, who is Exalted, is eternal, it is not consistent with his glory that he should be caused or created. In whomsoever are found the proofs of createdness, such as eating, drinking, cessation and passing from place to place, he is only created (and) a subject, and the raising of the dead at his hand does not show that he is a God to be worshipped. Instances of that in the case of one who claims the Prophecy only show that he is a true Prophet, because the qualities of createdness in him do not make absurd his being a Prophet. If it were permitted to say that Jesus, on whom be peace, was the creator of instances of miracle and unique in his action, we could say that Adam, Abraham, Moses, Muhammad and the rest of the Prophets, on whom be peace, were unique in creating instances of miracle, that it was all their creation and that in consequence they are Gods to be worshipped. Which is absurd. There is no Creator but God and no object of worship save him. These (others) are honoured Prophets and favoured Apostles, confirmed by God, who is Exalted, in these instances of miracle, which are only possible for him, nor is it true to say that any but he created them.

***

Now we have knowledge of your law and the disagreement of your doctors in regard to your religion and what each sect advances of your doubts in regard to the hypostases, the creation, the meaning of "divinity" and "humanity," the substance, and other brayings of your asses . . . which if we had displayed to them a small part, we should have stupefied and dazzled them, and they would have known that we possess of its aggregate and details what not one of the people of your religion has attained or succeeded in deducing and following its meanings, first and last of you. But we preferred to be mild with them, to use discretion and be pleasant to them, so we tempered our words to them, showing them a slight portion of the matter, from which our souls were not averse and their minds were not vexed to hear in this accepting the instruction of God, through their compliance.

We have seen that in your letter you differ from all the people of your religion, for there is no man among the sects of the Christians who says that one need have faith only in Christ. Rather it is faith in the Father which is necessary with you, and the Father is not taken with you in (the meaning of) humanity. Only the Son is so taken, and anyone who believes only in the Son, disbelieves in the Father. Previously you had said in your letter that Christ is the son of God, and this contradicts your statement that faith is necessary only in Christ, who is the Son. If we were to follow out the contradiction, dislocation and absurdity which appear in your letter, only a trifling portion would remain intact. But—may God give success to us and you—we ascribe that in you, in view of what we are accustomed to in people of your religion, to lack of knowledge, unfamiliarity with the aims of dialectic and neglect of study and discussion besides (your acceptance of) untrue views and stories which are unfounded in fact and do not help. I trust that God may grant you success by our guiding you to leave falsehood and clinging to deception and lies, and that he may give you in exchange knowledge of the truths and soundness of aim and instruction in dialectic, which will bring you to the plain paths and the evident truths.

***

God, who is Exalted, has made the present world the House of trouble and temptation and trial, that he might test us (to see) which of us would do good, and he has made the after-life the House of reward and punishment, to reward the believers who have done well and to punish the infidels who have associated (other deities) with him. Among the causes of temptation he has made the accursed Devil, and he has sent the Prophets to guide to the straight path, "lest mankind might have an argument against God, after the Apostles." He has guided by the Prophets whom he would, through his grace, and has cut off by the accursed Devil whom he would, through his justice.

The first of the Apostles to the people of the earth was our father Adam, on whom be peace. He summoned to the worship of God alone, who has no associate and no son, and so the Apostles after him. Whenever a law was forgotten and its covenant became old, God sent an Apostle to the people of the earth, to renew it and confirm it, till God, who is Exalted, sent a Prophet whose name was Jesus, on whom be peace. So (Jesus) called his people to the worship of his Lord and Maker and Creator. A few believed in him, a small number who were unable to defend him from his enemies who sought him—those who disbelieved and denied what he brought from (God)—till God raised him to himself and chose for him what was in store for him. "They did not kill him nor crucify him, but likeness was made for them." He gave his blood freely, according to what you say, desiring to save mankind from error, and only a small number believed in him. Yet people believed in other Prophets who did not go so far as this, just as they believed in Jesus. Moses, on whom be peace, did not die till a large number believed in him, a great multitude, nor did Muhammad—may God bless him and give him peace—die till a huge number believed in him, who thereby gained possession of the lands and conquered the horizons, and God made him victorious over every religion, "even though the polytheists were unwilling." Then, immediately after his death, his Companions conquered the land of Persia, in spite of its remoteness from his place, the strength of its ruler and its greatness and power. They conquered the land of Syria, which was the most excellent of your lands, the place of (the appearing of) your Law, and the end of your pilgrimage and worship. He whom you [assert] is your God, in spite of his having shed his blood, achieved less than the Prophets who were the subject sons of Adam, with God helping and guarding them. If Jesus had been a powerful God, he would not have needed (to do) that. He would have created them believers. And if God had wished that there should be no rebellion, he would not have created the temptations or the accursed Devil. But God has created for the Garden those worthy of the Garden, acting by the favour of God, who is Exalted, and he has created for the Fire those worthy of the Fire, acting without God's favour. If Jesus, on whom be peace, knew the Unseen, why did he give his blood through a desire for that which was not accomplished, and from which he gained nothing?

***

Among the strangest things which you people bring forward is your statement that (Jesus) gave his blood for the salvation of men. How could the Lord have blood, when blood belongs to caused (and) created bodies? If you defined the expression, you would say that it was the blood of humanity, not divinity, and you would have to say that what was crucified was the humanity, not the son of God, who is Exalted. But you are convinced that your God was crucified and died. This description is not right except for a caused, created being, because the negation of everlasting life is not admissible. If this were possible for him, it would certainly be possible for his father, according to what you say, because he has the same quality as his son. But he belonged to one of your communities. How then could he be a God, everlasting, living, self-existent [forever], to whom death was possible and whose life was subject to negation? Why did (Jesus) not remove death from himself and was not able to defend himself against it, when he had done away with (death) as you say, according to what you have mentioned in your letter? And if it is possible [that] he died and was nevertheless a God, what prevents our saying that all whom we have seen or heard of are everlasting and [forever] Gods, though they had a father or died or their life passed away and was negated? Can it be that anyone would reach this pitch of plain ignorance, admitting the reversal of truths and making ridiculous pretensions, whose speech had not stumbled, whose ignorance was not deep-rooted and whose eyes were not blind?

***

One of the curious things you advance, raising thereby the laughter of your hearers, is your saying that Jesus is the son of God, who is exalted above such a thing, and (at the same time) you say that he is of the sons of David, on whom be peace. This is stated in your Gospel and read from your sacred book. And you claim that Gabriel, when he brought the announcement of him to Mary, said to her, Truly, he shall be powerful with God, and his name shall spread abroad, and he shall be called the son of God, and God shall make him inherit the kingdom of his father David. You do not apply this in the sense that David was his father on the side of Mary, because she was not one of the descendants of David. You apply it only in the sense that (David) was his father on the side of Joseph the carpenter, whom you suppose was the husband of Mary, since Joseph was of the sons of David. David was a servant, who came into existence after he was not, and died after he had lived. How was Jesus, the son, the Creator and God of David, his father? And how is he son of David, who was created, and son of God, the Creator? Is this anything else than ignorance of the difference between son and father, eternal and caused, Creator and created? He who is so extremely ignorant cannot have right belief in a divine law. How can he call to it and speak about it? But deficient reflection and love of victory (in argument) necessitates extravagance and occasions folly and confusion—we ask God for protection.

***

Now our Lord has revealed in his noble book that Jesus announced our prophet Muhammad—may God bless him and give him peace. Either this information is known to you, or your religious leaders have concealed it and expunged it from your Gospels. We have read them in Arabic and know enough of their discrepancy and confusion to show us that distortion and alteration, addition and omission have affected them. . . . How can it be right for you (to have) faith in what differs and fails to agree, and varies and is not corroborative of itself? Our preserved book is preserved by small and great. No one can possibly add to it or take away from it, and what is read therein by people in the farthest East is read by those in the farthest West, without the addition of a letter or a phrase and with no difference in a vowel or a point.

And I am surprised, O monk, in view of what is reported to us of your superiority among your people and your precedence among those of your religion, at the appearance of excessive carelessness and want of knowledge in you, as regards what your letter contains on the subject of the accursed Devil being able to lead astray those whom God wills to lead to the eternal religion, though we say, or (indeed) you say in your book, that God is all-powerful. What is his power, if he shed his blood to annul what the Devil and others whom he had created began, and was unable to set right what (the Devil) had put wrong, make good what he had caused and straighten what he had laid awry? The accursed Devil, in what he achieved, did not go so far as to shed his blood, did not alter his condition, did not assume another corporeal form and did not change into something else. This surely must be impossible (to believe) for the least of your pupils and the youngest of your followers, as it must be impossible (to believe) for the most ignorant of mankind and the least of them in understanding.

But of what you say is not this strangest of all, that the Devil appeared to Jesus—God, according to you—and went up with him to the top of a mountain and showed him the glory of the present world, saying to him, If you worship me, I shall make you king of all this? When Christ heard that wile of the accursed Devil, he turned from his evil and sought refuge from his temptation by fasting 40 days and 40 nights, and the Devil let him go. Is there a grain of intelligence in one who admits this against his Lord and announces it of him? Does any relation remain between him and the attainment of truths and religious knowledge? Is not God the Creator of the Devil, able to destroy him when he wills, and Ruler of the earth and the heavens and what is between them, without partner or distinction?

**

God, who is Exalted, by his grace and wisdom and kindness and favour has sent Muhammad—may God bless him and give him peace—and thereby has set a seal on the Apostolate and perfected the Prophecy, making him the last of the Apostles. He has sent him to all the worlds and rendered him superior by these high prerogatives. He has made his Law to remain till the Day of judgement. . . . [Muhammad] summon[ed] them to the worship of the Merciful and the disavowal of idols. Near and far, foe and friend opposed him in that, and he produced for them miraculous signs in which no deception or fraud was seen, no pretence and no falsifying. . . .

Then God, who is Exalted, honoured him with the miracle by which God distinguished him above all Prophets and Apostles, namely the Qur'an, by which are guided men and *jinn* [i.e., supernatural beings], all of them. . . . But till the present day no one has been able to bring a [chapter] like its [chapters] or a verse of its verses.

This is the greatest miracle performed by a Prophet, because all previous miracles could not be witnessed, their time being past. . . . But the miracle of the Qur'an remains among us and continues with us, its time will not be cut off nor pass away, till God inherits the earth and those who are upon it.

**

You, O monk, whom we wish to free from error, if you listen to our advice to you and obey us in what we command you, will reach the after-life in our company of the followers of Muhammad, on whom be peace, the honoured Prophet, will ascend by his intercession, will drink of his fountain, and will dwell in the Garden with him.

Dialogue against the Jews (1110)

Petrus Alfonsi (ca. mid-eleventh century–ca. early-twelfth century)
Language: Latin
Source: Irven M. Resnick, *Dialogue against the Jews* (Washington, D.C.: Catholic University of America Press, 2006).

Alfonsi was born Moses, a Jew, in al-Andalus and trained in both Hebrew and Arabic. He was familiar with Hebrew literature and Arabic science, medicine, and philosophy. In 1106, he converted to Christianity, taking the name Petrus Alfonsi.

In order to defend his conversion to his former Jewish community, he wrote the Dialogue against the Jews, *constructed as a conversation between himself and Moses, his former Jewish self. Alfonsi also devotes a chapter to Islam as a defense for his choice to convert from Judaism to Christianity, not the Muslim religion. With this in mind, the* Dialogue *could also function as a kind of polemical sourcebook that Christian readers might refer to in debate with non-Christians or as a means for reassuring themselves of the strength and rationality of their faith.*

Not only does Alfonsi defend Christian doctrine in his text, but in his chapter on Islam he also launches vehement attacks against Muslim religious practice, the Qur'an, Muhammad, and Islamic history. Despite this polemic, Alfonsi's work represents some of the most accurate information about Islam available in the Latin West at the time. As such, his work was read and copied widely. In fact, Alfonsi's summary of Muslim beliefs, which he gives in the voice of Moses, is reasonably detailed and accurate. Of course, this summary merely serves as a focal point for Alfonsi's attacks as he twists accurate information about Islam to fit his appraisal of Christianity as a superior faith.

***

Moses: . . . I wonder why, when you abandoned your paternal faith, you chose the faith of the Christians rather than the faith of the Saracens, with whom you were always associated and raised. . . . For you were always, as I said, associated with them and you were raised among them; you read [their] books, and you understand the language. You ought to have chosen this [part] before the rest, which is known to be more pleasing and more suitable than the others, so that I would take their role for myself. Indeed [their] law is generous. It contains many commands concerning the pleasures of this present life, by which fact divine love is shown to have been greatest toward them.

***

Since childhood, no less, you have known that these [basic points of Muslim belief] and many others, which would take too long to enumerate, were written and were held in the greatest veneration by the entire race of the Saracens, then why have you followed the Christian rather than the Muslim [*Muzalemitica*] religion? Will you better enjoy the felicity of the present life and equally enjoy that of the future life as well?

Petrus: Although the web of your discourse, which has so much elegance and sweetness, is not less convincing than if [Muhammad] himself were present, for those who consider the delights of the body the highest good, nevertheless it is strange that you hope to instruct me in this, in order to convince me of that in which you believe I can in no wise be deceived. For you are certain that it is not unknown to me who [Muhammad] was, how he falsely fashioned himself a prophet with a clever deception, and who his advisor was in contriving this. One thing remains uncertain to you, I reckon: how useless I will judge that doctrine that they call [Muhammad's].

When, though, you have heard his life and character summarized in my narration, then you will easily be able to discern whether I do or do not know what is true about him.

***

Petrus: Muhammad then, after he was orphaned, passed the years of childhood under the protection of his uncle, Manephus [i.e., Abdu Manaf, the family name of Abu Talib], serving the worship of the idols of the time, with the entire race of the Arabs, as he himself testifies in his Qur'an, saying that God said to him: "You were an orphan wandering aimlessly, and I received you and I guided you; you were poor, and I enriched you." After the passage of a few years as a hired servant with a certain most noble widow named Khadijah, he so possessed, in a brief time, the mind of his mistress, that he would take possession by law of marriage both all the goods and the mistress of the goods herself. Once he was transformed from the humblest pauper into a very rich man by this wealth, he burst forth into such arrogance that he expected that the kingdom of the Arabs would be offered to him, except that he was afraid that his kinsmen would not accept him as king, since they were his equals and his betters. Nevertheless, devising a path by which he could be made king, he chose to fashion himself a prophet, relying upon that wit for eloquence which, when he exerted himself in business dealings among various nations, he had received by the facility of his intelligence. He relied, too, on the fact that the greater portion of the Arabs at that time were common soldiers [milites] and farmers, and almost all were idolaters, except for some who embraced the law of Moses in a heretical way, following after the Samaritans, and others who were Nestorian and Jacobite Christians.

The Jacobites, however, are heretics named after a certain Jacob. They preach the circumcision, and believe that Christ is not God but only a just man, conceived of the Holy Spirit and born of a virgin; nevertheless they do not believe that he was crucified or that he died. Moreover, there was at this time in the region of Antioch a certain archdeacon named Sergius, a Jacobite and a friend of [Muhammad's];

he was called from there to a council and condemned. Saddened by the shame of his condemnation, he fled from the region and came to [Muhammad]. [Muhammad], supported by his advice, brought to a conclusion what he contemplated but still was unable to fulfill on his own. There were also two Jews among those heretics of Arabia whom we mentioned, named Abdias ['Abdallah b. Salam] and Chabalahabar [Ka'b al-Ahbar], and these, indeed, attached themselves to [Muhammad] and offered their assistance to complete his foolishness. And these three mixed together [*contemperaverunt*] the law of [Muhammad], each one according to his own heresy, and showed him how to say such things on God's behalf which both the heretical Jews and the heretical Christians who were in Arabia believed to be true; whereas those who were unwilling to believe of their own free will nevertheless were forced to believe for fear of the sword. But we do not know of any other prophecy of his nor any miracles, as we heard about Moses, Joshua, Samuel, Elijah, and Elisha, who, we read, performed many miracles.

***

Petrus: . . . The indications of a true prophet are these: probity of life, a display of miracles, and the firm truth of all [their] teachings. Violence was the good quality of life in [Muhammad], by which he had himself proclaimed a prophet of God by force, rejoicing in theft and rapaciousness, and burning so much with the fire of lust that he did not blush to befoul another man's bed in adultery just as if the Lord were commanding it, just as is read about Zanab [Zaynab] the daughter of Ias, the wife of Zed [Zayd]. "The Lord has commanded," he said, "that you, Zed, send away your wife." Once she was sent away, he copulated with her himself regularly. The dishonor of his wife, Aissa ['A'isha], brought to light very clearly how empty his prophecy was when, after she had been caught in adultery by the testimony of many people, he confirmed with a message of the false Gabriel that she had not been caught in adultery, because he did not want to send her away. One reads that he had praised God for the power of his own vice, that is, lust, because the power abounded in him forty times beyond human measure, and he gave thanks that the sweet odor and beauty of women attracted him a great deal, with God granting it.

***

Petrus: [You, Moses,] say that [Muhammad] commanded prayer five times a day, and that certainly he did this for this reason, that—on his mentors' advice—he wanted his law to be established as a mediator between the law of the Christians and that of the Jews, and not for its probity nor from divine inspiration [*adiutorium*]. For the Jews, according to their law, pray three times each day, and the Christians seven times, but he established as a limit between each of them neither three nor seven, but instead five times for praying. What you praise—that, before they pray, they wash the hands and arms and other members of the body—is not important to prayer. For prayer it is important to be cleansed inwardly, not outwardly. A purity resulting from the ablution of the members, however, was important to the worshipers of the planet Venus, who, wanting to pray to her, prepared themselves as if they were women, coloring [their] mouths and eyes. He commanded this for the reason that he became king at the minute of the planet Venus.

. . . That [Muhammad] commanded [his followers] to despoil, capture, and slay the adversaries of God until they decided to believe or to pay tribute, is not among the acts of God, nor did any of the prophets command that anyone be forced to believe, but he commanded this himself out of a desire for money in order to destroy his enemies. As you know, however, this ought not be done; rather, if anyone wishes to convert someone else, he should not do this with violence, but diligently and sweetly, just as [Muhammad] himself attested in his Qur'an, saying, in the person of the Lord, "If the Lord your God were to will it, the peoples of the entire world would believe. Why, then, do you compel them to believe? Because no one believes except by the will of God."

***

Petrus: The Qur'an was not written by [Muhammad's] hand, for if it had been, it would be sequentially arranged [*ordinatus*]. Indeed, his companions who had dwelled with him composed the Qur'an after his death, each one declaring his own reading, so to speak; as a result, we do not know which was the earlier and which the later arrangement. Moreover, [Muhammad] ordered [them] to despoil, capture, and slay the nations for this reason: so that the Arabs, who dwelled in the desert but were ignorant of God, would find pleasure in the predations and so that they especially would believe him.

***

Petrus: If he had done all things with divine help, he would not have been defeated so often, nor, as we said above, would his teeth have shattered in battle; like other kings, sometimes he was conquered and sometimes he conquered. Moreover, after his death, they all wanted to abandon his law. For he himself had said that on the third day his body would be raised up to heaven. When they knew that he was a deceiver and saw that the cadaver stank, with the body unburied, the greater part [of his followers] departed. Haly ['Ali], however, the son of Abytharius [Abu Talib], one of [Muhammad's] ten companions, obtained the kingdom after his death. He preached flatteringly and cleverly admonished the people to believe, and told them that they did not properly understand [Muhammad's] expression. He said, "[Muhammad] did not say that he would be raised up to heaven before burial, nor while people watched. Indeed, he said that after the burial of his body the angels would bear him off to heaven, with none being aware of it. Therefore, because they did not bury him immediately, certainly he began to stink, in order that they might bury him right away." Therefore, by this argument he held the people a little while in their earlier error. Two brothers, sons of the secretary of [Muhammad], Hazan [Hasan] and Hozam [Husayn], tormenting their bodies severely with fasts and vigils, almost killed themselves. Their father often admonished the sons, lest they fatigue their bodies with a torment that lasted too long. When he himself saw, however, that they were stupid and had already arrived at death's door from too much effort, he revealed [to them] the truth about [Muhammad]. Once they became aware of his wickedness from their father, they began to eat and drink wine, and, just as they had bravely persisted in his law previously, so at last they began to abandon the law, although not totally. But also a certain part of this people followed them in their practice. In all these ways, then, O Moses, we can know that he was not a true prophet and that neither are his words true. Although we pass over many things that we can say about him, let us merely introduce one which both we and you believe, namely, that he denied Christ, whom we believe both to be dead and crucified. For he says, "They neither slew nor crucified Christ, but it only seemed so to them." Moreover, you will find him a deceiver not only in this matter, but reread all the books and sayings of the prophets, and in everything that he said about them you will find him to be a liar. How, then, do you exhort me to believe that liar, when you will find [him] deceitful in everything? I entreat the piety of almighty God to free me from his error and to complete the fulfillment of the law that I chose. Amen.

The Book of Denuding or Exposing
(ca. 1050–1132)

Author unknown

Language: Latin

Source: Thomas E. Burman, *Religious Polemic and the Intellectual History of the Mozarabs* (Leiden, Neth.: Brill, 1994), 240–385.

We do not know the identity of the author of The Book of Denuding or Exposing, *and we know very little about him beyond what can be surmised from his text. He claims to be a convert from Islam, though this claim may be a rhetorical device the author uses in order to add strength to his argument. It appears that he originally wrote his text in Arabic, though the only surviving manuscript is in a Latin translation. It is likely that he wrote from Toledo in present-day Spain.*

The text is a fine example of Arabized Christian writing from medieval Toledo. As such, the text demonstrates familiarity with the Qur'an and Islam. It also seems to draw on earlier Arab Christian anti-Muslim works in the author's unrelenting attacks upon Muhammad and the Qur'an. Significantly, the text was an important resource for later works devoted to Islam that were written by Latin Christians.

***

Muhammad says in the Chapter of the Cow, *God said, "Do not inquire regarding those who are in hell,"* that is, regarding the forefathers of the first Muslims. Whence he is reported to have said about [his] father and mother: *Would that I knew what their work is* (cf. 2:134, 41).

We ask, therefore, about their prophet Muhammad. For they do not dare to say that he prophesied until after forty years. What, therefore, was he doing for those forty years? Now they will not be able to say anything except that he instructed the people in the worship of idols, teaching them according to those usages—[all of] which the accounts whose truth cannot be doubted say. If they say that Muhammad never was an infidel, we will prove this to be false through the text of the Qur'an. For it is said to Muhammad himself in the Chapter of *Ebroha, Did not God find you an orphan, and gather you in when you were in error, and guide you* (93:6, 7)? This statement proves that your prophet had been in error.

Again in the Chapter of *Elfecep*, that is "Acquisition": *Certainly we*, says God, *opened for you a clear opening*—that is we acquired an acquisition—*for you in order that we might forgive you your past and future sins* (48:1-2). Bearing on the same point is the fact that Muhammad successively gave his daughter to two idolaters. Secondly, after the religion of Islam had begun, he took [her] from [one] husband until he became a Muslim. It is clear, therefore, that he was of the same sect at that time when he had given [his daughter] to an [idolater]. For he himself prohibits sexual intercourse with an infidel in the Chapter of *Elbaqara*, that is "The Cow," where it is said, *Do not fornicate with participators*—that is Christian women—*until they believe*; and do not have sex with male participators until they believe; *for the believing servants are better than participators* (2:221). And note that he here completely allows sodomy, the most shameful, arrogant, and false of all mortal sins. Through these things, nevertheless, he demonstrates that he had handed his daughter over to an infidel when he was equally an infidel.

On the other hand, let us see, therefore, what the Qur'an proclaims about Christ. Now it says that Christ Jesus is the word of God, and that He was sent by God. Whence it is said in the Chapter of *Elmaran*, *O Mary, God is giving news to you of a word from Himself whose name is Christ* (3:45). And again he said in the Chapter of The Women, that is *Elnessa, that,* he said, *Jesus son of Mary is a messenger of God and a word of Him, and He infused it into Mary, and He is a spirit from Him* (4:171). The Qur'an also says that Mary herself conceived as a virgin, and gave birth, and was [still] clean and holy; and there was no filth or [uncleanliness] mixed with her.

Let us, therefore, compare Muhammad your prophet, whom you dare to prefer to all others, to Christ word for word. If he descends from Ishmael, Muhammad is related to Abraham through a maid-servant. While Abraham prays to God saying, *Would that Ishmael lived in your presence* (Gen. 17:18), he will hear the Lord adding this also: *He will beget twelve princes* (Gen. 17:20); and again, *He will be a wild man, his hand against all, and the hand of all against him* (Gen. 16:12). But Christ [descended] from Abraham to whom it is said, *In your seed will all nations be blessed* (Gen. 22:18). He descends through Isaac, to whom was conceded the inheritance of the promises from which God excludes Ishmael.

Muhammad sends no prophet before himself nor any book witnessing to him. Before Christ comes, he provides before himself all the proclamations of all the prophets. The father and mother of Muhammad, unclean and [idolaters], burn in the eternal fire. Mary, [remaining] pure and holy, conceived Christ. Muhammad existed as an infidel for forty years. Christ, born sinless from a virgin, remained faithful to God always. For the Spirit and Word of God was not able to contract sin, much less perpetrate it. As you say, God forgives the sins of Muhammad. For Christ, however, it was more noble not to have sins than to be forgiven.

Muhammad, when asked to give certitude of his prophecy by means of miracles, produced nothing. Christ illuminated the blind, cleansed the lepers, [and] raised the dead in order to demonstrate not only that he was a prophet, [but] . . . that he was the Son of God. Christ also gave *power over unclean spirits and over all sicknesses to his apostles* (cf. Matt. 10:1), and also [power] that they might raise the dead. But Muhammad never gave sight to the blind, nor life to the dead, nor did he cast out demons, since he would have undoubtedly cast one from himself. Christ always and everywhere worked through the Holy Spirit. About your prophet you say that divination befell him, and that he himself was bewitched which is indeed a Satanic work. Likewise your prophet says that he does not know what will happen to him. Knowing everything which was to happen to him regarding His being handed over, His crucifixion, and His resurrection, Christ often intimated [these things] to the disciples before they came to be.

Finally, he says, *[Jesus] is the word of God which He infuses into Mary, and a spirit from Him* (4:171). If he had abided by this statement, and not added another, the Blessed Trinity would have been verified among men, and they would have received the religion of Christ. But he nullified this by the following statement in which he said that *Jesus in the eyes of God is just like Adam whom He created from clay, and He said to Him "Be!" and He was* (3:59). Note that the author [appears to be a] Christian according to the words which he sets forth thus: *and a Spirit from Him*. And [note], because he adds [this], that the Trinity would be verified among men. He appears to desire that what is called "spirit" be taken personally for the Spirit who is from God, that is, for the Holy Spirit who *overshadowed the Virgin* (cf. Luke 1:35) and filled out Christ as a man when God the Father transfused His Word into Mary, that is, made [the Word] to be incarnate from Mary.

And what the same one says later—that God transfused His word and spirit into Mary—this is said with various meanings: "He transfused the word" as that which is to be incarnate; "He transfused the spirit" as that which is about to prepare the Virgin or material of flesh to be assumed [by the word], or in order that [the spirit] fill out [Christ] according to [his] human nature. Now if it is said that Jesus is the word of God and a spirit of Him, that is, of God, it is necessary that what is called "spirit" be taken essentially, as the Son is called God from God and Spirit from Spirit. (And we would not attack so forcefully the word of the infidel here, except that Christians use this word against Muslims for the purpose of destroying the divinity of Christ.)

Now just as the word which goes out from the mouth of a corruptible man necessarily is corruptible, so also the Word which went forth from eternity, through which He *created heaven and earth and the things in between* (50:38)—as I might use the word of the Qur'an—must necessarily be eternal: It is the wisdom proceeding from Him. Neither did God use any created word before [the existence of any] creature. But for the infidel, even if truth compels in some measure, what was written will be said to be true in an exterior sense; but still on the interior unfaithfulness led to bad understanding.

Whence he added that *Jesus in the eyes of God is just like Adam whom He created from clay, and He said to him, "Be!"* (3:59). Now since you have confessed that God infused His word and spirit into Mary, and from this Christ came to be, and you will opine after this that Christ was like Adam whom He created from clay, how is it suitable that you say that the word of God and His spirit be clay? For then, since clay is not [made] but from clay, you propose that the nature of the deity is clay. It is not proper! It is not proper! For a god who has neither a word nor a spirit is a statue which neither sees nor breathes.

But our God who *is blessed in the ages* (Rom. 7:25) sees, hears all, and has a Word which was incarnate from the most holy Virgin. And He has a Spirit who overshadowed the Virgin and filled out the humanity of the Word.

If you were to opine that the Word of God was in Adam in the same way [that it was in Jesus, then] similarly his spirit [would be there] in substance. In this there is obvious falsity since if the Word were united to his flesh or his clay, and the Spirit of God had filled Adam, then Satan never would have deceived or cast down Adam. By His Word, however, God said to Adam, "Be!"—by this same Word through which He made all things, which from eternity was with God, which was incarnate in the most holy Virgin. Now this Word, embodied from the Virgin, remained visibly among men and walked on the earth; for if the Word and Spirit had been without flesh, no one would seek to discern this or see that which here joined the Spirit to the Word. Notice that the Word was not without flesh, that is humanity, to which the Word (and not the Spirit) was united, through which the Word was visible to the eyes of both the flesh and the mind. And neither was that flesh or humanity without the Spirit which presided and worked miracles in that [flesh]. Through [those miracles] the Holy Spirit appeared to the eyes of the mind.

. . . [Christ] was, therefore, the perfect and one God incarnate with two natures and two wills, a divine and a human; and [he was] one person within the womb of the Virgin, and after the Virgin's giving birth, and [during] His dwelling among men, and [during] His ascension into heaven, without separation of the deity from the nature or person: the true son of God born impassibly, and coeternally proceding from God, just as the birth of heat from a fire, light from the sun, intellect from the soul, [and] the precious stone's lustre [radiating] from it, in all of which one thing does not precede the other. Through Him, therefore, we have the certain promise of the kingdom of God, if we continue as worshippers of Him. And we will not be like you who affirm that the Spirit of God and His Word, which is from Him, are clay, and who give your adversaries to understand that the Highest God is a Spirit and Word, and [then] do not worship a [god] of this kind, but rather you worship a god without a word and spirit.

***

Now if someone should say, "How is it possible to understand that the one whom heaven and earth are not able to contain, the one who, rather, contains all things Himself, was able to be circumscribed in the womb of a virgin?" But the response to this is that the boundless God united to flesh in the womb of the Virgin was circumscribed by flesh alone, the infinity of His own divinity in no way having been diminished.

But let us bring forth some commoner examples for the ruder senses, and first from the Old Testament: God entered paradise after Adam had sinned saying, *Adam, where are you* (cf. Gen. 3:9)? and Adam heard the sound of His feet. He entered the house of Abraham, even though the house of Abraham could not hold Him, and nevertheless He did not cease [to] be boundless (cf. Gen. 18:1-8). So also when He spoke to Moses in the tree—the bush—when nevertheless neither the bush grew, nor was the boundlessness of God diminished (cf. Exod. 3:1-10 and Qur'an 28:29-30). Do not wonder, therefore, if, while remaining boundless, in the womb of the Virgin [God] was circumscribed by flesh alone.

But you, infidel, do you not read in the Qur'an that *God is sitting upon a seat* (cf. 40:15), and the seat is described as on a throne, and the *width of the throne is heaven and earth* (2:255)? And again the throne is said to be within the seat, and all this is above the heavens and the earth. Now how will the heavens and the earth be within the measure of the seat, and the seat be greater, and all at the same time be over the heavens?

But also according to an account which none of you doubt, [we know] that on the day of the general resurrection when God orders the sons of perdition to be thrown into the fire, the fire itself will cry out, and will say, "Are there not more?" And as often as it says, "Are there more?" so often will more be thrown into it. And it will continue to call out until The Most High extends His foot to it and then it will be full. And then the Highest God will thrust his finger into hell and extract from it whom he desires. If, therefore, hell will be able to grasp the foot or finger of God, which, nevertheless, is above your understanding, there is little wonder if your understanding cannot grasp that the womb of the Virgin held the Eternal Word within itself.

***

But how did the glorious God deign to be mocked or [how was He] able to be crucified or die . . . ? To this we will respond that Christ in suffering and death redeemed His [followers] from eternal death, and [His divinity] did not sustain any of the injury which lay hidden in the flesh—just as a pearl in a shell: If [the shells] of it are divided or broken accurately, the pearl is preserved white.

But again if a king hands over some condemned person to the fire in a place where no breathing can occur, [and] an angel is sent to him for protection and enters [the fire] with him, will [the angel] be able to be injured by the fire? By no means. Much less, therefore, the divinity which is wholly impassible. Whether, therefore, Christ was in the womb of the Virgin according to the flesh, or on the cross, or under the earth, God was always seated upon His throne and was watching over everything while ruling all.

But the Jews by their power did not inflict disgraceful and savage torments upon an unwilling or unforeseeing Christ, since He forsaw all things and predicted them to the Apostles: *I have the power*, He said, *of laying down my soul and of raising it up again, and no one takes it from me, but rather I lay it down by myself* (cf. John 10:17-18). Anyway everything which Christ suffered was foretold by the prophets, and these same noble prophets suffered at the hands of the ancestors of crucifiers of Christ, such as were Isaiah, Jeremiah, Ezechial, and Zacharaiah son of Jehoiada, Jehu son of Hanani, and Uriah the prophet, who all had prefigured the passion and death of Christ, by which the Devil lost [his] dominion of death.

Whence also afterward the witnesses of His death, resurrection and ascension into heaven, the blessed Apostles, who are much praised in the Qur'an—they are called the triumphs of God and His outstanding ones—died for Christ. Afterward, [endless] thousands of martyrs suffered for justice on the example of the passion and death of that Christ. Neither to die nor to suffer was a disgrace to Christ, since to suffer for justice is, rather, glory, and to die for the salvation of all is the chief privilege of charity, and especially because after the humiliation of the passion immediately followed the glory of resurrection and ascension to the heavens.

We do not accept that which is written in your narratives, that the Jews did not kill Christ, but only appeared to do this. Far be it from God to be the author of so great a deception! Indeed you write that Eba Horeire [Abu Hurayrah] asked of Muhammad, "How did the Jews crucify Christ?" And, laughing, Muhammad said that the cursed Jews were planning to crucify Christ who came to a crowd and said, "Who among you will take my likeness and be crucified for me, and he will immediately have paradise?" A certain one from the crowd took it. And while he suffered the *sun was darkened, and rocks were split, and many rose from [their graves] and went to the Holy House, Jerusalem* (Matt. 27:45, 51-53). In this, rather, is proved that which we hold in the firmest faith, for God never at any time would make such wonderful miracles for someone who, indeed, was not a prophet or an apostle, but rather a man of the people. But these things were done, rather, because while the Lord of the world suffered, the most noble creatures suffered with Him. And the dead would not arise from graves, death having now been conquered in them, unless He who was suffering had been the giver of life to all.

5

Questions and Answers

Christian-Muslim Theological Exchanges (Thirteenth to Fourteenth Centuries)

Reasons for the Faith against the Saracens, Greeks, and Armenians, to the Cantor of Antioch (ca. 1274)

Thomas Aquinas (1225–1274)
Source: Joseph Kenny, "Saint Thomas Aquinas: Reasons for the Faith against Muslim Objections," *Islamochristiana* 22 (1996): 31–52.
Language: Latin

Thomas Aquinas was a well-known philosopher and theologian. He wrote on topics ranging from biblical commentaries to philosophical and theological works. Uniquely, he was familiar with the philosophical works of Jewish and Muslim contemporaries, Moses Maimonides and Ibn Sina (Avicenna) respectively.

While his Summa theologiae *and* Summa contra gentiles *are reasonably well-known, many works are less familiar, such as a relatively small work written for a cantor in Antioch. The cantor had asked Aquinas to provide him with a defense of Christian faith against objections posed by Muslims and Eastern Christian groups. Aquinas identifies the Muslim objections and offers concise responses that are based largely on reason and logic. Notably, Aquinas's reason is not used to prove Christian faith—to attempt this would diminish the faith—but it can be used to address opposing objections.*

***

The following are the things you say the Muslims attack and ridicule: They ridicule the fact that we say Christ is the Son of God, when God has no wife (Qur'an 6:110; 72:3); and they think we are insane for professing three persons in God, even though we do not mean by this three gods.

They also ridicule our saying that Christ the Son of God was crucified for the salvation of the human race (Qur'an 4:157-8), for if almighty God could save the human race without the Son's suffering he could also make man so that he could not sin.

They also hold against Christians their claim to eat God on the altar, and that if the body of Christ were even as big as a mountain, by now it should have been eaten up.

. . . Concerning merit, which depends on free will, you assert that the Muslims and other nations hold that God's fore-knowledge or decree imposes necessity on human actions; thus they say that man cannot die or even sin unless God decrees this, and that every person has his destiny written on his forehead.

On these questions you ask for moral and philosophical reasons which the Muslims can accept. For it would be useless to quote passages of Scripture against those who do not accept this authority. I wish to satisfy your request, which seems to arise from pious desire, so that you may be prepared with apostolic doctrine to satisfy anyone who asks you for an explanation. On these questions I will make some explanations as easy as the subjects allow, since I have written more amply about them elsewhere [in the *Summa contra gentiles*].

***

First of all we must observe that Muslims are silly in ridiculing us for holding that Christ is the Son of the living God, as if God had a wife. Since they are carnal, they can think only of what is flesh and blood. For any wise man can observe that the mode of generation is not the same for everything, but generation applies to each thing according to the special manner of its nature. In animals it is by copulation of male and female; in plants it is by pollination or generation, and in other things in other ways.

God, however, is not of a fleshly nature, requiring a woman to copulate with to generate offspring, but he is of a spiritual or intellectual nature, much higher than every intellectual nature. So generation should be understood of God as it applies to an intellectual nature. Even though our own intellect falls far short of the divine intellect, we still have to speak of the divine intellect by comparing it with what we find in our own intellect.

. . . But besides this, the Word of God is not an accident or a part of God, who is simple, nor something extrinsic to the divine nature, but is something complete, subsisting in the divine nature and coming forth from another, as any word must be. In our human way of talking, this is called a son, because it comes forth from another in its likeness and subsists in the same nature with it.

Therefore, as far as divine things can be represented by human words, we call the Word of the divine intellect the Son of God, while God, whose Word he is, we call the Father. We say that the coming forth of the Word is an immaterial generation of a son, not a carnal one, as carnal men surmise.

. . . We call this Word of God a Son, as said above, because he is of the same nature with the Father, and we profess that he is co-eternal with the Father, only-begotten and perfect.

***

. . . We fittingly call [God's] love not simply Spirit, but the Holy Spirit, since holiness refers to his purity.

. . . We call the Word of God the Son; so it is clear that the

Holy Spirit comes from the Son. Just as God's act of knowledge is his very being, so also is his act of loving. And just as God is always actually understanding, so also he is always actually loving himself and everything else by loving his own goodness. Therefore, as the Son of God, who is the Word of God, subsists in the divine nature and is co-eternal with the Father and perfect and unique, likewise we must profess the same about the Holy Spirit.

. . . Three human persons are three men and not one man, because the nature of humanity, which is common to them, belongs to each separately because they are materially distinct, which does not apply to God. So in three men there are three numerically different human natures, while only the essence of humanity is common to them. But in the divine persons there are not three numerically different divine natures, but necessarily only one simple divine nature, since the essence of God's word and of his love is not different from the essence of God. So we profess not three gods, but one God, because of the one simple divine nature in three persons.

***

A similar blindness makes Muslims ridicule the Christian Faith by which we profess that the Son of God died, since they do not understand the depth of such a great mystery. First of all, lest the death of the Son of God be misinterpreted, we must first say something about the incarnation of the Son of God. For we do not say that the Son of God underwent death according to his divine nature, in which he is equal to the Father who is the foundational life of everything, but according to our own nature which he adopted into the unity of his person.

***

When we say that God became man, let no one take this to mean that God was converted into a man, as air becomes fire when it is turned into fire. For God's nature is unchangeable. Only bodily things can be changed from one thing into another. A spiritual nature cannot be changed into a bodily nature, but can be united to it somehow by the strength of its power, as a soul is united to a body. Although human nature consists of soul and body, the soul is not of a bodily but a spiritual nature. But the distance between any spiritual creature and God's simplicity is much more than the distance between a bodily creature and the simplicity of a spiritual nature. Therefore, as a spiritual nature can be united to a body by the strength of its power, so God can be united to a spiritual or a bodily nature. And in that way we say that God was united to a human nature.

. . . Christ is one because of the unity of his person or hypostasis, and he cannot be called two; rather he is properly said to have two natures. Although the divine nature can be predicated of the hypostasis of Christ, which is the hypostasis of the Word of God, which is his essence, nevertheless human nature cannot be predicated of him abstractly, just as it cannot in the case of anyone having a human nature: Just as we cannot say that Peter is human nature, but is a man having a human nature, so we cannot say the Word of God is a human nature, but that it has taken on a human nature and for this reason can be called a man.

. . . Whatever belongs to a nature can be attributed to the hypostasis of that nature, while a hypostasis of both a human and a divine nature is supposed in a name signifying the divine nature as well as in a name signifying the human nature; this hypostasis is single having both natures. Consequently both human and divine things can be predicated by that hypostasis, whether it is referred to by a name signifying the divine nature or by a name signifying the human nature. Thus we can say that God, the Word of God, was conceived and born of the Virgin, suffered, died and buried, attributing to the hypostasis of the Word human things because of the human nature. Inversely we can say that man is one with the Father, that he is from eternity and that he created the world, because of the divine nature.

In predicating such diverse things of Christ a distinction can be made according to which nature they are predicated. Some things are said according to his human nature and others according to his divine nature. But if we consider whom they are said about, they apply indistinctly, since it is the same hypostasis of which divine and human things are said. It is like saying that the same man sees and hears, but not according to the same power; he sees with his eyes and hears with his ears. Likewise the same apple is seen and smelt, in the first case by its colour, in the second by its smell. For this reason we can say that the seeing person hears and the hearing person sees, and that what is seen is smelt and what is smelt is seen. Similarly we can say that God is born of the Virgin, because of his human nature, and that man is eternal, because of the divine nature.

***

The foregoing shows that there is no contradiction in our professing that the only-begotten Word of God suffered and died. We do not attribute this to him according to his divine nature but according to his human nature, which he assumed into the unity of his person for our salvation.

But if someone objects that, since God is almighty, he could have saved the human race otherwise than by the death of his only-begotten Son, such a person ought to observe that in God's deeds we must consider what was the most fitting way of acting, even if he could have acted otherwise; otherwise we will be faced with this question in everything he made. Thus if it is asked why God made the heaven of a certain size and why he made the stars in such a number, a wise thinker will look for what was fitting for God to do, even if he could have done otherwise.

I say this supposing our belief that the whole disposition of nature and all human acts are subject to Divine Providence. Take this belief away and all worship of the Divinity is excluded. Yet we argue presently against those who say they are worshippers of God, whether Muslims or Christians or Jews. As for those who say that everything comes necessarily from God, we argued at length elsewhere [Contra gentiles, II, ch. 23]. Therefore if someone considers with a pious intention the fittingness of the suffering and death of Christ, he will find such a depth of knowledge that any time he thinks about it he will find more and greater things, so that he can experience as true what the Apostle says (1 Cor. 1:23-24): "We are preaching a crucified Christ: to the Jews an obstacle they cannot get over, to the gentiles foolishness, but to those who have been called, whether they are Jews or Greeks, a Christ who is both the power of God and the wisdom of God." He continues (v. 25): "God's folly is wiser than human wisdom."

The Letter from the People of Cyprus (ca. 1316)

Author unknown
Source: Rifaat Ebied and David Thomas, *Muslim-Christian Polemic during the Crusades* (Leiden, Neth.: Brill, 2005), 54–147.
Language: Arabic

Few details are known about this author beyond what can be gleaned from a letter he wrote in the early-fourteenth century. It appears he lived in Cyprus, though his familiarity with Arabic, the Qur'an, and leading Muslim scholars suggests that he may have been from Syria. Further, he structured his letter around another letter (Letter to a Muslim Friend), which was written by Paul of Antioch, Melkite Bishop of Sidon, sometime around 1200. This suggests that the author was also a Melkite Christian.

The author was intimately familiar with the Qur'an—so familiar, in fact, that he corrects quotations of the Qur'an in the letter he used as a source and is even able to add appropriate chapter (surah) titles. The author uses an appreciative tone throughout and is keen to acknowledge that both the Qur'an and Muhammad were legitimately sent to the Arabs. However, he argues that this scriptural and prophetic legitimacy only applied to the Arabs, and as such, Christians were not obligated to follow either of them. In fact, the Qur'an only confirms beliefs to which Christians already adhered,

163

according to the author. Even Christian doctrines like the Trinity and the incarnation could, with proper exegesis, be supported by the Qur'an. The Bible, then, is the proper lens through which the Qur'an should be read.

The author sent his letter to Ibn Taymiyyah (see below) in 1316 and to Muhammad b. Abi Talib al-Dimashqi in 1321 (see below), leading Muslim scholars in Damascus. Both Muslims, as I discuss in their introductions below, responded to the letter in great detail.

***

The people say: We heard that a man by the name of Muhammad appeared among the Arabs, saying that he was the messenger of God and bringing a book which he said had been revealed to him from God the exalted. So we did not rest until this book was obtained for us.

I said to them: If you have heard about this man, and made efforts to obtain for yourselves this book which he brought, then for what reason do you not believe in him, especially since in the book it says in *The Family of 'Imran*, "And whoso seeketh a religion other than the Surrender it will not be accepted from him, and he will be a loser in the Hereafter"? They replied, saying: For many reasons. I said: What are they?

They said: One is that the book is in Arabic and not in our language, according to what is stated in it, "And we have revealed it, a Lecture in Arabic." Also, we have found what is said in *The Poets*, "And if we had revealed it unto one of any other nation than the Arabs, and if he had read it unto them, they would not have believed in it. . . ."

When we noticed this in it, we knew that he had not been sent to us but to the pagan Arabs, about whom it says that no messenger or warner had come to them before him, and that it was not obliging us to follow him because messengers had come to us before, addressing us in our own tongues and warning us about our religion, to which we adhere today. They delivered to us the Torah and Gospel in our languages, in accordance with what the book brought by this man attests about them. For in *Abraham* it says, "And we never sent a messenger save with the language of his folk"; in *The Bee*, "And verily we have raised in every nation a messenger"; and in *The Romans*, "Verily we sent before thee messengers to their own folk. They brought them clear proofs." So it has been shown correctly according to this book that he was sent only to the pagan Arabs. Its words: "And whoso seeketh as religion other than the Surrender it will not be accepted from him, and he will be a loser in the Hereafter," according to the demands of what is just it means: his people to whom he brought it in their language, and not others to whom he did not come, as is stated in it.

We know that God the exalted is just, and it is not part of his justice to require on the day of resurrection that any community should have followed a man who had not come to them, or whose book they were not familiar with in their language or without the authority of any summoner preceding him.

***

There are also the testimonies to the lord Christ in the miracles, that he was conceived not through the intercourse of a man but by the annunciation of an angel of God to his mother, that he spoke in the cradle, brought the dead back to life, healed those born blind, made lepers whole, created from clay the likeness of a bird, breathed into it, and it was a bird by the permission of God.

***

Then we also find him extolling our Gospel, favouring our hermitages, honouring our churches, and bearing witness that the name of God is mentioned in them often. This is his word in *The Pilgrimage*, "For had it not been for Allah's repelling some men by means of others, cloisters and churches and oratories and mosques, wherein the name of Allah is oft mentioned."

This and other things oblige us to keep to our religion and not to neglect our doctrine, abandon what we have or follow anyone other than the lord Christ, the Word of God, and his disciples whom he sent to us to warn us in our languages.

***

As for the Word of God, which is creator, uniting with a created human, the exalted Creator never addressed any of the prophets except through revelation or from behind a veil, as is given in this book where it says in *Counsel*, "And it was not (vouchsafed) to any mortal that Allah should speak to him unless by revelation or from behind a veil, or (that) he sendeth a messenger to reveal what he will by his leave. Lo! He is exalted, wise." So the Qur'an approves of God appearing through a veil, and Christ in his humanity is God's veil, through whom God spoke to creation.

. . . If refined things are only made manifest in physical things, then the Word of God the exalted, by which refined things were created, could not possibly be made manifest in anything other than a physical thing. Thus it was made manifest in Jesus, son of Mary, because humankind is the most noble thing that God the exalted has created, and in this way he spoke to creation from him and they beheld something of him.

***

If this is our view concerning God, holy be his names and great his divinity, no blame or offence attaches to us for not abandoning what we have received, or rejecting what we have been given to hold, and following something else, especially since we have these clear witnesses and obvious proofs from the book which this messenger brought.

Our most important proof is the witness in our favour that we find in it, that God has placed us above those who disbelieve until the day of resurrection because we follow the Lord Christ, God's Spirit and Word.

On the matter of the uniting of God's creative Word, by which God created all things, with the created man taken from the Virgin Mary, the chosen one who was honoured "above the women of creation," it united with him in a union free from mixing or altering, and addressed people from him as God the exalted addressed the prophet Moses from the thorn bush. He performed miracles by his divine nature and exhibited weakness, such as pain, death and so on, by his human nature, both actions being in the one Christ.

Furthermore, in this book which this messenger brought occur his words in *The Family of 'Imran*, "O Jesus! Lo! I am gathering thee and causing thee to ascend unto me"; and it also says in *The Table Spread* when Jesus son of Mary said, "I was a witness of them while I dwelt among them, and when thou tookest me thou wast the watcher over them"—by his being taken it means the death of his human nature which was derived from the Virgin Mary; it also says in *Women*, "They slew him not nor crucified, but it appeared so unto them"—by these words it refers to the divine nature which is the creative Word of God, by analogy with which we say that Christ was crucified in his human nature and not crucified in his divine nature. There also occurs in this book in agreement with our statement what is said in *Women*, "The Messiah, Jesus son of Mary, was only a messenger of Allah, and his word which he conveyed unto Mary, and a spirit from him." In another place it says, "Lo, the likeness of Jesus son of Mary is as the likeness of Adam"—by his word "Jesus" he intends to refer to the human nature derived from Mary the pure one; just as Adam was created without intercourse or intimacy, so the human body of Christ was created without intercourse or intimacy; and just as the body of Adam tasted death, so the body of Christ tasted death.

***

I said to them: If your belief about the exalted Creator is that he is one, what has made you say "Father, Son and Holy Spirit"? You have made those who hear think that you believe that God is three composite individuals, or three gods, or three parts, and that he has a son. Someone who did not know your belief might imagine that by this you mean a son by intimacy and reproduction, laying you open to a charge of which you are innocent.

They said: The Muslims as well, since their belief about the Creator, great is his might, is that he has no body, limbs or organs, nor is limited in one place, what has made them say that he has two eyes by which he sees, two hands which he spreads wide, a leg, a face which he turns in every direction, and a side, and that he comes in the darkness of clouds, so that people hearing might imagine that God the exalted has a body, limbs and organs, and that he moves from place to place in the darkness of clouds? Someone who did not know their belief might think that they give a body to the Creator—indeed, people among them have believed this and taken it as their doctrine—and someone who had not verified their belief might charge them with things of which they are innocent.

I said, They say: The reason for our saying this, that God has two eyes, two hands, a face, leg and side, and that he comes in the darkness of clouds, is that the Qur'an speaks of it, though the intention in this is not literal. Anyone who takes it literally and believes that God has two eyes, two hands, a face, a side, limbs and organs, and that his essence moves from place to place, etc., as corporealism and anthropomorphism entail, we condemn him and declare him an unbeliever. And if we declare as an unbeliever anyone who believes this, our opponents are not in a position to impose it upon us, since we do not believe it.

They said: It is exactly the same with us. The reason we say that God is three hypostases, Father, Son and Holy Spirit, is that the Gospel speaks about it. What is intended by "hypostases" is not composite individuals, parts and divisions and so on, as partnership and plurality entail. For the Father and Son are not the fatherhood and sonship of wedlock, procreation or reproduction. We excommunicate, curse and accuse of unbelief everyone who believes that the three hypostases are three different or coincident gods, three physical objects brought together, three separate parts, three composite individuals, accidents or powers, or anything entailed by partnership, plurality, division or anthropomorphism, sonship through wedlock, intimacy, procreation, reproduction or birth from a wife, or a physical object, an angel or a creature. And if we curse and accuse of unbelief anyone who believes this, our opponents are not in any position to impose upon us what we do not believe.

Thus, if they force us to acknowledge polytheism and

anthropomorphism on account of our teaching that God the exalted is one substance and three hypostases, Father, Son and Holy Spirit, because this literally entails plurality and anthropomorphism, we in turn force them to acknowledge corporealism and anthropomorphism because of their teaching that God has two eyes, two hands, a face, a leg and a side, that his essence moves from place to place, that he was seated on the throne after not being on it, and other things that literally entail corporealism and anthropomorphism.

The Correct Answer to Those Who Have Changed the Religion of Christ (ca. 1316)

Ibn Taymiyyah (1263–1328)
Language: Arabic
Source: Thomas Michel, *A Muslim Theologian's Response to Christianity* (Ann Arbor, MI: Caravan Books, 1985).

Ibn Taymiyyah is one of the most prolific Muslim scholars and jurists to emerge from the medieval period. He wrote extensively, critiquing Islamic movements that did not accord with his vision of the central tenets of Islam. Similarly, he denounced Christianity in his writings in addition to authoring texts prescribing the ways in which Muslims and Christians might interact.

In 1316, as I note in the previous introduction, he was sent a version of a letter from an anonymous Christian in Cyprus. He responded with an extensive and very lengthy refutation in which he quotes the Christian's letter in sections. As I observe, the Christian's letter was a re-working of an earlier letter written by Paul of Antioch. Interestingly, Ibn Taymiyyah is also aware of the latter letter.

In his response, Ibn Taymiyyah addresses the universality of Muhammad's prophethood and the Christian doctrines of the Trinity and the incarnation. He also attacks Christian scripture, arguing that is was corrupted. In all of this, he does more than simply refute the Christian letter from Cyprus: he seeks to demonstrate that Islam is the superior religion.

***

There is no god but God, and Muhammad is the messenger of God. Praise to God, the Lord of the universe, the merciful, the compassionate, the Master of the Day of Judgment. Praise to God who created the heavens and the earth and made the darkness light. Those who disbelieve in their Lord wander astray.

Praise to God who did not take a son, who has no partner in governance, nor has any associate from lower creation whom He has exalted in greatness. Praise to God who sent down upon His servant the Book, and did not permit any deviation in it, but established it in order to warn of a severe chastisement from Him, to make the believers who do good works rejoice so that for them there would be a fine reward, and to warn those who say that God has taken a son. They have no knowledge of that, nor did their forefathers; dreadful is the word that goes forth from their tongues. In any case, what they speak is but a lie (Qur'an 18:1-5).

As for what follows (*amma ba'd*): God—may He be blessed and exalted!—made Muhammad the Seal of the prophets, and perfected His religion for him and for his community. He sent him during an interval between the messengers, at a time when unbelief was manifest and the [correct] paths blotted out. Through him He gave life to the characteristics of faith which had been studied. By him He restrained the people of idolatry and unbelief and doubt from their service of idols and fires and crosses. By him He conquered the unbelievers of the People of the Book—the people of idolatry and doubt—and he erected the lighthouse of His religion which pleased Him.

Through him He celebrated the memory of His servants whom He chose. He elected [Muhammad], and by him He manifested what the People of the Book had kept hidden. Through him He showed where they had gone astray from the correct path. By him He confirmed the trustworthiness of the Torah, the Psalms, and the Gospel. In him He disclosed what was not true in them by way of the falsity of corruption and replacement.

***

These people have claimed that Muhammad was not sent to them but to the Arabs of the Jahiliyya [i.e, the time of ignorance before Muhammad]. This claim has two alternatives: either they hold that he himself did not claim that he was sent to them and that only his community has made that claim, or they hold that he claimed that he was sent to them, and that he was lying in this claim. Their claim in the beginning of this book demands the first alternative.

About other works it may be said that they have suggested the other alternative [that he was lying]. Here they do not really deny his messengership to the Arabs, but only reject his having been sent to them. As for his mission to the Arabs, they make no firm statement about confirming or rejecting it, although it is evident that their formulation demands a confirmation of his messengership to the Arabs. Actually they confirm what agrees with their view while rejecting that which opposes it.

We will show that their argumentation is not correct in anything of that which the Prophet brought. Subsequently we will address two questions. We will show that in the Qur'an there is no proof for them, nor does it contradict itself or any of the previous books of the prophets. That from which they argue is an argument against them, and even if Muhammad had not been sent, it would not have been in any respect an argument for them. How could it have been an argument for them when the Book which Muhammad brought is in agreement with the rest of the teaching of the prophets, as well as with sound reason, in showing the falsity of their religion—their view of the [Trinity], divine union, and other things.

This is in contrast to Muslims, for their argumentation against the People of the Book—the Jews and Christians—is consistent with what was brought by the prophets before Muhammad. But the argumentation of the People of the Book is not acceptable if they argue from what Muhammad brought. The reason is because Muslims admit the prophethood of Moses, Jesus, David, Solomon, and the other prophets, and according to them they must put faith in every book which God revealed and in every prophet whom God sent. This is the basis of the religion of the Muslims. Whoever disbelieves in one prophet or in one book is, according to them, a disbeliever. Among them whoever even insults any of the prophets is a disbeliever worthy of death (2:136-37; 2:285; 2:177).

"The Book" is a generic term for every book revealed by God, and includes the Torah and the Gospel, just as it includes the Qur'an (42:15; 2:285; 2:1-5). In these passages God has stated that this Book which He has revealed is a guidance for the god-fearing who believe in the unseen, who undertake the prayer (al-salah), who pay the poor tax, who believe in what God has revealed to him [Muhammad] and in what He has revealed to those before him, and who are certain of the afterlife. God then disclosed that it is these people who will prosper. He has encompassed these people with prosperity, and no one will be among the prosperous unless he be from those whom God called, "those who believe in what was revealed to you [Muhammad] and what was revealed to those before you" (2:4).

It is not permitted for any Muslim to reject a single thing of what was handed down to those who preceded Muhammad, but any argumentation from that demands that three prerequisites [be fulfilled].

[First:] Its being established as [having come] from the prophets.

[Second:] The correctness of its translation into Arabic or into the language in which it appears—e.g., Greek or Syriac. The language of Moses, David, Jesus, etc., of the Israelite prophets was Hebrew, and whoever says the language of Jesus was Syriac or Greek is in error.

[Third:] Exegesis of the passage and knowledge of its meaning. Muslims have not rejected a single one of their arguments by denying what any one of the prophets said. They may, however, reject the transmitter [of prophetic statements] or they may misinterpret what has been handed down from the prophets by some other meaning which they desire. Even though Muslims may err in rejecting some transmitted information or in their interpretation of something handed down from the prophets, it is like someone among them or among the people of the other religions who errs in respect to something of what was handed down from him whose prophecy he accepts or in interpreting that which was handed down from him.

This is different from rejecting the prophet himself; blatant (sarih) disbelief is not the same as that of the People of the Book. Their intention is only achieved by rejecting some of what God has revealed. When someone rejects one word of what a person who declares himself to be a messenger of God has disclosed, that person's argumentation from the rest of his teaching is invalid, and their argument for what they are trying to prove is untenable. The reason is that someone who says he is the messenger of God either is truthful in his calling himself messenger of God and in everything else which he discloses from God, or he is false if he lied in even one word from God.

If he is truthful in that manner [in his claiming to be the messenger of God], he is prevented from lying concerning God in a single thing which reached him from God. Whoever lies about God, even in one word, is someone perpetrating falsehood against God and is no messenger of God. It is clear that whoever perpetrates a lie against God is a lying pseudo-prophet, and it is not permissible to make an argument from the information he has disclosed from God. It can be known that God did not send that person. If he said that something was merely a statement [of his own] and it was correct, it could be accepted, not because he received it from God nor because he was a messenger from God, but rather just as something true is acceptable from [idolaters] and other unbelievers. If idol worshipers speak what is true concerning God, like the affirmation of the idolatrous Arabs that God created the heavens and the earth, we do not accuse them of lying on such a matter, even though they are unbelievers. Thus if an unbeliever holds that God is living, omnipotent, a creator, we do not reject him for (holding) this opinion.

However, anyone who has lied about God in even one word and said that God revealed it to him—when God did not reveal it to him—that person is one of the liars nothing of whose statements which they claim to have received from God may be used as argumentation. They are like other people in whatever they say other than that, and even like other liars similar to them. If the truth of their statement is known from a source other than them, this is acceptable for establishing an indication of its correctness, rather than for their having said it. But if its correctness is not known from a source other than them, there is no proof for it in their saying it after it is established that they have lied about God.

Therefore, if these people affirm the messengership of Muhammad and hold that he was trustworthy in the Book and the Wisdom which he received from God, they must place faith in everything in the Book and the Wisdom which is proven to be from him, just as faith must be placed in everything which the [other] messengers brought.

If they reject him in even one word or if they doubt his truthfulness in it, they are prevented by that from affirming that he is a messenger of God. If they do not affirm that he is messenger of God, then their argumentation from what he said is like their arguing from the statements of the rest of those who are not prophets or even of those who are liars or whose truthfulness is doubtful.

Obviously a person who is known to have spoken lies about God in what he claims to have received from Him or whose veracity is doubtful is not known to be the Messenger of God or that he is truthful in all of what he says and [claims] to have received from God. If that is not known about him, it is not known that God revealed a thing to him. On the other hand, if his falsity is known, it is known that God did not reveal a thing to him, nor did He send him.

. . . If his truthfulness is doubted in even one word—if it is possible that a single word be incorrect either intentionally or inadvertently—then it is not possible at the same time to confirm him in the rest of what reached him from God. Confirmation in what someone discloses from God is only [possible] if he is a faithful messenger who lies neither intentionally nor inadvertently. Everyone whom God sent must be truthful in every thing which he receives from God and lie neither intentionally nor accidentally.

This is a matter on which all people—Muslims, Jews, Christians, and others—agree. They agree that the messenger must be truthful and that he lie neither intentionally nor accidentally. Without that [infallibility] the goal of prophethood is not attained (7:104-05; 69:44-47; 16:101-02; 10:15). This is elaborated elsewhere.

The point here is that their arguing from even one word of what Muhammad brought is inadmissible in any respect. If he was a truthful messenger in everything which he disclosed from God (and everyone knows that what he brought is opposed to the religion of the Christians), it is necessary that the religion of the Christians be false. If they hold that one word of what he brought is false, it is necessary that he [cannot be] for them a truthful prophet receiving information from God.

Whether they say that he is a just ruler, a scholar, an upright man, or whether they make him a great saint among the very greatest saints, however much they extol him or praise him when they see his dazzling virtues, his obvious favors, and his spotless Law, when they reject or doubt him in one word which he brought, they have rejected his claiming to be messenger of God and [his claim] to have received this Qur'an from God. Someone who was false in his claiming to be the messenger of God is not one of the prophets or messengers. The statement of anyone who is not one of them is no proof at all, but his situation is the same as other people like himself. If the truth of what he says is known by detailed argument, his statement is accepted because his truthfulness is known from a source other than himself, not because he said it. If the truth of the statement is not known [from external reasons], it is not acceptable. Thus it is clear that someone who does not profess about a person who has stated that he is the messenger of God and infallibly preserved from establishing intentional or inadvertent error cannot properly use any statement of that individual as an argument.

This principle disproves the view of the insightful among the People of the Book, and against the ignorant among them it is even more confounding. Many or most intelligent People of the Book extol Muhammad for his calling on people to [affirm] the oneness of God, for his prohibition against the worship of idols, for his confirmation of the Torah, the Gospel, and those sent as messengers before him, for his manifesting the wonder of the Qur'an which he brought, for the good qualities of the Law which he brought, for the superior characteristics of the community which believed in him, for the signs, proofs, miracles, and favors which were manifested at his and their hands.

Nevertheless, in spite of this they hold that "he was sent to others than us," or else that he was [merely] a just ruler with a just government, and that he attained kinds of knowledge like those of the People of the Book and others, and that through his knowledge and his rituals he laid down and systematized for them a Law just as their own leaders had imposed on them the canons and laws which they possessed. Whenever they say this, they do not thereby become believers in him, and simply from their saying that it is not permissible for them to use a thing of what he said as an argument. It is known by overwhelming transmission that which all groups of people from all religious traditions admit as true, that is, that he said that he was messenger of God to all people, and that God sent down upon him the Qur'an. If he was truthful in that, anyone who rejects him in a single word has rejected the messenger of God, and whoever rejects the messenger of God is an unbeliever. But if he was not truthful in that, then he was not God's messenger, but rather a liar. It is not possible to use as an argument anything in the statements of someone who lies concerning God by saying "God sent me with this [message]" when God did not send him.

Reply to the Letter of the People of Cyprus (1321)

Muhammad b. Abi Talib al-Dimashqi (1256–1327)
Language: Arabic
Source: Rifaat Ebied and David Thomas, *Muslim-Christian Polemic during the Crusades* (Leiden, Neth.: Brill, 2005), 149–497.

Al-Dimashqi was a well-known imam (Islamic religious leader) in Damascus. His interests ranged widely, from mathematics and history to theology and geography. As I note in the introduction to The Letter to the People of Cyprus, *in 1321 al-Dimashqi was sent a letter from an anonymous Christian in Cyprus with an apology for Christian doctrine, details about the Christian's view of Muhammad and the Qur'an, and an explanation for how the Qur'an supported Christianity.*

Al-Dimashqi replied with a lengthy and detailed rebuttal. In fact, al-Dimashqi quotes the Christian's letter and responds to its claims systematically, attacking Christian scripture and the history of its formation. It is clear that he is familiar with Christian liturgical practice, but at times his understanding of Christian history is mistaken. At other times, he offers descriptions that are simply meant to make a mockery of Christianity. Al-Dimashqi also spends much time defending the prophet Muhammad's universality, a key point in response to the Christian's accusation of Muhammad's ethnic limitations as a prophet.

***

In the name of God, the Compassionate, the Merciful.

Praise be to God, who has illumined the hearts of chosen mortals with the blaze of his unity, and chased the shades of polytheism from them, so their star beams out at the zenith of honour and good fortune; they have been made to see by the brilliance of Muhammad's apostleship, so their tongues declare that he who made them is too exalted for partners and companions; the [angel Gabriel] has inspired their spirits, so they confess he is too holy to unite with spouses and sons; he is too blessed and exalted to dwell in or unite with the essences of ephemeral things, or to combine with a humanity composed of all the many races, which intellect rules is prone to change and decay; his most perfect majesty is too great to seek help in executing his will and attaining his purpose from those he created and formed.

***

I witness that Muhammad is his servant and messenger, whose apostleship the Torah and Gospel announced; the rays of its proofs spread abroad when the evidence was made plain to the leading minds by its dazzling miracle; it radiated with the brightness of its purpose over west and east; and the banners of the most perfect human souls billowed over land and sea when they proclaimed that the One, the Creator was free from faults.

***

The bishops and patriarchs, priests and monks, the foremost in the faith of Christ and leaders of the community of Jesus, had sent two copies of it from the Island of Cyprus, one to the Shaykh, the Imam the model of humanity [Ibn Taymiyyah], may God always afford benefit through him and give delight by his continuing life, and the second to one whom they thought might have some knowledge.

When this poor soul read it and reflected upon it, he realised they were looking for a response to what it contained. For they were opening up means of seeking a confrontation through it, under the impression that they had mastered what they had been assured was teaching, or that this might lead straight to their religion by the mention of it. But this poor soul found that everything they clutched at was dust, or "as a mirage in a desert, which the thirsty one supposeth to be water." So I thought it right to send back responses to what they had written, and to provide a proof that what they believed was false. After dividing their letter into sections, I have given as a confirmation of truth a clear response to each section for anyone who desires a way to the truth, observing the religion of God and following his pleasure, hoping that in return God will give me a place in the abode of safety.

★★★

. . . You claim that the appearance of our lord Muhammad (may God bless him and give him peace) was sudden and surprising to people, because no earlier prophet or messenger announced him, the jinns did not hail his qualities nor the soothsayers rhyme his traits, nor likewise were his name and mission written in seven places in the Torah and the Gospel. Even so, you and the Jews read even today in the Torah, what in Arabic translation is, "God came from Sinai and shone out from Seir and towered over the mountains of Paran." You know that what is meant by Sinai is Moses and the Torah, since Sinai was the mountain of direct address, that what is meant by Seir is Christ and the Gospel, since Seir is the town of Nazareth, the place of the annunciation of Christ, and that what is meant by the mountains of Paran is Muhammad and the Qur'an, since Paran is Mecca and the mountains of Paran are those of the Hijaz.

Similarly, you and the Jews read in the Torah, what in translation is, "God said to Moses: Say to them (that is to the people of Israel), God will raise up for you from your brothers a prophet like me, and God will put his own word in his mouth." You know that the people of Israel have no brothers except the people of Isma'il, and that no one has arisen among the people of Isma'il and the people of Kedar who upheld the general law and the supreme revealed Law in the way that Moses did except Muhammad. And since it is stated in the Torah: "A prophet like Moses will not come from among the people of Israel," God said, "I will raise up a prophet from your brothers," not saying "from you" so as not to contradict his own words. Hence our Prophet rose up from the people of Isma'il. God's word was in his mouth, and he delivered it orally for he was illiterate, he had not studied, he could not write, and he had not gone on journeys for anyone to think he had studied on a journey.

Similarly, there occurs in the Torah what again in translation is, "God said to Isma'il: I have heard you; listen, I will bring him up and bless him, and make him into a great nation. Mudhmadh will beget twelve princes." Both you and the Jews know that no one has been brought up, or been blessed, or sent forth to the great nation, or has engendered twelve princes other than Muhammad, who is called "Mudhmadh" and "the very greatly blessed" (may God bless him and give him peace).

Similarly, in the fifth book of the Torah there occurs what in translation is, "God said to Moses: I will raise up for the people of Israel a prophet like you; let them hear him and obey him. And whoever opposes him, I shall punish him and turn away from him." This is what the Samaritans and Jews read, and you yourselves know it, and that it was only put at the end of the Torah as an assurance and promise. And there has come no one like Moses except Muhammad (may God bless him and give him peace).

Part of the description and declaration about him that was given by Christ (peace be upon him) are his words in the four Gospels to the disciples on the night of the Passover, the meaning of which is, "I am going from you, and it is good for you that I go, because God will send to you the Paraclete who will teach you all things." The meaning of "the Paraclete" is the messenger. He also said, what in translation is, "When I have gone, the ruler of the world will come to you; he will rebuke the world about justice, about sin on my account and about judgement." No one has come after Christ who has rebuked the world about these three and has been ruler of the world except Muhammad (may God bless him and give him peace). Christ also said, its meaning being, "Truly, truly I say to you, the Paraclete who will come after me, from his mouth will pour forth the spirit of truth; he will rebuke the world because they held me in derision and were wilfully hateful towards me. So listen to him and obey him."

And when he was passing through Bethany and its headman questioned him saying, "Are you Elijah or Akmad?," Christ also said, "I am neither Elijah nor Akmad; I am only the Son of Man and no more." And you know that Akmad is Ahmad in Latin, because it does not have the letter *ha'*. This is the meaning of what appears in our Book in the words of Christ, "And bringing good tidings of a messenger who cometh after me, whose name is Ahmad."

***

There is the story of the monks Bahira and Nestorius with [Muhammad] at Bosra, when they saw him before he had grown up with a caravan of Quraysh and with his uncle Abu Talib. They came to him and kissed his hand, and they asked him about the birthmark on his back, and about things that he was able to relate to them. They gave his uncle the good news of prophethood, kingship and great status, and they told the caravan about the tree near which they had halted sprouting green because of him, and about clouds shading him throughout his journey. They said that Christ had announced him, and that he was the ruler of the world, so they should guard him against the Jews, because they were his enemies.

***

Thus, the sending of Muhammad (may God bless him and give him peace) was not surprising or sudden without any previous announcement or intimation about him. The tokens of his prophethood and signs of his apostleship appeared throughout the earth: prophets, sages and soothsayers announced him; the jinn hailed him; the Jews living in the Hijaz most eagerly awaited his appearance in order to overcome the pagan Arabs through him, though when he appeared they were the first to disbelieve in him and the fiercest of all enemies.

***

The Paraclete was the true messenger, the giver of elucidation, instruction, legislation and just words, to whom Christ pointed. He was not the Holy Spirit, for that is a spiritual, immaterial force, angelic and divine, without body, limbs, or mouth with which to speak or from which the spirit of truth could proceed, or tongue with which to rebuke the world. He spoke just as Christ said the ruler of the world would, the messenger who would utter the word of God, sent from God and rebuking the world with his tongue, making plain the truth to them by his elucidation, an honoured human to whom revelation was sent, a noble prophet (may God bless him), not an imaginary force which in the intellect is similar to many forces and which adversaries might object to and oppose.

***

In short, you should follow this Arabian Prophet in accordance with your statement that you know he did not come to you but to the pagan Arabs. For you do acknowledge that God sent him to the Arabs. A prophet confirms what is truthful and trustworthy, and this Arabian prophet, who confirmed what is truthful and trustworthy and whom you recognise was a messenger from God to the Arabs, declared that God the exalted sent him to all people. So you should follow him in accordance with your statement.

The argument by which you have sought to prove from the noble verses the restricted nature of Muhammad's apostleship can be proved against you, against your lying claim. For you imagine that "the nations," in the words of the exalted One, "And if we had revealed it unto one of any other nation" and the rest of the verse, excludes the Arabs, so that the sending down is restricted to the Arabs. But it is not thus: "the nations" is the plural of "nation," and "nation" is anyone who has incorrectness in his speech, whether Arab or foreigner from among the non-Arabs, even though he may be an eloquent speaker. Also that the words of the exalted One, "Even as we have sent unto you a messenger from among you," is an address to the Arabs alone; though it is not thus: the "you" in "unto you" is a plural pronoun for those who are addressed, and they are all people, and the meaning of "you" in "from among you" is "a man from your kind," rather than an angel or a jinn. And similarly his words, "By sending unto them a messenger of their own, *min anfusihim*"; the reading *min anfasihim* with a vowel "a" on the "f," meaning "from the most distinguished among them," gives strength to this. And that the exalted One's words, "That thou mayest warn a folk unto whom no warner came before thee," are the Arabs alone; though it is not thus: "the folk" are all who were living at the time he was sent (may God bless him and give him peace), as is proved by the words of the exalted One, "To warn whosoever liveth," which also confirms that it was to everyone living at his time, for no warner had come to them when his mission (may God bless him and give him peace) occurred, at an interval after the messengers. Similarly, the exalted One's words, "That thou mayest warn a folk whose fathers were not warned, *ma undhira aba'uhum*" and the rest of the verse, for he spoke truly to their fathers that no prophet had warned them in his language. This is so if we accept that *ma* is the negative "not." But if we do not accept this then it is the affirmative, so that its meaning becomes "what," and the sense of the words is, "That you may warn a folk what their fathers had been warned," "That you may warn a folk what warners had brought them before you," the verb being used transitively alone without a preposition. This also confirms that Adam and those after him were fathers to them, and so it affirms the messengers, and bears out what they brought, according to the proof of the exalted One, "Alif. Lam. Mim. Allah! There is no god save him, the alive, the eternal. He hath revealed unto thee the scripture with truth, confirming that which was before it." Furthermore, we might allow that "the folk" here are the Arabs, but it does not follow from this that he was only sent to them alone, because he did not include any restrictive particle in it. So how could it be [that Muhammad was sent only to the Arabs], when the exalted One has said, "O mankind! The messenger hath come to you with the truth from your Lord," "Say: O mankind! Lo! I am the messenger of Allah to you all," "And we have not sent thee save unto all mankind," "O people of the scripture! Now hath our messenger come unto you, expounding unto you much of that which ye used to hide in the scripture, and forgiving much," "O people of scripture! Now hath our messenger come unto you to make things plain unto you after an interval of the messengers," and other verses that prove the universality of his call[?]

As for the words of the exalted One, "And we never sent a messenger save with the language of his folk," "And verily we have raised in every nation a messenger," and "Verily we sent before thee messengers to their own folk," these are notifications from God the exalted that the above contains no proof to support you, but is rather an argument against you. For what the messengers brought was an announcement of Muhammad (may God bless him and give him peace) and an incitement to follow his religion. For the exalted One has explained the above by the attestation of his words, "And whoso seeketh a religion other than the Surrender it will not be accepted from him, and he will be a loser in the hereafter." "Whoso" refers to everyone, by agreement of all who are reasonable, and not to the particular few that you spuriously make them out to be.

***

How many verses in this esteemed book witness that the messenger of God was sent to the whole world? You have read it and reflected upon it and, as you say, you know all about its references to Christ and his mother, the description of them as perfect, noble, chosen and near to God, great and mighty. And you also know all about the stories of the prophets in it, and the accounts of bygone nations. If you were to apply your minds and consider without deflecting or distorting, then you would find in it reports of what had been, news of what was to be, and an announcement to the community of what was to happen to it, namely the triumph of the religion of Islam over every other religion, the destruction of unbelievers and the ignorant pagan polytheists, the clearing of idols out of Arabia, the entry of masses of people into the religion of God, the community inheriting the earth both east and west and God's appointing them as successors there, the exacting of the tribute from hostile People of the Book in surrounding areas, and other things that had taken place and were to take place as are reported in it.

***

So reflect on it, you who claim you have obtained it, read it and comprehended it, according to your immense knowledge about it, and accept with fairness among yourselves what I have mentioned and explained to you about some of what is in the glorious Qur'an.

Letter of [Gregory Palamas] Which, as Captive, He Sent from Asia to His Church (1354)

Gregory of Palamas (1294/1296–1357/1359)
Language: Greek
Source: Daniel Sahas, "Captivity and Dialogue: Gregory of Palamas (1296–1360) and the Muslims," *Greek Orthodox Theological Review* 25 (1980): 409–36.

Gregory was born in Constantinople to a senator and imperial tutor. He grew up surrounded by royalty, but he left the city at about twenty years of age to become a monk at Mount Athos and was eventually ordained a priest. In the spring of 1354, while traveling from Thessaloniki to Constantinople, his ship was forced to take refuge in an area controlled by the Ottomans. He was taken captive with the demand of a ransom. He was released a year later.

Gregory wrote a letter about his captivity that was eventually sent to his church in Thessaloniki. In the letter, Gregory gives a colorful and detailed account and notes that the Muslims and Christians where he lives in captivity mix with one another, an observation that concerns him. He also gives descriptions of Islam along with an account of a religious discussion he had with a Muslim concerning Christ and the prophethood of Muhammad. Detailed accounts of similar disputations are included as well, one of which involves a group of Turks and Muslim scholars who were converts to Islam and who approached Gregory with questions for him to answer. In another exchange, Gregory approaches a local religious scholar after observing him officiate a Muslim funeral.

***

When the other captives and I arrived there was sent to us a grandson of the great Emir. He invited me apart from the rest of the captives, and he sat down with me on the soft grass with a few leaders surrounding him. After we sat down they brought to me fruits and to him meat. At his signal we began eating, myself the fruits and he the meat. As we were eating he asked me if I ever eat any meat and for what reason. As soon as I gave the proper answer to the question, somebody came in from outside apologizing for his tardiness. "Only now," he said "was I able to finish the distribution of alms which the great Emir has ordered to take place every Friday." Thence we began a long discussion on almsgiving. "Do you also practice almsgiving?" asked Ishmael; that was the name of the grandson of the great Emir. I said to him that the true almsgiving is the one which derives from the love towards the true God, and that the more one loves God, the more and truly benevolent he is. Then he asked me again whether we also accept and love their prophet Muhammad. When I answered in the negative, he asked for the reason. I offered a sufficient defense on this matter also, as it was appropriate to the interlocutor who did not believe in the teaching of the Teacher, and who said that one should not love the Teacher as teacher. "But," he said, "on the one hand you love Isa (this is how he called Christ), and on the other hand you believe that he was crucified!" I agreed with this assertion and bringing forth the matter of the voluntary character, the way and the glory of the passion, and the matter of the impassibility of the divine nature, I explained with a few words what he thought to be a contradiction. As I did this he asked me again, "Why do you venerate the wood and the cross?" I gave him to this also the response which God had provided, adding "Would you not accept those who would honor your insignia, and punish severely those who would dishonor them; Christ's banner of victory and His sign are the cross." He, however, wanted to ridicule further and defame our beliefs as inappropriate, and said, "At any rate, you believe that God has had a wife, for you proclaim that He gave birth to a son." Then I said to him again, "The Turks say that Christ is the word of God, and that he was born from the virgin Mary, whom we glorify as Theotokos. Therefore, if Mary, who gave birth to Christ insofar as the flesh is concerned, did not have a husband, nor did she need one—since she gave birth, physically, to the Word of God—much more it is so with God, Who, in giving birth to His own word, incorporeally (being Himself incorporeal) and in a God-like manner, has had no wife, nor did He need any, as you wrongly presume."

***

[The group of Muslim scholars said,] "But tell us this, how do you confess Christ to be God since he was a human and was born as human?" Again the bishop, "God is not only sovereign and all-mighty, but righteous as well, as David the prophet says: 'The Lord our God is righteous, and loves righteousness; there is no injustice in him.'There is no work of God, therefore, that does not have in it the righteousness of God. As the ray of the sun has also the life-giving power, as well as light and warmth, so does the divine energy have in itself the divine power and the righteousness. God created man to do good deeds and commanded him to live according to His own divine will. When, therefore, this man obeyed and submitted himself to the devil willingly, and he sinned by transgressing the divine will and he was, justly, sentenced to death, it was not congenial to God to redeem man from him [the devil] by force; that way He would have been unjust to the devil, to have pulled out from his hands by force man whom he did not get by force. Also the free will of man would have been destroyed by the force and the power, as God would have been freeing man; and it is not like God to destroy His own work. It was, therefore, necessary that a sinless man be made, who would be without sin and who would live without sin and who, this way, would help the man who had sinned willingly."

... The Turks became disturbed, and they interrupted him, saying, "How can you say that God was born and that the womb of a woman contained him, and many such things? God only said and Christ, too, was made." He then said to them, "God is not a big body that cannot fit because of its size into something small. On the contrary, by being incorporeal He is able to be everywhere, beyond everything and in one single thing. He can fit even into the smallest possible thing that one can imagine." They, however, protested again noisily, saying that "God only [spoke] and Christ, too, was made." The bishop said again: "You confess that Christ is the word of God. A word, then, is made again by another word? In such a case it will mean that the word of God is not co-eternal with God Himself. But I showed you this at the beginning and you, too, confessed that God has a Word and a Spirit co-eternal with Him. That is why you call Christ not only word but also spirit of God. God said and things were made, like this stone—pointing to a stone nearby—the herb and even the reptiles. Therefore, if Christ is the word and spirit of God because he was made by the word of God, then the stone, the herb and everyone of the reptiles is also word and spirit of God because in their case also He said and they were made! You see how absurd it is to say that 'God [spoke] and Christ, too, was made'? The pre-eternal Word of God, even though he became human and took up flesh, without mixture [of the two] nor in the manner of flesh, is spirit and word of God. It was later, as we said, that he took up from us and for our sake the human nature. He was always in God as His co-eternal Word 'through whom God created the world.'"

. . . [Then one of the Muslim scholars said,] "The master demands from you to answer the question how we accept Christ, love him, respect him, confess him to be God's word and breath, and we also place his mother near to God, and yet you do not accept our prophet nor do you love him?" Then the bishop said: "He who does not believe in the words of a teacher cannot love the teacher himself; that is why we do not love Muhammad. Our Lord God Jesus Christ has said to us that he will come again to judge the entire world. He also commanded us not to receive anyone else until He will come back to us again. He also said to those who disbelieved in him: 'I have come in my Father's name, and you do not receive me, nor did you accept me; if another comes in his own name, him you will receive.' That is why the disciple [sic] of Christ writes to us: 'But even if an angel preaches to you contrary to that which you have received from us let him be accursed.'"

. . . [Then they said,] "Circumcision was handed down by God from the very beginning. Even Christ himself was circumcized. How then, you do not circumcize yourselves?" Then the bishop: "Since you are referring to the old law and to what was handed down by God to the Hebrews at that time—for traditions of God also were the keeping of the Sabbath, the Jewish passover, sacrifices which were to be offered exclusively by the priests, the altar in the interior of the temple, and the dividing curtain—since all these and other such things have also been handed down by God, why do you not cherish any of them and you do not practice them?"

. . . [After interrupting the bishop, they asked,] "Why do you place many representations in your churches and you venerate them, even though God wrote and said to Moses: 'Thou shalt not make a likeness of anything, whatever things are in heaven above, and whatever are in the earth beneath, and whatever are in the sea'?". . . [The bishop answered them,] "Friends are venerated by each other, but they are not made gods. It is evident to everyone that this is, indeed, what Moses learned from God and this is what he taught the people then. However, this same Moses again and at that time, left almost nothing of which he did not make a representation. He made the area beyond the curtain to be like and represent the celestial [reality]. Also, since the Cherubim are in heaven, he made representations of them and placed them into the innermost sanctuary of the temple. As to the exterior of the temple, he made it to represent the earthly [reality]. If anyone, then, had questioned Moses 'Why have you made anyway such things, since God forbids the icons and the likeness of things in heaven and of things on earth?,' he would have, certainly, answered that 'icons and representations are forbidden so that one may not worship them as gods. However, if one is to be elevated through them toward God, this is good!' The Greeks, too, praised created things but they did so as if they were gods. We praise them too, but we elevate ourselves through them to the glory of God." Then the Turks said again: "Did, indeed, Moses make these things then?" Answered many, "Yes, he did all these things."

***

[As a crowd gathered to listen, the local Muslim religious scholar] began saying that [Muslims] accept all the prophets including Christ, as well as the four books sent down from God, one of which is also the gospel of Christ. When he finished he turned the speech to me saying, "Why then, do you not accept our prophet or do you not believe that his book came down from heaven?" I said to him again: "Your custom and our custom, that has been confirmed by antiquity and law, is to accept or consent to nothing as true without witnesses. And there are two kinds of witnesses: either those of their works and deeds, or those of trustworthy persons. Thus Moses disciplined Egypt with signs and marvels. With his rod he split the sea into two and he united it again. He also brought down bread from heaven. But what is the use of mentioning the rest since you also believe in Moses? He has also been witnessed to by God as a trustworthy servant, although not as a Son and Word. Later on, at God's commandment, he ascended the mountain and died, and he added himself to those who had preceded him. On the other hand, Christ, in addition to the [extraordinary] things that he did, which are many and great, is witnessed to by Moses himself and the other prophets; He is also the only one who is called eternal Word of God by you, as well. He is the only one ever born of a virgin; the only one ever who ascended into heaven and remains there immortal; the only one ever who is hoped to come back thence to judge the living and the dead who will rise—to say about him only what you, too, the Turks confess. It is, therefore, for these that we believe in Christ and His Gospel. As far as Muhammad is concerned we do not find that he is either witnessed to by the prophets, or that he did anything unusual or worthwhile leading to faith. That is why we do not believe in him or his book."

. . . [The religious scholar responded,] "There was reference to Muhammad in the Gospel but you cut it out. Moreover, setting out from the farthest East he progressed victoriously, as you can see, all the way to the West." I, then, said to him: "Insofar as the gospel is concerned nothing was ever cut out from it by any Christian, or altered in any way. There are heavy and most shivering curses for such an act, and he who dares to either cut out or to alter anything, is cut off actually from Christ. How is it possible then, that a Christian did such a thing, or how could he be still a Christian, or in anyway acceptable among the Christians if he had erased off what has been divinely engraved and what Christ himself imprinted or foretold? Witnesses to this are also the many and various dialects in which the gospel of Christ was conveyed from the very beginning; it was not written originally in only one [dialect]. If anything was distorted, how did this pass unnoticed, and how was such an agreement kept in the minds of various nations until today? Also many people of a different faith have the Gospel of Christ, whom we call heretics, among whom there are some who agree with us on some issues, and yet they, too, do not have any such thing to show in the Gospel of Christ. Even among those who were adversaries from the beginning—and there are many of these—there is no such thing [to be] shown. The opposite, rather, can be found clearly in the Gospel. How is it then that the Gospel confirmed something to the opponents which itself does not contain and which was not told before to the divine prophets? If there were anything good about Muhammad written in the Gospel it would have also been written in the prophets. On the contrary, you may rather find not wiped out but written that 'many false Christs and false prophets will arise and lead many astray.'

". . . Muhammad marched from the East and he progressed victoriously to the West. He did so, however, by the means of war and the sword, with pillage, enslavement and executions, none of which has its origin in God, the righteous One, but he is advancing the will of him who from the beginning was the destroyer of man. How about Alexander? Did he not, starting from the West, conquer the East? There have also been other men at other times who, after repeated campaigns over-ruled the entire world. However, no nation entrusted their souls to any of them, as you did with Muhammad, who, although he resorted to violence and allowed licentious things, did not take into his fold even a whole portion of the world. On the other hand, the teaching of Christ although it directs one away from almost all the pleasures of the world, has embraced the universe to its ends. It endures even among its enemies without instigating violence, but rather every time winning the adversary force."

6

Old Strategies for a New Era

Muslims and Christians at the Dawn of Modernity
(Fifteenth Century)

The Cultured Man's Gift, in Refutation
of the People of the Cross (ca. 1420)

Fray Anselmo Turmeda (ca. 1352–ca. 1424–1430)
Language: Arabic
Source: Jean-Marie Gaudeul, *Encounters and Clashes: Islam and Christianity in History*, vol. 2 (Rome: Pontificio Istituto di Studi Arabi e Islamici, 1984), 106–115; see also, Mikel de Epalza, *Fray Anselm Turmeda ('Abdallah al-Taryuman) y su polemica islamo-cristiana* [Madrid: Hiperión, 1994], 192–497).

Anselmo Turmeda was born in Mallorca, an island off the western coast of present-day Spain. From an early age he studied the Bible and Greek. He became a Franciscan friar and, while continuing his study of theology, converted to Islam. He travelled to Tunis in order to formally convert.

Taking the name 'Abdallah, he settled in Tunis and worked as an official translator.

One of his main works was a lengthy refutation of Christianity that includes an account of his conversion. In his refutation, he covers many of the standard topics of Muslim anti-Christian literature: the corrupt nature of the Christian scriptures, the superiority of Islam as a religion, the prophet Muhammad as the promised Paraclete, and an attack upon Christian Christology. What follows is Turmeda's account of his conversion.

***

You should know that I come from the town of Majorca—God bring it back to Islam!—a big town on the sea-side, placed between two mountains, and divided by a little river.

. . . My father was among the notabilities of the town of Majorca, and I was his only son. When I was six, my father put me in the care of a learned priest under whose direction I studied the Gospel so that at the end of two years I knew most of it by heart. Then I began to learn the language of the Gospel and Logics and did so during six years.

At the end of these studies, I left Majorca for Lerida in Catalonia, a town well-known for its learning among the Christians of that region.

. . . It is in that city that Christian students come together in great numbers, a thousand or one thousand and five hundred, following no other law than that of the priest under whom they study.

. . . I stayed in that city at the church of a very old priest who enjoyed a great prestige among them whose name was Nicolau Fratello.

. . . It is with that priest that I studied the principles and foundations of the Christian religion, while I went on serving him, defending his interests, so that he finally received me among his most intimate friends.

. . . At the end of that period, it happened that he was struck by an illness one day, and was prevented from attending the lecture, so that the students kept waiting for him. They began to remind one another of the questions of (religious) sciences until the time came when the conversation came on the word of God—Praise and Glory to Him—that came on the lips of Jesus—Peace be upon him—which says: "After me will come a prophet called the [Paraclete]." They began to determine who was that prophet, which one was he among the other prophets. Each of them spoke according to his knowledge and understanding, and the discussion became animated, and even turned to a quarrel. At the end they went away without solving the question.

I returned to the house of the old teacher whom I described. He asked me:

—What was the subject of your discussion [today] during my absence?

I informed him of the difference of opinions in the group concerning the word Paraclete. . . .

—And you, he said, what answer did you give?

—The answer of Doctor So-and-so, I replied, as found in his Commentary on the Gospel.

—How far, and how near the truth you are, he exclaimed. So-and-so erred, So-and-so almost found. None however has found the real meaning.

. . . On hearing this, I fell at his feet and kissed them, and said:

—Sir, you see that I came to you from a distant country; for these past ten years I have been at your service, and, thanks to you, I have acquired a great amount of knowledge. Now, will you please bring to perfection your goodness to me by letting me know this noble name?

At this he wept, and said:

—My child, you are very dear to me because of the service you have offered me, and the affection you have for me. In knowing this noble name, there is a great advantage, but I fear that, if you revealed it, the Christians would kill you at once.

—Sir, I replied, by God the Most-High, and by the truth of the Gospel, and by Christ who came with it, I will say nothing to anyone of what you will tell me, unless you command me to.

—My child, he replied, as soon as you arrived here I asked information about your country. I wanted to know whether it was situated near the Muslims, if your fellow-countrymen were at war with them, or if they were at war with you, in a word, I wanted to know your feelings as regards Islam. Know then, my child, that the Paraclete is one of the names of the Prophet of the Muslims, Muhammad, to whom has been revealed the fourth book mentioned by the prophet Daniel—God bless him—who predicted that "this book would be revealed to him, and his religion would be the true religion," and his community is the immaculate community mentioned in the Gospel.

—Sir, I said, what is your opinion about this religion, I mean, the religion of the Christians?

—My child, he answered, if the Christians had remained faithful to the original religion of Jesus—Peace be upon him—they would be in God's religion, for the religion of Jesus and of all the prophets—may God bless them all—is God's religion.

—Sir, I asked him, what is "the way out" of all that?

— . . . My son, he said, you must enter Islam!

—Is one saved who enters it, I asked?

—Yes, he said, he is saved in this world and in the next.

—Sir, I asked him, the clever man chooses for himself the best thing he knows. Well, then, you yourself know the excellence of the religion of Islam, what prevents you from joining it?

—My child, he answered, God the Most-High—Praise and Glory to Him—has only revealed to me what I passed on to you concerning the truth of the religion of Islam, the dignity of its prophet—God bless him and grant him peace—after I had grown old in years, and weak in body (I find no excuse for him in these words of his, on the contrary, God's condemnation still stands against him!). If God had guided me to this discovery when I was young as you are, I would have left everything. But you see yourself my situation among the Christians: high rank, consideration, respect and comforts of this earthly life. If I showed in any way that I incline towards Islam the whole people would kill me at once. And even if I escaped from their hands and took refuge among the Muslims, and I told them: "In truth, I have come to you as a Muslim," what if they answered me: "Your soul has benefited by your entrance into the true religions; do not ask us for any favour on account of your conversion: you saved your soul from God's punishment through this action." And I would be left among them, an old man, weak and poor, over 90 years of age, not knowing their language, unable to make them understand me, and I would die of starvation in their midst, while, on the contrary—praise God for it—I keep following the religion of Jesus and its precepts, and this God knows about me.

—Then I said: Sir, are you telling me that I should go to a Muslim country and embrace their religion?

—He answered: If you know what is good for you and look for salvation, do that, and do it promptly: this world and the next will be yours. But, beware, my child, let no one know of it now except the two of us. Hide your intention with all your strength. If any of it became known, the people would kill you at once, and I could do nothing for you, and it would not help you at all to involve me saying that you learnt it from me: I would deny it, and my word against yours would be believed while yours would not be accepted. I will have no responsibility in your fate if you can understand what I mean.

—Sir, I retorted, God save me from even thinking on those lines.

And I promised him anything that would satisfy him. I then began to prepare for my journey and came to take leave of him. He blessed me as I was leaving him, and he provided me with fifty dinars in gold.

I sailed towards my country, the city of Majorca, and stayed there six months.

Then I traveled from there to the island of Sicily, where I remained five months, waiting for a ship that would be directed towards a

Muslim country; finally a ship came that was going to the city of Tunis. I joined it and left Sicily on it as the sun was setting down, and we arrived at the harbour of Tunis towards noon.

When I disembarked, some people who belonged to the Christian troops heard of me and came for me with a mount and offered me a ride to their quarters which they shared with some traders residing in Tunis like them. I stayed with them and enjoyed their hospitality in the most pleasant way for a period of four months.

At that time I asked them whether there was at the court of the Sultan someone who understood the language of the Christians. The Sultan, at that time, was Our Lord Abu l-'Abbas Ahmad—God rest his soul. The Christians told me that at the court of that Sultan lived a gentleman of high rank among his courtiers whose name was Yusuf the Physician, and indeed he was a physician and belonged to the household of the Sultan. On hearing this I was filled with a great joy.

I asked for that man, that physician, and I was shown where he was. I went to meet him, and explained to him my situation, and the reasons why I was presenting myself to enter Islam. At this he [rejoiced] greatly seeing that it was given to him to bring this affair to its conclusion.

He then mounted his horse and brought me with him to the palace of the Sultan, entered it and told him my story, asking on my behalf for the permission to enter. And I found myself in the presence (of the Sultan).

The first thing that the Sultan asked me was my age. I told him: 35. Then he asked me about the studies I had made, and I told him. Then he said: You have come for a good purpose! He then provided me with fifty dinars in gold. You have sailed the seas to come to this country, now become a Muslim (or feel safe) with God's blessing.

Then I told the interpreter, I mentioned him already, Yusuf the Physician:

—Tell Our Lord the Sultan that no one leaves his religion without seeing his friends turn against him spreading rumours about him. In your goodness, deign send for those traders and Christian soldiers who live at your court, and ask them about me, hear what they have to say on my behalf, and at that very moment I will become a Muslim, God willing.

He answered through the [interpreter]:

—You asked from me the very thing that 'Abdallah b. Salam asked from the Prophet—God bless him and grant him peace—when he became a Muslim.

He then sent for the Christian soldiers and some of the traders, making me hide in a room next to the audience hall. When the Christians came into his presence, he told them:

—What is your opinion of this new priest who came in that ship?

They told him:

—Our Lord, this man is great scholar in our religion, to the point that our elders told us that they had never seen in our religion anyone with a higher degree of learning and piety.

—What would you say, he told them, if he became a Muslim?

—God forbid, they answered, he will never do that!

When he heard what the Christians were saying, he sent for me; I stood in his presence, and recited the true "shahada" in front of the Christians. At that they crossed themselves on their faces, and exclaimed:

—It is only the desire to get married that led him to do that. For the priest among us does not get married.

And they left the palace in deep grief and distress.

The Sultan—God rest his soul—assigned to me a salary of four dinars a day, and a room in his own palace. He married me to the daughter of Al-hajj Muhammad al-Saffar. On the day of our wedding, he gave me one hundred dinars in gold and a complete set of beautiful clothes. I had from her a child whom I called Muhammad when he was born in order to be blessed through the name of our prophet Muhammad—God bless him and grant him peace.

On the Peace of Faith (1453)

Nicholas of Cusa (1401–1464)
Language: Latin
Source: Jasper Hopkins, *Complete Philosophical and Theological Treatises of Nicholas of Cusa*, vol. 1 (Minneapolis: Arthur J. Banning Press, 1994), 633–70.

Nicholas was a priest and a prolific author with expertise in a wide range of fields such as philosophy, theology, philology, and history. He worked fervently in the Church, especially promoting conciliarism. He also took interest in Islam and the Qur'an, a Latin translation of which he acquired and later annotated.

Nicholas's interests in conciliarism and Islam are reflected in his work On the Peace of Faith. *Written just after the Ottoman sack of Constantinople, the work takes the form of a heavenly dialogue between the Word, Peter, Paul, and seventeen wise men representing different religions. Instead of a multifaceted disputation of doctrinal differences, the heavenly dialogue focuses on pursuing a universal religion. This religion essentially has a Christian reference point as the competing truth claims and objections represented by the seventeen wise men are smoothed over so that each one can essentially accept the basic tenets of Christianity. The result is a universal religion with a diversity of rites. According to Nicholas, pursuit of this kind of belief could lead to peace among the different religions.*

***

There was a certain man who, having formerly seen the sites in the regions of Constantinople, was inflamed with zeal for God as a result of those deeds that were reported to have been perpetrated at Constantinople most recently and most cruelly by the King of the Turks. Consequently, with many groanings he beseeched the Creator of all, because of His kindness, to restrain the persecution that was raging more fiercely than usual on account of the difference of rite between the [two] religions. It came to pass that after a number of days—perhaps because of his prolonged, incessant meditation—a vision was shown to this same zealous man.

. . . The King of heaven and earth said that from the kingdom of this world sorrowing messengers had conveyed to Him the moanings of the oppressed, that for the sake of religion very many [men] were in armed conflict with one another, and that by physical force men were either compelling [their fellow-men] to renounce their long-adhered-to religious sect or were inflicting [upon their fellow men] death. From the whole earth there were very many message-bearers of the laments; and the King commanded them to present their accounts amid the full assembly of the saints. All these message-bearers seemed to be known to the heavenly inhabitants, for [these messengers] had been established by the King of the universe, from the beginning, over each of the mundane provinces and over each of the religious sects.

***

. . . Upon summoning the angels who were in charge of all the nations and tongues, he commanded each [of them] to bring to the Word-made-flesh one very experientially knowledgeable [man]. And straightway there appeared in the presence of the Word the most judicious men of this world—as if caught up unto ecstasy. To them the Word of God spoke as follows: "The Lord, King of heaven and of earth, has heard the moaning of those who have been killed, those who have been imprisoned, and those who have been reduced unto servitude—[the moaning of those] who suffer on account of the diversity of the religions. All who either inflict or suffer this persecution are motivated only from their belief that such [action or passion] is expedient for salvation and is pleasing to their Creator. Therefore, the Lord has had mercy upon His people and is agreeable that henceforth all the diverse religions be harmoniously reduced, by the common consent of all men, unto one inviolable [religion]. To you select men He entrusts the burdensome responsibility of

[this] commission, giving you from His own court assisting and ministering angelic spirits who will watch over you and guide you. And He designates Jerusalem as the most fitting place for this [work]."

***

At this point an Arab spoke up: "Nothing can be said more clearly or more truly."

Word: Just as by virtue of your being lovers of Wisdom you declare that there is Absolute Wisdom, do you think that there are men of sound understanding who do not love Wisdom?

Arab: I think it altogether true that all men by nature desire Wisdom. For Wisdom is the life of the intellect, which cannot be sustained in its own vitality by any other food than by truth and by the Word of life (i.e., by the intellect's intellectual bread, viz., Wisdom). For just as every existing thing desires whatever it cannot exist without, so the intellectual life [desires] Wisdom.

Word: Therefore, all men declare together with you that there is one Absolute Wisdom, which they presuppose and which is the one God.

Arab: So it is. And no one who has understanding can affirm anything different.

Word: Therefore, for all those who are of sound understanding there is one religion and worship, which is presupposed in all the diversity of the rites.

Arab: You [Yourself] are Wisdom, because [You are] the Word of God.

How is it, I ask, that the worshippers of more than one god are in agreement with the philosophers [with regard to belief] in one God? For never at any time are the philosophers found to have believed otherwise than the following: viz., that it is impossible that there be a plurality of gods over whom there is not pre-eminent a single super-exalted God who alone is the Beginning from which the others have whatever they have ([having it] in a way that is much more excellent than [the way in which] oneness is present in number).

202

Word: All who have ever worshiped a plurality of gods have presupposed there to be deity. For in all the gods, they adore the deity as [one and] the same in [all] its participants. For just as there are no white things if whiteness does not exist, so if the deity does not exist, there are no gods. Therefore, the worshiping of [a plurality of] gods bespeaks the deity; and he who says that there is more than one god says [implicitly] that there is, antecedently, one Beginning of them all—just as he who maintains that there is more than one holy [man] admits that there is one Most Holy, by participation in whom all [these] others are holy. For no race was ever so obtuse that it believed there to be a plurality of gods each of whom was the universe's First Cause, Beginning, or Creator.

Arab: I agree. For he [who says] that there is a plurality of First Beginnings contradicts himself. For since the Beginning cannot be originated (because it would be originated from itself and would exist before it existed—something which reason does not accept), the Beginning is eternal. Moreover, it is not possible that there be a plurality of eternal things, because oneness is prior to all plurality. Thus, necessarily, there will be [only] one Beginning, and Cause, of the universe. Accordingly, I have not yet found that any race has deviated from the way of truth with regard to this [teaching].

Word: Therefore, if all those who worship a plurality of gods look unto that which they presuppose, viz., unto the deity, which is the cause of all [the gods], and if, as reason dictates, they accept this deity into their overt religious practices (even as, implicitly, they worship it in all whom they call gods), then the dispute is dissolved.

Arab: Perhaps this [dissolution] might not be difficult [to effect]. But it will be hard to eliminate the worshipping of gods. For the people hold it to be certain that help is afforded to them from [such] worshipping; and, consequently, they are inclined to these gods for the sake of their own salvation.

Word: If the people were informed about salvation—[informed] in a manner comparable to the aforesaid one—then they would rather seek salvation in Him who has given being and who is Saviour and

Infinite Salvation than [seek it] in those who of themselves have nothing unless it is conceded [to them] by the Saviour. But [take a case] where the people flee for refuge unto gods who in everyone's opinion are holy because they have lived in a Godlike manner. [Suppose the people are fleeing] as if to an esteemed intercessor vis-à-vis a certain infirmity or other distress. Or [suppose] they either adore this intercessor by means of a veneration that is appropriate to holy creatures or reverently honor his memory because he is a friend of God and his life is to be imitated. Provided they were to give to the one, unique God complete and true worship as Sovereign, there would be no contradiction of the one religion; and, in this manner, they would be easily calmed [if the foregoing were explained to them].

***

Turk: There still remains no small difference, since Christians maintain that Christ was crucified by the Jews, whereas others deny it.

Peter: The fact that certain deny that Christ was crucified and assert that He still lives and will come at the time of the Antichrist results from their being ignorant of the mystery of His death. And because He is going to come, as they [rightly] maintain, they believe that He will come in mortal flesh. [They believe this] on the supposed ground that otherwise He could not subdue the Antichrist. As for their denying that He was crucified by the Jews, they seem to do so out of reverence for Christ—on the supposed ground that such men could not have had any power over Christ. But note that the historical accounts, which are numerous, and the preaching of the Apostles, who died for the truth, ought assuredly to be believed: viz., [the testimony] that Christ died in this manner. For the Prophets, too, foretold of Christ that He was to be condemned to a most shameful death—which was death on the Cross. And here is the reason [that He died]: Christ came, as one sent by God the Father, to proclaim the Kingdom of Heaven; and regarding that Kingdom He made claims which were able to be proved by Him in no better way than by means of the witness of His own blood. Hence, in order to be most obedient to God the Father and in order to furnish complete certainty for the truth that He Himself was proclaiming, He died, by a most shameful death, so that no man would refuse to accept the truth for the sake of whose attestation Christ was known by him to have voluntarily accepted death. For [Christ] preached the Kingdom of Heaven, proclaiming that man could attain unto it, being capable of receiving it.

In comparison with that Kingdom, the life of this world—[a life] which is loved so tenaciously by all—is to be esteemed as nothing. And in order to make known the fact that truth is the life that is present in the Kingdom of Heaven, He gave the life that He had in this world—[gave it] for the sake of truth—so that in this way He might most perfectly proclaim the Kingdom of Heaven, might free the world from the ignorance by which it prefers this life to the future one, and might give Himself as a sacrifice for many. [Indeed, He sacrificed His life] so that, being lifted up on the Cross in the sight of all, He might draw all [men] unto belief, and might glorify the Gospel, strengthen the faint-hearted, give Himself freely for the redemption of many, and might do all [these] things in the best way in which they could be done, so that men might attain unto saving faith and unto the hope of obtaining salvation and unto a love of keeping God's commandments.

Suppose, then, the Arabs were to attend (1) to the benefit of Christ's death, and (2) to the fact that it pertained to Christ, as one sent by God, to sacrifice Himself in order to fulfill His father's desire, and (3) to the fact that nothing was more glorious for Christ than to die for the sake of truth and of obedience—[to die] even by a most shameful death. [In that case,] they would not take away from Christ the glory of the Cross—[a glory] through which He merited to be the loftiest [man] and to be super-exalted in the glory of the Father.

Moreover, if Christ preached that men after their deaths would obtain immortality through resurrection, how was the world able to be made certain of this [fact] in a better way than [by] His freely having died and His having arisen and presented Himself as alive? For the world was made certain, by means of an ultimate certification, when it heard of the man Christ having died openly on the Cross and having arisen publicly from the dead and being alive—[heard of these things] through the testimony of many who saw Him alive and who themselves died in order to be faithful witnesses to His resurrection. Therefore, the most perfect proclamation of the Gospel was that which Christ exhibited in Himself and which was [so] perfect that it [was not] able to be more perfect, but which without His death and resurrection could always have been more perfect. Hence, whoever believes that Christ most perfectly fulfilled the will of God the Father ought to confess all those things without which the proclamation of the Gospel would not have been most perfect.

. . . Therefore, everyone's faith—[being a faith] which confesses that holy men are present within the eternal glory—presupposes that Christ died and ascended into Heaven.

***

Paul: Where conformity of mode cannot be had, nations are entitled to their own devotions and ceremonies, provided faith and peace be maintained. Perhaps as a result of a certain diversity devotion will even be [increased.] Since each nation will endeavor with zeal and diligence to make its own rite more splendid, in order that in this respect it may excel some other [nation] and thereby obtain greater merit with God and [greater] praise in the world.

. . . Therefore, in the loftiest domain of reason a harmony among the religions was reached, in the aforeshown manner. And the King of kings commanded that the wise [men] return and lead their nations unto a oneness of true worship and that administering spirits guide and assist them [in this undertaking]. Moreover, [He commanded] that thereafter [these wise men], having full power [to speak] for all [in their respective nations], assemble in Jerusalem, as being a common center, and in the names of all [their countrymen] accept a single faith and establish a perpetual peace with respect thereto, so that the Creator of all, who is blessed forever, may be praised in peace.

Sifting the Qur'an (1461)

Nicholas of Cusa (1401–1464)
Language: Latin
Source: Jasper Hopkins, *Complete Philosophical and Theological Treatises of Nicholas of Cusa*, vol. 2 (Minneapolis: Arthur J. Banning Press, 2001), 965–1096.

After obtaining a Latin translation of the Qur'an and studying it along with various anti-Muslim works, Nicholas set himself to the task of writing a work that could sift bits of truth from the Qur'an. By doing so, he hoped to find a way in which the Qur'an would support Christian doctrine. In a manner similar to his work On the Peace of Faith, *he minimizes some of the Qur'an's rejections of doctrines like the incarnation. Such rejections were, for Nicholas, the result of ignorance or misunderstanding in the context of Muhammad's desire to preach truth. While Nicholas's sifting is distinct in its relatively positive tone, he retains some of the polemical antagonism of his forebears.*

***

There is a book of Arab law which is called the [Qur'an], because of its collection of precepts, and which is called the Furkan [i.e., *al-furqan*, or criterion, is a title given to the Qur'an as it is seen as a means for discerning good and evil; Nicholas misunderstands the term here], because of its distinct separation of chapters. It has other names as well. Some adherents to [this] book say that it is divided in one way in the East and in another way in the Western regions. For Westerners state that after the prefacing prayer, called the mother of the book, the complete book has 123 surahs, or chapters. But the Easterners say that the first surah lasts until Surah Amram, which is Chapter 5 in the book [used] in Spain. I saw [a copy of] this book (as it is read in Spain) translated into Latin; and where I mention anything from this book of the law, I intend to indicate that it is contained in that Latin [translation].

The author of this [book] seems to be apocryphal. For some Arabs say that a certain Muhammad of Arabia, of the Ismaelites, composed it. But others say that according to Muhammad this book came down from God by means of seven men, whom they name. Still others claim that after Muhammad's death four different and mutually inconsistent [Qur'ans] were composed by four [men]—whom they name—who were adversaries of one another. Moreover, certain [people] affirm that the book presently in use was composed by Merban, son of Elheken, and that Merban committed the other versions to the fire. It is also reported that Elgag, a powerful man, deleted eighty-five statements from the book and added just as many others. In the Chronicles of Muhammad and of the kings who were his successors [i.e., the *Chronica mendosa*, a twelfth-century polemical work] we read that Gomar, the second king after Muhammad, ordained that prayers be made in individual temples during the month of Ramadan and that the [Qur'an] be read through by the end of the month. Gomar was succeeded by Odiner, who with the help of others first collected the entire [Qur'an]. From these [foregoing considerations] it is certain that although Muhammad collected from the Testament and from the Gospel certain precepts, which were called the precepts of God, or the [Qur'an], nevertheless that book was collected in its entirety [only] after Muhammad's death.

Now, in its first chapter that book states the following: "Every adversary of Gabriel, who by [the will of] the Creator revealed this book to your heart—indeed, a book entrusted to your hands by divine commandment . . . ," etc. These [words] are read as being the words of God to Muhammad; and in [that] book [this] same statement is very often repeated—[a statement] which claims that

God alone, the Creator, is the author of the book. But as the wisest Arabs and the true historical accounts maintain, and as the book itself and the [very] name "[Qur'an]" show, it is a collection of certain precepts. But, indeed, this collection cannot at all be ascribed to the true God. Whence would He who is Wisdom itself make a collection? Therefore, it is necessary that the collection, which can only be made in the course of time, not at all be ascribed to God, whose meaning is beyond all time and is without succession. To whom, then, should the collection be ascribed except to the man who makes the collection from various scriptural passages and entitles, as he chooses to, that which he has collected (even as this collection is called [*Qur'an*])? And so, certain wise defenders of the book say that the collection is human but that the revelation is of God by way of Gabriel. It is true that the collection is of man; but it cannot be true that God, the Creator of the universe, revealed this book to the heart of Muhammad through Gabriel. For in the book there are contained teachings which—because of their turpitude, injustice, and flagrant lies and contradictions—cannot without blasphemy be ascribed to God.

Therefore, the author of the book will be someone other than the true God; but he cannot be [anyone] except the god of this world. For this god is he who blinds the minds of unbelievers, so that the light of the Gospel of the glory of Christ, who is the image of the invisible God, does not shine [in them]; and since the Gospel is concealed from them, they perish—as the Apostle writes to the Corinthians. This god, or prince, of this world, who from the beginning is a liar, encountered the man Muhammad through [the person] of some *one* of his own angels who assumed the appearance of light and perhaps the name "Gabriel." [This god found] that the idolater [Muhammad], who was worshiping Venus and lusting after all the things of this world, was most suitable for his purpose. And through Muhammad, chiefly, and his successors he put together the deceitful [Qur'an]. Moreover, to Muhammad he attached heretical Christians and perverse Jews as counselors suitable for his purpose.

For example, there were Sergius the Nestorian, Bahira the Jacobite, and the Jews Phineas and Abdia-called-Salon (but later called 'Abdallah)—as the Arabs' true historical accounts of this matter are found [to indicate]. And although [the Qu'ran] is seen to contain many testimonies of praise for the Testament, for the Gospel, and for the Prophets Abraham, Moses, and especially Jesus Christ, the son of the Virgin Mary, nevertheless since it contradicts all these [writings and writers] with respect to [its account of] the true and salvific end (as will be evident subsequently), these praises are [best] believed to have been placed [in the Qur'an] in order to deceive.

***

Unless the Gospel is included in the [Qur'an], one cannot say that the [Qur'an] suffices and is the right way; moreover, it is evident that, within the [Qur'an], only that which agrees with the Gospel ought to be called the light of truth and of the right way. Furthermore, the author of the [Qur'an] did not have any doubts about the Gospel; for he cited passages and contents of the Gospel regarding the fact that some [men] turned away from Christ when He expounded the parables regarding the grain of wheat, regarding the man born blind, and regarding other matters. For that Gospel of which he spoke and which was cited by him is found perhaps even today in parts of Arabia and thereabouts; and it was written down in an ancient volume before the [Qur'an] was composed.

From the beginning of the Christian faith and throughout so many centuries prior to Muhammad, the Gospel was made known to the world; and until the present day it remains unchanged. Moreover, we do not read that even Muhammad then entertained doubts about it. Therefore, we must wonder why in order to understand the [Qur'an], the Arabs have not generally adduced the Gospel for reading and study (even as many wise [men] among them secretly embrace the Gospel with supreme devotion). For without a knowledge of the Gospel [the Arabs] cannot perfectly extract from the [Qur'an] any [teaching]. But as a certain knowledgeable [man] states, there is no other reason [for this failure to study the Gospel] than that the wise among the Arabs know that the falsity of the [Qur'an] would easily be detected if [the people] were permitted to read the books called sacred and truthful. Hence, if one considers the matter rightly, [he will realize that] an envoy to the nation of Arabs was not necessary for teaching any other [faith and law] than the faith and law of the Gospel. For subsequent to Christ (the highest of all the prophets, even according to the [Qur'an]) and subsequent to the book of the Gospel (the most perfect of all books), nothing better remained to be expected from God.

Hence, if any beauty or truth or clarity is found in the [Qur'an], it must be a ray of the most lucid Gospel. And this [fact] is seen to be true by anyone who, after having read the Gospel, turns to the [Qur'an]. From where does contempt for this world and a preference for the future age come? [From where does] the persuasion to justice, to works of mercy, and to love of God and of neighbor [come]? Whence comes the conviction that the selling to God of all one's possessions and even of one's soul is of maximum profit? Whence comes the view that to die for God is to live eternally? Whence did both the [Qur'an's] love of virtue and its prohibition of usury, murder, perjury, fornication, adultery, and lusting for married women receive the splendor of their brightness except from the Gospel's perfection and fittingness? Why are many other things which are promised in the [Qur'an] regarding sensual pleasure and impurity of flesh deemed by all the wise (even by wise Arabs) to be shady and abominable and vile?—[why] except because they are at variance with the Gospel's promises (as will be discussed later).

Therefore, in the [Qur'an] the splendor of the Gospel shines forth to the wise, i.e., to those who are led by the spirit of Christ—[shines forth] even beyond the intent of the [Qur'an's] author. But [the Gospel's splendor does] not [shine forth] to lewd Muhammad and to those antichrists who prefer the present age to the future one and who judge that nothing is good unless it is conformed to this world and to their own lusts. They think that God, as author of the

[Qur'an], confirms their corrupt desires; and they do not recognize that whatever in the [Qur'an] contradicts the Gospel is not true.

***

It is evident that Arabs must confess that there is this trinity in God. For unless they confess [it], then—since they believe that the [Qur'an] is the Book of Truth—they are convicted of ascribing to God a participant. For it is written in the [Qur'an] that God said to Muhammad: "Indeed, upon you, who did not know the Book and the Law, we have bestowed light, in sending our Spirit." And elsewhere: "Having been sent to you from Heaven with this [Book], the Blessed Spirit, who is altogether just, has penetrated your heart, in order that with this [Book] you may administer reproof in Arabic." And, again, [the Qur'an] elsewhere says regarding Christ: "Jesus is the son of Mary and is the messenger of God and is God's Spirit and is the Word sent to Mary from Heaven." And still elsewhere: "For God Himself and His blessed Spirit wrote this most true Book, the [Qur'an]." In many other places the [Qur'an] contains similar [statements].

Hence, since the Blessed Spirit of God cannot be said to be a creature and since the Spirit that is sent is not sent from Himself, then unless you affirm that He is the third person in God and is sent by the Father and the Son (for [the Qur'an] speaks, in the plural, of *senders* [of the Spirit]), you will have to posit more than one God—viz., the Gods who send and the God who is sent. Moreover, Jesus the son of Mary is the Word-of-God sent from Heaven. But the Word of God cannot be a creature, since all things are created by the Word of the Lord. Therefore, the Word of God is God. Therefore, if [the Word of God] is God but is not the second person, which is called Son, i.e., Word of the Father, then you will have to posit that there is more than one God and that the Word of God is a participant in God. Note that while wanting to deny that the Word of God is the Son of God, who is of the same nature as the Father—[deny it] lest you seem to ascribe to God a participant—you really are ascribing to God a participant! And this [point] is also proven from the authority [of the Qur'an, when it states]: "God and His Spirit wrote the Book." If God and His Spirit are not two Gods, then it follows that the Spirit is a person in God. Therefore, Arabs must confess the Trinity. Otherwise, they are unbelievers who ascribe to God a participant.

Furthermore, [we can argue] in the following way: You [Arabs] confess that the Gospel is a most clear and most truthful book. In it is contained [the view] that the one God is Father and Son and Holy Spirit. Therefore, nothing to the contrary can be claimed by you when this [view] is pointed out to you from the Gospel. (For the Gospel is of no less authority than is the [Qur'an]—as the [Qur'an] itself teaches.) Now, it is certain that [this view] is found in the Gospel. For we read in the Gospel that Christ said: "There is one who is good, [viz.,] God." Likewise: "God so loved the world that He gave His only begotten Son." Likewise: "the Comforter, the Holy Spirit, whom the Father will send . . ." Elsewhere: "the Spirit of truth, who proceeds from the Father . . ." And, again, Christ commands [the Apostles to] baptize in the name of the Father and of the Son and of the Holy Spirit. From these and other passages of the Gospel it is clearly inferred that the one God is Father and Son and Holy Spirit.

Let [it suffice that] the foregoing points have been made regarding the Holy Trinity.

Conclusion

Mapping Some of the Literary Topoi of
Christian-Muslim Relations

One of the most common kinds of maps in the medieval world was the T-O map, so called because it was made by placing the shape of a capital *T* within a circle, or an O. The *T*, which represents both a Christian cross and the Mediterranean Sea, separates the three known continents with Asia in the top portion of the circle, Africa in the lower right quadrant, and Europe in the lower left quadrant. The encircling O represents the ocean. More elaborate maps based on the T-O design also depict Christ's hands, feet, and face. Such a depiction reminded viewers in the medieval world that the earth was "contained within the body of Christ."[1]

Obviously, viewers of these maps looked at them not necessarily so they could discern by what route to arrive at a certain destination but because the map told them something about how to view the world. In keeping with this mindset, some Christian authors or cartographers placed Jerusalem at the very center of maps (for Muslims, Mecca is known to have been placed at the center). By identifying a "sacral center" like Jerusalem or Mecca, cartographers and authors could establish "an anchor about which the parts of the world are arranged, deriving their significance from their distance

1. Suzanne Conklin Akbari, *Idols in the East: European Representations of Islam and the Orient, 1100–1450* (Ithaca, NY: Cornell University Press, 2009), 28.

from and relationship to the central point."[2] In other words, a sacral center became the point from which everything around it was viewed, measured, and assessed. Furthermore, by establishing a center, one could, in turn, establish a periphery. As a result, an area could be defined based on its proximity to or distance from another area.[3]

Much of what can be said of medieval maps can also be said of the kinds of medieval texts introduced in the previous chapters. Consider Eulogius, the ninth-century Cordovan priest mentioned briefly in the introduction. He chastised Christians who were seemingly comfortable with Islamic culture and language. In their cultural accommodation, Eulogius fulminated, they "willingly abandoned the line of sound doctrine . . . with their dim-witted rabbit trails."[4] For Eulogius, a set of boundaries, or a line (*lineam*), distinguished who was adhering to "sound doctrine" from who was not. By delineating these boundaries in his texts, Eulogius essentially charted the territory of what he thought constituted a properly defined Christian community. By looking at his map, that is, by reading his texts, Eulogius's readers could see the borders they needed to avoid or stay safely within. They could also use Eulogius's texts to police these borders, warning or chastising others who wandered too close to boundaries. Likewise, they could condemn those who might haphazardly cross the boundaries that distinguished one religious community from another.[5]

From Eulogius's stern remark, it is clear that other Christian communities were charting the boundaries of religious identity differently than Eulogius. Thus, different authors created different borders with their texts. At times, these borders were straight and

---

2. Ibid., 51, 52.

3. Cf., ibid., 22, 29–31.

4. "Per deuios intelligentiae suae calles . . . lineam sanae doctrinae propio electionis iudicio derelinquunt." Eulogius, *Memoriale sanctorum*, I.19 in Ioannes Gil, ed., *Corpus scriptorium muzarabicorum*, 2 vols. (Madrid: Instituto Antonio Nebrija, 1973).

5. Of course, just because Eulogius's texts *could* be used in this way does not indicate that they *were* used in this way. In fact, the minimal manuscript witness of his texts suggests that they were not widely read.

uncompromising, prohibiting any sort of accommodation or contact with the other. At other times, borders were relatively permeable, bending in order to show readers what aspects of another's culture or language could be embraced and what religious tenets the other clung to that they should avoid. In either case, authors often used their texts as maps, trying to help their communities navigate contexts where other religions played a role in shaping lives and beliefs.

Seeing medieval religious apology and polemic like this helps in two ways. First, it helps us understand one of the essential purposes of such texts. In many cases, Christian texts about Islam, for example, were not necessarily meant to educate Christian readers about the intricacies of Muslim beliefs. Neither were they necessarily intended to convince Muslim readers of the alleged insufficiency of their beliefs. Instead, many of the texts I introduce in this book were intended to remind Christian readers of what distinguished them from Muslims. Similarly, many Muslim texts were intended to shore up Muslim readers' beliefs, working to assure their religious convictions and allegiances, not necessarily to convince Christian readers of their theological shortcomings.

Second, the view of medieval religious apologetic and polemic I describe above provides a helpful way in which to summarize the texts in this book. Like medieval maps and medieval apologetic and polemic, it may be helpful by way of conclusion to chart the territory covered in these texts. As an exercise in literary or rhetorical criticism, the map can be thought of as a collection of literary topoi (sing. topos): standardized and commonly used categories that indicate a certain genre of writing and are strategically deployed in texts in order to reinforce a specific argument. So, if many of these texts were used as a means for defining or reinforcing religious borders, then what were the indicators—the literary topoi—that authors used to highlight the boundaries they hoped would distinguish Muslim communities from Christian ones (whether by drawing them closer together or pushing further apart)? For modern readers, what are the markers—at least the ones that are presented by the texts selected in this book—that let them know the kind of literary territory they are in and, in turn, how to read that literature and interpret the arguments contained therein? With these questions in mind, what follows can be seen as a kind of literary map of the medieval texts presented in this book.

Muslim Comments on Unity and Trinity

From the Muslim texts surveyed in this book, it seems clear that these authors were most concerned to address the central theological claims of Christianity. If it is not a main feature of their texts, then nearly all of them at least turn to the topic of God's nature at some point. Of course, they took their cues from the Qur'an, in which the nature of God, alongside the person and work of Christ, are topics that feature widely. Accordingly, the Muslim authors defend God's absolute oneness (*tawhid*) and attack the notion that, as Christians saw it, he was a Trinity in Unity. According to Muslim authors, such a theological doctrine did not conform to reason or logic.

Muslim Concern over the Person and Work of Christ

Discussing the logical pitfalls of Trinitarian doctrine also led most of the Muslim authors included in this book to attack Christian Christology. These authors are particularly keen to address the incarnation—not only the idea that Christ was God but also the means by which Christians claimed this to be so and the way in which he became present on earth. For Muslims, this doctrine failed to conform to reason and logic as well. In fact, it was, in Muslim minds, theologically contradictory.

Even more, Muslims believed that Christian Christology led Christians to stumble into polytheism and idolatry. As a result, their doctrine was deemed foolish by many Muslim authors. Some, like al-

Jahiz and al-Tabari, go so far as to consider Christian theology, based on Christological articulations, to be uncultured. For others, like al-Jabbar and al-Dimashqi, Christian views of Christ were disgusting. This was especially the case in light of their accusation that Christians believed God cohabited with Mary in order to father Jesus.

Other Muslims questioned aspects of the crucifixion and the work of salvation it allegedly wrought. Of course, there were questions of logic applied to this doctrine, but on a deeper level, some Muslims wondered about the purpose of such an act. Thus, the means by which Christ was crucified—whether such an act applied to his divine nature or his human nature—and the work it accomplished missed for Muslims the question of whether or not it was even really necessary. If Christ was crucified, which the authors deny, then why was this the required means? Are humans really flawed in such a way that requires this kind of (unthinkable) sacrifice? These more primary questions forced those like al-Baji to look at Christian doctrine and, in his case, the Christian monk who invited him to salvation, and judge them to be rather impotent.

Of course, Christian authors were keen to articulate the ways in which God was a Trinity in Unity or the nuances of the incarnation and crucifixion in their texts. Some of them attempted these arguments in Arabic and by using Islamic thought forms and qur'anic language; Christian use of the qur'anic description of Christ as a "spirit of God" and "word of God," seen repeatedly in treatises like *On the Triune Nature of God*, is one such topos in this kind of literature. Frequently, these authors also resorted to analogies for explaining the Trinity or the incarnation, comparing them to such things as the sun and its rays or a fire and its heat.

Muslim Comments on the Church

Adding insult to injury was the Muslim observation that not even the Christian community could agree on its views of Christ. Most of the Muslim authors surveyed are not only able to point out the main Christian traditions in their midst, but many of them quite intelligently articulate the ways in which they differ over aspects of, say, the incarnation.

Besides this ecclesial division, some Muslim authors reflect on the personal character of Christians in their midst. Al-Jahiz notes that some Christians are rather scheming and manipulative in their dealings with Muslim neighbors. Al-Jabbar attacks elements of hypocrisy among the clergy, noting that some of them have children despite their vocational commitments to celibacy.

Christian Scripture Is Corrupt

The argument that Christian scripture was somehow corrupted and changed by Christians appears in both Muslim and Christian texts. Sometimes we see it in the context of Christian-Muslim debate, such as the disputation between Timothy and al-Mahdi or the conversation between Gregory of Palamas and his Muslim interlocutors. At other times, Christian authors like Abu Rai'tah include the charge in their treatises for the purpose of responding to it. For their part, many Muslim authors like al-Tabari, al-Jabbar, and Ibn Taymiyyah give space to the accusation in their texts in order to render inert Christian arguments based on biblical texts. But it is perhaps Ibn Hazm who gives the most attention to the notion of Christian scripture as having been made corrupt. This occurs over the course of lengthy passages filled with numerous examples where Ibn Hazm suspects biblical contradictions and errors.

Muhammad as the Paraclete and a Biblical Figure

Whether or not the Bible is corrupt is particularly important when our authors discuss the Prophet Muhammad. Some Muslims felt that Muhammad was foretold in the Gospels, an argument responded to by Timothy and raised by al-Dimashqi. Many other Muslims argued that Muhammad was the Paraclete, the helper that Jesus promised would come. This prophecy, or even ones in other parts of the Bible, is said by some Muslims to have been removed by Christians, or at least not properly understood by them—an argument especially significant for Turmeda that becomes the basis for his conversion to Islam.

Attacking the Prophet Muhammad

It should come as no surprise that the Prophet Muhammad is a significant feature of Christian texts devoted to Islam. In some cases, he is given a relatively positive assessment. This can be seen in Timothy's responses to al-Mahdi and in the anonymous *Letter from the People of Cyprus*. For Timothy, Muhammad "walked in the path of the prophets and trod in the track of the lovers of God." In both texts, Muhammad is given some legitimacy as a prophet to Arabs, particularly in regard to his message of monotheism. It is important to note that relatively positive assessments like this must be seen in context. Accordingly, it should be noted that Timothy never explicitly calls Muhammad a prophet. Both authors restrict Muhammad's ministry to Arabs and argue that the truth of his message is already contained and better explicated in Christian doctrines. Even in these assessments, then, Muhammad is of only peripheral and secondary importance.

Nevertheless, these assessments are markedly positive when seen in the wider literary context of authors like John of Damascus, al-Kindi, Petrus Alfonsi, and others in whose works Muhammad is often assaulted as a violent false prophet, a forerunner of the Antichrist, and a licentious, power-hungry glutton. In one case among the texts in this book—*The Book of Denuding or Exposing*—he is even thought to have been demon possessed.

These sorts of assessments of and attacks upon the Prophet are widespread in Christian texts devoted to Islam. But even more significant in terms of literary topoi are attacks upon Muhammad that focus on the nature of prophethood, Muhammad's early formation, and marriage. Many of the Christian authors included in this book point out to their readers that Muhammad produced no miracles. Associated with this accusation is their claim that Muhammad could not predict the future and was left unprotected by angels in the context of danger or battle. In Christian eyes, these deficiencies, especially the lack of miracles, are unbecoming of anyone who might claim to be a prophet.

Additionally, whether or not Muhammad had any prophetic legitimacy among Arabs is not the point for many of the Christian authors in this book. In their eyes, Muhammad had a parochial ministry. He spoke only Arabic and was sent only to Arabs. These deficiencies also strain Muhammad's claim to prophethood, for true prophets, in these Christian authors' works, are those with a universal message proclaimed in a multiplicity of languages. As a result of these kinds of attacks, one of the marks of Muslim texts like those of al-Tabari, al-Dimashqi, and Ibn Taymiyyah is a defense of the Prophet, whereby the nature of his prophethood and its universality is supported. Likewise, the importance of miracles in downgraded by Muslim authors, and some are quick to point to the miraculous Qur'an (*i'jaz al-qur'an*) as the greatest miracle wrought through the Prophet.

Many Christian authors also focus on Muhammad's early theological formation. According to some, Muhammad was recognized and taught by a Christian monk named Sergius or Bahira, depending on the text. Many authors who discuss this history, stories of which are included in the Prophet's biography (*sirah*), point out that the monk was a heretic. As a result, not only did Muhammad have help in devising his message—and here he is made to appear rather inept—but his message had heretical roots as well.

Perhaps most significantly, Muhammad's multiple marriages appear in many Christian texts. In particular, his marriage to Zaynab catches the eye of Christian authors. For them, the circumstances surrounding this marriage make it appear as though Muhammad essentially claimed Zaynab for himself and then gave the relationship a divine stamp of approval. To Christian authors, such an affair characterizes the inherent immorality of Muhammad.

Attacking the Qur'an

In much the same way that they attack Muhammad, many Christian authors are keen to demonstrate the true nature of the Qur'an. Authors like al-Kindi, Alfonsi, and Nicholas of Cusa claim that the book is full of lies, violence, sexual license, and simple foolishness. Others doubt whether the Qur'an was truly from God and note that the book, unlike true Scripture, was not confirmed by miracles. In any case, as al-Kindi notes, any truth or goodness in the Qur'an could be found in other books, notably the Bible. Similarly, Nicholas suggests that the Qur'an, in its most articulate expressions, is merely "a ray of the most lucid Gospel."

Attacking Muslims

If Muhammad and the Qur'an are, for many of the Christian authors in this book, dubious at best, then his followers are similarly questionable. Muslims often appear in Christian texts as carnal simpletons, and their heritage of idolatry is frequently highlighted. Al-Kindi, Alfonsi, the author of *The Book of Denuding or Exposing*, and Nicholas of Cusa all discuss pre-Islamic worship of pagan deities. John of Damascus even connects Arab pre-Islamic worship of Aphrodite to a god called "Chabar" (which he may have confused with the Arabic phrase *Allahu akbar*).

Christ vs. Muhammad

In a number of Christian texts devoted to Islam—in this book, the excerpts from Abu Qurrah and the author of *The Book of Denuding* or *Disclosing* in particular—the literary topoi I have discussed are collected into a kind of zero-sum game that compares Christ and Muhammad (Abu Rai'tah takes a similar approach, but makes a comparison with Christ's disciples). In these comparisons, a point won for Christ is a point lost for Muhammad. The result is that Christ emerges as true and Muhammad is revealed to be false. For example, Christian authors are keen to point out Christ's many miracles, the purity of his life on earth, and the universality of his message spreading over all the known earth. The authors often do this in explicit, or at times subtle, comparison to Muhammad's alleged lack of miracles, probity of life, and universality. For their part, the Muslim authors' defense of Muhammad can be seen in the context of such "Christ vs. Muhammad" motifs.

Discerning the True Religion

Some authors attempted to discern the uniquely true religion among Christians, Muslims, and Jews (and sometimes others). In order to do so, they gathered many of the topoi described above and collected them into lists that would distinguish the one true religion. Along these lines, Abu Qurrah argues that three characteristics of the true religion are that its messengers have been sent to all nations of the world, speak to the nations in their indigenous languages, and perform signs and wonders in order to validate their message. The implication is that only Christianity can lay claim to these characteristics.

Others, like Abu Ra'itah, focus on the reasons one might choose to belong to a religion or to convert to a religion. Reasons that are foolish suggest a false religion. Reasons that are wise, such as an uncoerced response to miracles and clear proofs, are deemed legitimate and becoming of the true religion.

Apocalypticism

Other kinds of texts that fit within or alongside this religious or apologetic literature may elicit other topoi. For example, apocalyptic texts, such as the one written by Pseudo-Methodius, are characterized by arguments that highlight internal sin as an explanation for Muslim ascendency and Christian repentance as a solution and harbinger for God's victorious judgment. Additionally, authors of apocalyptic texts often attempt to locate their enemies in sacred text as a means for characterizing them, interpreting their actions, and predicting an outcome. Thus, Muslims can be read into the biblical book of Daniel, and an author can subsequently suggest to readers what might be going on in their midst and what they might do to bring a return of God's blessing or safety.

A Few Concluding Words

Of course, texts not included in this book may evince further examples of literary topoi, but a good many of them are detailed here. While it is helpful to know what information authors used in these texts, it is quite another matter to consider *how* they used this information. For example, if an author had accurate information about another religion in his possession, why were tired myths and disinformation sometimes perpetuated? It could be that the author was depending on a source for the material he used, but it could also be that the author strategically set accurate information aside in order for his text to achieve a certain goal. However, deeper analysis of the purpose lying behind these topoi remains beyond the limitations of this book. That task is left to other studies, some of which are found in the "Suggestions for Further Reading" at the end of this book.

With that in mind, it is hoped that introducing readers to these texts has opened up one of the ways of telling the story of Christian-Muslim relations. More importantly, by reading these authors in their own words, it is hoped that readers will be encouraged to learn even more about this history, to read about it in the company of those who have gone before, and to let as many voices speak as they can so that the story of Christian–Muslim relations can continue to be known in its fullness.

Glossary

‘Abbasid	Relating to the second dynasty of Sunni Islam after the first four Caliphs (Islamic rulers) from 750–1258, the political center of which was Baghdad.
anthropomorphism	A figure of speech whereby a human characteristic is applied to God or something inhuman in order to illustrate a point. For example, referring to God's "eye" in order to illustrate something he sees.
Ash‘ari	Describes a school of Islamic thought that arose mainly as a response to Mu‘tazili thought (see below); characterized by its subordination of reason to revelation found in the Qur'an and the Sunnah (tradition) of the Prophet Muhammad.
corporeal	A term used to indicate a body; of or relating to a physical body.
dualism	A system of thought that describes the nature of something as being comprised of two distinct realities, such as good and evil.
hypostasis (pl. hypostaseis/ hypostases)	A Greek word used by Christians to indicate the three distinct persons of the Trinity who share the same essence of substance (ousia). God is said to be one ousia in three hypostaseis.
incorporeal	A term used to indicate lack of a body; having no physical or material existence.
Jacobite	An ancient Christian tradition adhering to a monophysite Christology—the belief that, after the union of the divine and human natures of Christ in the incarnation, Christ retained a single, undivided nature.

227

Magian	An adherent of Zoroastrianism, an ancient religion from Persia.
Manicheism	The third-century form of dualistic Gnosticism (from the Greek gnosis, meaning "knowledge") founded by Mani and distinguished by its notion of salvation by knowledge.
Melkite	An ancient Christian tradition in opposition to monophysitism, referring to Eastern Christian communities in communion with Constantinople and adhering to the Chalcedonian Creed (451). The term is no longer used by Arab Orthodox Christians and is instead used by Arabic-speaking Eastern Catholics in communion with Rome since 1724.
Mu'tazili	Describes a school of Islamic thought distinguished by reason and rationalism.
mysterion	A sacred mystery that defies concrete interpretation.
Nestorian	An ancient Christian tradition attributed to Nestorius (ca. 386–450), which emphasizes that Christ's two natures existed separately. For Nestorians, Mary was Christotokos, the mother of Christ in his human nature, not Theotokos, the mother of God Incarnate.
ousia (pl. ousiae)	A Greek word, meaning "substance" or "being," used by Christians to indicate the one substance shared by the three persons (hypostaseis) of the Trinity.
Sabian/ Sabean	Also known as Mandaean; a follower of a Judeo-Christian sect practicing the rite of baptism.
Shi'a	A significant, though minority, group among Muslims who believe that the subsequent leaders of the Muslim community should come from the Family of the Prophet Muhammad (Ahl al-Bayt).
Sunni	The largest group of Muslims who believe they are the people of the tradition (sunnah) of the Prophet Muhammad.
syllogism	A process of reasoning in which a conclusion is arrived at by drawing upon two propositions.

Suggestions for Further Reading

Overviews of Texts on Christianity and Islam

Gaudeul, Jean-Marie. *Encounters and Clashes*. Rome: Pontificio Istituto di Studi Arabi e d'Islamistica, 2000.

Hoyland, Robert G. *Seeing Islam as Others Saw It: A Survey and Evaluation of Christian, Jewish and Zoroastrian Writings on Early Islam*. Princeton, NJ: Darwin Press, 2002.

Nadim, Ibn al-. *The Fihrist: A 10th Century AD Survey of Islamic Culture*. Edited and translated by Baynard Dodge. New York: Columbia University Press, 1970.

Noble, Samuel and Alexander Treiger, eds. *The Orthodox Church in the Arab World, 700–1700: An Anthology of Sources*. DeKalb: Northern Illinois University Press, 2014.

RELMIN, The Legal Status of Religious Minorities in the Euro-Mediterranean World (5th–15th Centuries). The website includes a database of medieval texts that define the legal status of religious minorities in medieval Europe. http://www.relmin.eu.

Thomas, David, ed. *Christian-Muslim Relations. A Bibliographical History*. 6 vols. Leiden, Neth.: Brill, 2009–.

Christian Views of Islam

Daniel, Norman. *Islam and the West: The Making of an Image*. Oxford, UK: Oneworld, 1993.

Griffith, Sidney H. *The Church in the Shadow of the Mosque: Christians and Muslims in the World of Islam*. Princeton, NJ: Princeton University Press, 2008.

Michel, Thomas F. *A Christian View of Islam: Essays on Dialogue*. Edited by Irfan Omar. Maryknoll, NY: Orbis Books, 2010.

Quinn, Frederick. *The Sum of All Heresies: The Image of Islam in Western Thought*. Oxford: Oxford University Press, 2008.

Tolan, John V. *Saracens: Islam and the Medieval European Imagination*. New York: Columbia University Press, 2002.

Muslim Views of Christianity

Ayoub, Mahmoud. *A Muslim View of Christianity: Essays on Dialogue*. Edited by Irfan Omar. Maryknoll, NY: Orbis Books, 2007.

Goddard, Hugh. *Muslim Perceptions of Christianity*. London: Grey Seal, 1996.

Lewis, Bernard. *The Muslim Discovery of Europe*. New York: Norton, 2001.

Robinson, Neal. *Christ in Islam and Christianity*. Albany: State University of New York Press, 1991.

Waardenburg, Jacque. *Muslim Perceptions of Other Religions: A Historical Survey*. Oxford: Oxford University Press, 1999.

General studies on Christian-Muslim Relations and Dialogue

Bulliet, Richard W. *The Case for Islamo-Christian Civilization*. New York: Columbia University Press, 2004.

Cheetham, David, Douglas Pratt, and David Thomas, eds. *Understanding Interreligious Relations*. Oxford: Oxford University Press, 2014.

Goddard, Hugh. *A History of Christian–Muslim Relations*. Chicago: New Amsterdam Books, 2000.

Renard, John. *Islam and Christianity: Theological Themes in Comparative Perspective*. Berkeley: University of California Press, 2011.

Roggema, Barbara, Marcel Poorthuis, Pim Valkenberg, eds. *The Three Rings: Textual Studies in the Historical Trialogue of Judaism, Christianity and Islam*. Leuven, Belg.: Peeters, 2005.

Siddiqui, Mona. *Christians, Muslims, and Jesus*. New Haven: Yale University Press, 2013.

Siddiqui, Mona, ed. *The Routledge Reader in Christian-Muslim Relations*. New York: Routledge, 2013.

Smith, Jane Idleman. *Muslims, Christians, and the Challenge of Interfaith Dialogue*. Oxford: Oxford University Press, 2007.

Troll, Christian W. *Dialogue and Difference: Clarity in Christian-Muslim Relations*. Maryknoll, NY: Orbis Books, 2009.

Volf, Miroslav, Ghazi bin Muhammad, and Melissa Yarrington, eds. *A Common Word: Muslims and Christians Loving God and Neighbor*. Grand Rapids, MI: Eerdmans, 2010.

Zebiri, Kate. *Muslims and Christians Face to Face*. Oxford, UK: Oneworld, 1997.

Index